Teaching and Learning History Online

Teaching and Learning History Online: A Guide for College Instructors offers everything a new online history instructor needs in one package, including how to structure courses, integrate multimedia, and manage and grade discussions, as well as advice for department chairs on curriculum management, student advising, and more.

In today's technological society, online courses are quickly becoming the new normal in terms of collegiate instruction, providing the ideal environment to "flip the classroom" and encourage students to hone critical thinking skills by engaging deeply with historical sources. While much of the attention in online teaching focuses on STEM, business, and education courses, online history courses have also proven consistently popular. However, due to the COVID-19 pandemic, new history instructors are rushed into online teaching with little or no training or experience, creating a need for a guide to ease the transition from classroom to online course development and teaching.

A timely text, this book aims to provide both new and experienced college history teachers the information they need to develop dynamic online courses.

Stephen K. Stein is an Associate Professor of History and Department Chair for online programs at the University of Memphis, USA.

Maureen MacLeod is an Assistant Professor of History, Chair of the Humanities Department, and the History Program Director at Mercy College, USA.

Teaching and Learning History Online

A Guide for College Instructors

Edited by
Stephen K. Stein and
Maureen MacLeod

NEW YORK AND LONDON

Designed cover image: Melpomenem / Getty Images

First published 2023
by Routledge
605 Third Avenue, New York, NY 10158

and by Routledge
4 Park Square, Milton Park, Abingdon, Oxon OX14 4RN

Routledge is an imprint of the Taylor & Francis Group, an informa business

© 2023 selection and editorial matter, Stephen K. Stein and Maureen MacLeod; individual chapters, the contributors

The right of Stephen K. Stein and Maureen MacLeod to be identified as the authors of the editorial material, and of the authors for their individual chapters, has been asserted in accordance with sections 77 and 78 of the Copyright, Designs and Patents Act 1988.

All rights reserved. No part of this book may be reprinted or reproduced or utilised in any form or by any electronic, mechanical, or other means, now known or hereafter invented, including photocopying and recording, or in any information storage or retrieval system, without permission in writing from the publishers.

Trademark notice: Product or corporate names may be trademarks or registered trademarks, and are used only for identification and explanation without intent to infringe.

Library of Congress Cataloging-in-Publication Data
Names: Stein, Stephen K., editor. | MacLeod, Maureen, editor.
Title: Teaching and learning history online : a guide for college instructors / edited by Stephen K. Stein and Maureen MacLeod.
Description: New York, NY : Routledge, 2023. | "This book originated with two panels on online teaching organized...for the 2020 annual meeting of the American Historical Association." | Includes bibliographical references and index. |
Identifiers: LCCN 2022047477 | ISBN 9781032192710 (hbk) |
ISBN 9781032192727 (pbk) | ISBN 9781003258414 (ebk)
Subjects: LCSH: History--Web-based instruction--United States. | History--Study and teaching (Higher)--United States.
Classification: LCC D16.255.C65 T44 2023 |
DDC 907.1/173--dc23/eng/20221018
LC record available at https://lccn.loc.gov/2022047477

ISBN: 978-1-032-19271-0 (hbk)
ISBN: 978-1-032-19272-7 (pbk)
ISBN: 978-1-003-25841-4 (ebk)

DOI: 10.4324/9781003258414

Typeset in Baskerville
by Taylor & Francis Books

Contents

Acknowledgements viii
About the Contributors ix

Introduction 1
STEPHEN K. STEIN AND MAUREEN MACLEOD

PART I
Administrative, Legal, and Technical Issues of Online Teaching 5
MAUREEN MACLEOD

1 Overcoming Resistance to Teaching History Online and Methods of Engagement 7
   RACHEL J. MITTELMAN

2 Teaching to the Whole Class: Accessibility and Inclusivity in Teaching Online History Classes 15
   CHRISTINA GHANBARPOUR

3 Balancing Act: Offering History Online from a Department Chair's Perspective 25
   KATHLEEN A. TOBIN

4 Advising Online History Majors 33
   CHRYSTAL GOUDSOUZIAN AND AMANDA LEE SAVAGE

5 Working with Publisher-Produced Material 43
   DAVID L. TOYE

6 Instructor, University, and Other Contributors: Balancing Copyright Protections for Online Learning 49
   ELIZABETH F. BUCHANAN AND STEPHEN K. STEIN

PART 2
Innovative Pedagogy for the Online Class — 59
STEPHEN K. STEIN AND MAUREEN MACLEOD

7 More than a Mode of Delivery: Benefits and Challenges of Teaching History Online — 61
ELIZABETH F. BUCHANAN

8 Intercultural Learning Online: Using Students' Diverse Perspectives to Build Connections to History — 69
MOLLY J. GIBLIN

9 Using Technology in Pedagogy and Assessment: Timelines, Story Mapping, and Edpuzzles — 78
MAUREEN MACLEOD

10 Dynamic Video Content in the Online History Classroom — 85
COURTNEY LUCKHARDT

11 Assessment and Feedback as Instruction in the Online History Classroom — 94
CASSANDRA L. CLARK

12 Games and Gamification in Online History Classes — 101
MARY A. VALANTE

PART 3
Online Discussion and Interactive Learning — 109
STEPHEN K. STEIN

13 Creating Meaningful Online Discussions — 111
TONY ACEVEDO

14 Managing Online Discussions in Larger Sections — 123
J.M. WOLFE

15 Letting the Sources Guide the Way: The Dynamic Utilization of Primary Sources in the Online History Classroom — 133
MICKI KALETA

16 It's All Relative: The Importance of Scaffolding and Course Design in the Online History Classroom — 139
LEIGH ANN WILSON

17 Interactive Timelines as the Center of Class Discussion — 146
BRANDON MORGAN

18 Using Omeka to Bring Women's History to Online Learners   154
    BRIGITTE BILLEAUDEAUX AND CHRISTINE EISEL

Appendix 1: Sample Course Design Agreement and Related Documents   162
Appendix 2: Website and Additional Resources   169
Bibliography   173
Index   185

Acknowledgements

This book originated with two panels on online teaching organized by Brandon Morgan for the 2020 annual meeting of the American Historical Association. The editors are grateful to the panelists and the many attendees who asked wonderful and insightful questions at these panels and other presentations we attended on online teaching over the last few years, such as the "Teaching History with the Technology of the Future" at the 2021 Digitorium Conference organized by Leigh Ann Wilson. Brandon has continued to organize panels on online teaching at major history conferences. He helped recruit contributors for this anthology, provided feedback on early drafts, and contributed his own chapter.

Collectively, the contributors possess well over a century of online teaching and course design experience. We are grateful to all of them. In addition to imparting their experience and wisdom, they made assembling this volume a much less daunting process than is often the case when wrangling more than a dozen contributors. Elizabeth Buchanan was particularly generous; always ready to help with anything the editors needed. Brigitte Billeaudeaux, Christine Eisel, and Christina Ghanbarpour stepped in at the last minute to replace contributors who had to drop out, and we are especially thankful for the speed at which they produced such stellar chapters.

About the Contributors

Tony Acevedo is Assistant Professor of History and Program Coordinator at Hudson County Community College in Jersey City, NJ, where he teaches survey courses, including Honors seminars and online sections, on a variety of topics. Outside of his work at HCCC Tony has been an NEH Summer Scholar in Switzerland and Italy and a MetroCITI Fellow at Teachers College, Columbia University, where he developed pedagogical projects to improve general/liberal education curricula at high-diversity urban colleges and universities. He was recently awarded a Dale P. Parnell faculty distinction award by the American Association of Community Colleges.

Brigitte Billeaudeaux is an Associate Professor, Librarian and Archivist for the University of Memphis Libraries' Special Collections department. She has over 15 years' experience working with cultural heritage materials and studies best practices for using primary sources in classroom settings. She has published original research on incorporating primary sources into postsecondary educational seminars. She has also authored chapters on developing a private historical corporate archive with Omeka and the use of primary source materials as tools for outreach. More recently she acts as the archivist for the Mid-South LGBTQ+ Archive, housed at University Libraries' Special Collections department.

Elizabeth F. Buchanan received her DPhil from the University of Oxford, United Kingdom, in 2015, with a thesis entitled *Debt in Late Antique Egypt, 400–700 CE: Approaches to a Time in Transition*, which she is currently preparing for publication. She has been employed as an Assistant Professor at the University of Findlay since the fall of 2016, and teaches Introduction to History, the Global History series, and the History of the Late Antique and Medieval Eastern Mediterranean as well as Latin and Greek. Commencing in 2018, Dr. Buchanan created a new Museum Studies minor for undergraduates. She teaches in both on-campus and online capacities, often for the same classes, and so has a basis for comparing methodologies. Her principal pedagogical interests involve scaffolding and teaching increasingly sophisticated historical skills to undergraduate and graduate students.

Cassandra L. Clark is an Assistant Professor in the History Department at Utah Tech University. Dr. Clark has taught United States and Environmental History classes online and in person at several institutions of higher education, including Salt Lake Community College's prison education program, since 2010. She is also a public historian and has worked for the Utah Division of State History and the American West Center at the University of Utah. Her research focuses on the environmental history of insane asylums in the Intermountain West. She received her PhD in US history from the University of Utah, an MA in US history from the University of Northern Colorado, and a BA in history and a BA in secondary education from Adams State University.

Christine Eisel is an Assistant Professor of Teaching at the University of Memphis, where she teaches courses on early America, US women, and American ideas and culture. Eisel earned her PhD in Early American Policy History from Bowling Green State University. Her research focuses on women's gossip in early Virginia, bringing together her interests in women, law, and gender in the British North American colonies. Her essay, "'They make one very handsome Mirkin amongst them': Gossip and Church Politics in Early York County, Virginia" appears in *When Private Talk Goes Public: Gossip in American History* (Jennifer Frost and Kathleen Feeley, eds., 2014), and she is the editor of *The Schlager Anthology of Early America: A Student's Guide to Essential Primary Sources* (2022).

Christina Ghanbarpour is Professor of History at Saddleback College, where she has been employed since January 2012. She has also taught courses at the University of California Irvine, Chapman University, Santa Monica College, and Sophia University in Tokyo, Japan. Her publications include "Home Education in Rural Japan: Continuity and Change from Late Edo to the Early Postwar," published in the *US–Japan Women's Journal* (2011), and "Legacy of a Minority Religion: Christians and Christianity in Japan" for the multi-volume reference work, *The Changing World Religion Map: Sacred Places, Identities, Practices and Politics* (2014). She is currently preparing her book manuscript, *Changing Traditions: The Role of Rural Women in Creating Japan's Modernity*, for publication.

Molly J. Giblin is a historian, teacher, and international education professional. She is a former online skeptic who realized while teaching her first online course that the virtual format can allow instructors to engage more meaningfully with students who sometimes slip through the cracks in face-to-face settings. As Associate Director of Academic Integration and Global Learning at Northeastern University, she works with faculty to create both virtual and in-person intercultural experiences across a variety of disciplines.

Chrystal Goudsouzian is an Instructor/Advising Coordinator in History at The University of Memphis. She received her PhD in History, with a focus in Egyptology, at the University of Memphis in 2012. Her research focuses on gender, family, and identity in ancient Egypt. She teaches classes in the ancient Mediterranean world and directs the history department's advising program and undergraduate history writing center.

Micki Kaleta is an Associate Professor at Mitchell Community College. She received her PhD from The University of Memphis with a focus on 19th century US history. Her research centers on the enslaved family in the Antebellum Cotton Frontier of the United States. She has been teaching online for ten years.

Courtney Luckhardt is Associate Professor of History at the University of Southern Mississippi. She is a medieval historian who received her PhD in Medieval Studies from the University of Notre Dame. Her research focuses on the religious and cultural history of the early Middle Ages (ca. 400–1000 AD). Her first book, *The Charisma of Distant Places: Travel and Religion in the Early Middle Ages* (2019), explores ideas about power, holiness, identity, and mobility during the transformation of the Roman world in the global Middle Ages. She was named Mississippi Humanities Council Teacher of the Year for Southern Miss in 2020.

Maureen MacLeod is an Assistant Professor of History and History Program Director at Mercy College in Dobbs Ferry, NY, where she teaches courses in European, women's, and gender history. She is currently the William F. Olson Chair in Civic and Cultural Studies and a 2019 National Academy of Education Spencer Postdoctoral Fellow. She has served as the School of Liberal Arts Online Learning Coordinator and is a certified Quality Matters Peer Reviewer.

Rachel J. Mittelman is an Assistant Professor of History at Gordon State College in Barnesville, Georgia. Her areas of interest include Late Bronze Age / Early Iron Age Egypt and Libya, ancient Mediterranean ceramics, crisis migration and identity formation in antiquity, and fakes, forgeries, and pseudoscience in history. Over the past ten years, she has taught both survey- and upper-level online courses on various online platforms at a variety of colleges.

Brandon Morgan is the Chair of the History, Anthropology, Economics, Political Science, and American Studies cluster at Central New Mexico Community College in Albuquerque. He earned a PhD in Latin American and Borderlands History from the University of New Mexico and has been teaching History and Latin American History courses online for the past decade. His research focuses on the ways that violence and the development of the capitalist economy shaped small communities along the New Mexico–Chihuahua border between the 1880s and the 1930s and he has published articles in the *New Mexico Historical Review* and contributed chapters to *Just South of Zion: Mormons in Mexico and its Borderlands* and *Along these*

Ragged Edges: Histories of Violence Along the US–Mexico Border (forthcoming). He also published an interactive, digital textbook on the *History of New Mexico* for use with undergraduate students in the state.

Amanda Lee Savage is an instructor, academic advisor, and online program coordinator at the University of Memphis, located on the ancestral land of the Chickasaw, Choctaw, and Quepaw, among others. She teaches courses in early US history and social justice. She has advised online undergraduates since 2011 and has been involved in advising leadership on campus for almost a decade. She received the Dean's Award for Outstanding Advising in 2017 and 2021. She is the cofounder of Native RITES, a grass-roots organization committed to advocating for indigenous peoples in the Midsouth.

Stephen K. Stein has taught online for 20 years. He founded the online history program at the University of Memphis, which for many years was the university's largest online program. His publications include *From Torpedoes to Aviation: Washington Irving Chambers and Technological Innovation in the New Navy, 1877–1913* (2007); *The Sea in World History: Trade, Travel, and Exploration* (2017); *Sadomasochism and the BDSM Community in the United States: Kinky People Unite* (2021); "The Greely Relief Expedition and the New Navy" (*International Journal of Naval History*, 2006), which won the Rear Admiral Ernest M. Eller Prize in Naval History; and "Lessons Learned Building the Online History Program at the University of Memphis" (*History Teacher*, 2014).

Kathleen A. Tobin is Professor of History and Chair of the Department of History and Philosophy at Purdue University Northwest. She earned her PhD from the University of Chicago and currently teaches US social history with an emphasis on the mid-20th century. Her recent research addresses population issues and birth control history, and she recently published "People, Not Property: Population Issues and the Neutron Bomb," in *Cold War History* (2016) and a chapter entitled "Manning the Enemy: US Perspectives on International Birth Rates during the Cold War" in *Gender, Sexuality, and the Cold War: A Global Perspective* edited by Philip Muehlenbeck (2017). Her books include *The American Religious Debate over Birth Control, 1907–1937* (2001) and *Politics and Population Control, A Documentary History* (2004).

David L. Toye earned his PhD in Ancient and Medieval History from the University of California, Santa Barbara in 1991. He has been a Professor at Northeast State Community College in Tennessee since 1993. For the last 20 years, he has developed and taught online survey courses in United States and World History.

Mary A. Valante is a Professor of Medieval History at Appalachian State University and a former Scholar at the Dublin Institute for Advanced

Studies. In graduate school she studied medieval history, archaeology, and dead languages at the Pennsylvania State University. She is the author of *The Vikings in Ireland: Settlement, Trade, and Urbanization* (2008), co-editor with Lahney Preston-Matto of *Kids those Days: Children in Medieval Culture* (2021), and the author of numerous articles and book chapters including "Murder in a Viking Town" (2011) and "Castrating Monks" (2013). Her courses include "Experiencing the Middle Ages," "Gaming History," and "Urban Vikings." She is the recipient of the Southeastern Medieval Association's 2021 Award for Teaching Excellence.

Leigh Ann Wilson is an Associate Professor of History and Communications at University of Massachusetts Global. She holds an MA in Journalism & Mass Communication from Kansas State University and a PhD in US History from the University of Memphis. Voted Faculty of the Year for 2015 and 2021, she founded her university's chapter of Alpha Sigma Lambda, a national honor society that recognizes excellence in adult learners. She has taught history online for almost 20 years and has worked extensively outside the classroom in the areas of competency-based education, rubrics, and student assessment. She currently serves as Vice President for Teaching and Learning for H-Net: Humanities and Social Sciences Online and is the Secretary of the Immigration and Ethnic History Society, an affiliated society of the American Historical Association.

J.M. Wolfe is an Instructor of History and Coordinator of Dual Enrollment at Louisiana State University. He is also responsible for the development and implementation of online offerings for summer semesters and facilitates departmental workshops demonstrating tools and techniques for creating successful online courses. Research has taken him to Germany, South Africa, and Namibia in addition to special collections in the United States. His manuscript, *God's Children without a Nation: German missionaries, Settlers, and Africans in Southwest Africa, 1915–1960* (forthcoming) examines what modern-day is Namibia through the lens of German evangelists from the Rhenish Missionary Society, specifically their role in shaping cultural, religious, and political developments in what became a League of Nations mandate. He is the 2019–2020 recipient of the Tiger Athletic Foundation's Undergraduate Teaching Award.

Introduction

Stephen K. Stein and Maureen MacLeod

Around the world colleges have recognized the importance of online courses to their students and steadily increased online course offerings over the past two decades. By 2015, almost a third of college students had taken at least one online class. In 2021, a third of college students took at least one online course each semester. About half of those students took all their classes online. Online courses provide working students—who today account for the majority of college students—the flexibility essential for timely degree completion. More and more students take a mix of online and in-person classroom courses, and those who do often progress to graduation faster than students who rely solely on either classroom or online courses.[1]

While much of the attention in online teaching focuses on STEM (science, technology, engineering, and mathematics) courses, as well as business, criminal justice, education, and nursing, which attract many students, history courses have also proven consistently popular. This is true not only of the US and World History surveys that anchor general education curricula at most universities, but also elective courses in diverse fields, including ancient, African American, military, and women's history. The same is true of other fields in the humanities.

The demand for online courses is such that many new faculty are rushed into online teaching, often with the expectation that they develop their own online courses with little time to prepare and paltry institutional support and pedagogical guidance. Most soon discover that one cannot simply move traditional classroom techniques online. The result is often that students perceive the class and instructor as detached, remote, and impersonal. The result is often a class (and instructor) that students perceive as detached, remote, and impersonal.

Different learning environments call for different approaches. The online environment is unique, offering many advantages over traditional classroom teaching, but also constraints that teachers must address to produce effective online courses. This book aims to provide both new and experienced college history teachers the information they need to develop dynamic online courses. It will help online instructors incorporate these and other tools into their courses and offer guidance and suggestions to best engage online students and facilitate their learning.

While this book focuses on teaching history online, much of the material discussed is broadly applicable to other courses in the humanities, particularly conducting online discussions, scaffolding assignments, and incorporating a broad array of primary and secondary sources into online courses. Rich multimedia sources are available to online instructors, including audio, video, text, and games, but integrating these into courses often proves challenging. Similarly, many textbook publishers offer readymade components for online courses, but these come with their own problems. They require work to customize and integrate into existing or new courses and may tie instructors more closely than they would like to a particular publisher or textbook.

Technology continues changing, but basic concepts, such as the centrality of primary sources and student–student and student–teacher interaction to history courses will endure. Whether one approaches teaching and learning through constructivism (building on previous knowledge and experience), situated learning (acquiring and honing skills through participation in community of practice), or reflective practice (learning through trial and error and self-reflection), the online environment has much to offer. It provides an ideal place for students and instructors to build effective learning environments and encourage one another's research, writing, and learning.

Doing so, though, requires attention and work, both before a class launches and over the course of the semester. Online courses require careful organization to help students locate course materials, assignments, deadlines, and other information and work their way through the course efficiently. Online teachers themselves need to be flexible and compassionate toward diverse student populations. They need to clearly communicate expectations, encourage discussion and critical reflection, use active learning techniques, give prompt feedback on assignments, and encourage different styles of learning.

While students may only remember only about 20% of what they hear, they recall as much as 90% of what they do.[2] Online history courses are all about doing. History courses should encourage interaction and introspection, and the online environment is ideal for this. In well-designed courses, students get right to analyzing historical sources through questioning evidence, demonstrating understanding, explaining cause and effect, drawing conclusions, and developing arguments.

Students learn to think critically in online discussions. They re-read posts, seriously consider classmates' comments, and often spend more time in "class" than they would in a traditional course offered in a physical classroom. Online courses offer an ideal environment for building active, student-centered learning communities in which students take relationships built in one class to the next, and the next, growing a community of active, engaged learners. The intense focus on writing in online courses not only improves students' writing, but often that of instructors, as well. Interacting with students in a primarily text-based, online environment forces instructors to explain ideas and assignments clearly and precisely. It forces clarification.

This book is organized into three parts; the first covers administrative, technical, and legal issues; the second focuses on online pedagogy and teaching tools; and the third on managing discussions and interactive learning, which are central to teaching history online.

Online courses present some unique administrative challenges, such as protecting the intellectual property rights of both course developers and the authors and creators of any materials used in the course. This is as true for courses whose developers use just a few outside resources as it is for the off-the-shelf courses produced by textbook publishers. Students in online courses, particularly those taking all their courses online, often have different needs of which advisors should be aware. Ensuring the accessibility of online course materials to all students is critical.

Part 2 focuses on online pedagogy and a variety of teaching tools, old and new. How do you move your traditional courses online? What are the best ways to address diverse student populations online? How does one overcome the seemingly impersonal online environment to build connections with students and provide them with effective feedback? Growing numbers of instructors have enriched their classes with video and games. How can one apply these in an online environment?

Finally, Part 3 focuses on class discussions and interactive learning, which are central to teaching history online. How should one organize and manage online discussions? What about discussions in very large classes? What are the best ways to incorporate primary sources in online courses? How can one use discussions to help students complete assignments, scaffold assignments, and showcase their work?

Collectively, this book's authors have experience at small liberal arts colleges, community colleges, and large public universities. They have developed courses and taught online for many years, reaching diverse student populations across the United States. While their pedagogical approaches vary, they share a deep commitment to online teaching, student engagement, and adapting new technologies to suit their particular styles of teaching, rather than the opposite. They employ new technologies to reinforce and improve their courses, using the rich resources available to online teachers to add depth and enrich their courses. This book showcases their many years of online teaching experience.

Notes

1 Hobson, Tiffaney D. and Krista K. Puruhito, "Going the Distance: Online Course Performance and Motivation of Distance Learning Students," *Online Learning, 22*, no. 4 (2018): 129–140; and National Center for Education Statistics. "Fast Facts: Distance Learning." 2020. https://nces.ed.gov/fastfacts/display.asp?id=60 Accessed June 20, 2022.

2 Edgar, Dale, *Audio-Visual Methods in Teaching*. New York: Dryden, 1969; and Schneider, Vivian I., Alice F. Healy, Kenneth W. Carlson, Carolyn J. Buck-Gengler, and Immanuel Barshi, "How Much is Remembered as a Function of Presentation Modality?" *Memory* (2019): 261–267. As Schneider, et al. show, the exact numbers and ratios are disputed, but Dale's original claim that doing, as opposed to reading or listening, increases learning retention remains a bedrock of education theory.

Part I

Administrative, Legal, and Technical Issues of Online Teaching

Maureen MacLeod

Teaching online for the first time requires significant time and preparation. Instructors must create assignments, upload material, and organize online platforms. These tasks can seem daunting, but good planning and forethought can ease the stress and anxiety of producing a brand-new online course. Before instructors begin creating content in an online course, other pieces need to be thought about and decided that will help make course construction more fluid.

One of the biggest challenges to online teaching is faculty resistance, as many prefer the in-person teaching experience. Rachel J. Mittelman's chapter, "Overcoming Resistance to Teaching History Online and Methods of Engagement," addresses this issue by examining faculty reservations and offering solutions to have a positive online teaching experience. Christina Ghanbarpour takes the idea of a positive online experience to the students in her chapter, "Teaching to the Whole Class: Accessibility and Inclusivity in Teaching Online History Classes." Ghanbarpour discusses how history instructors can build a better online learning environment through advocacy, assessment, and addressing inclusivity.

As teaching history online becomes the norm in many departments, administrators face many obstacles regarding students and faculty. Kathleen A. Tobin examines the online history course as a department chair in her chapter, "Balancing Act: Offering History Online from a Department Chair's Perspective." Tobin discusses important issues such as budgetary concerns, student retention, class size, and computer literacy. In addition, Tobin emphasizes the importance of department chairs in supporting their faculty and regularly reviewing data to make changes or advocate for the department when necessary. Taking Tobin's discussion of student retention further, Chrystal Goudsouzian and Amanda Lee Savage delve into the issue of student retention and engaging with history majors in their chapter, "Advising Online History Majors." Goudsouzian and Savage outline best practices in advising and how to create a sense of community for those who are consistently in a virtual learning environment.

Turning to the physical construction of an online course, instructors need to decide what type of material they want students to use in their course.

Choosing course material is a normal part of the course design process, but how does it differ in an online course? Many instructors use publisher-produced material to ease the problematic course design and allow for more data-driven results, as David L. Toye discusses in his chapter, "Working with Publisher-Produced Material." Elizabeth F. Buchanan and Stephen K. Stein explore these issues further, examining copyright, intellectual property, and the ownership of online materials in their chapter, "Instructor, University, and Other Contributors: Balancing Copyright Protections for Online Learning." Buchanan and Stein offer an understanding of intellectual property and fair use of course material created by others, which often presents a challenge for instructors.

The chapters outlined above offer essential insight and guidance in creating an online history course. Examining the big picture issues is essential before beginning the construction of a specific history course. In addition, the authors hope that through these chapters, the course design process will be easier and more inclusive for instructors and students.

Chapter 1

Overcoming Resistance to Teaching History Online and Methods of Engagement

Rachel J. Mittelman

Introduction

History remains a pillar of academic learning. History not only teaches students about the past, but also provides students with a variety of essential skills to help them become successful in their other classes and in their careers. History's long-lived place in higher education, however, means that many consider it to be a "traditional" lecture class. Thus, some history faculty who maintain this perspective resist changes in their courses, despite online learning's commonplace role in the academe today. Faculty resistance to online historical instruction is well documented, despite great student interest in online classes and the increased shift to online learning.[3] However, the recent pandemic forced many reluctant historians to adapt, creating a unique opportunity to research and examine why some history professors continue to be reticent to adopt online teaching, and to determine ways of overcoming this resistance.

There are many common reservations towards online teaching: greater time investment and poor compensation for larger classes; more work/information/responsibilities; lack of face-to-face interaction; lower-quality content delivery; clarity about intellectual property ownership; lack of training, IT resources, and support; the effect on promotion and tenure; little or no experience; and perceived lack of standards.[4] Older faculty tend to be more resistant to online teaching than their younger colleagues, as older faculty are fully tenured and may place different weight on the importance of online classes.[5]

Compensation / Time / Responsibilities

Financial compensation is one of the largest factors in faculty resistance. Usually, course redesign occurs on one's own time, which means more effort for little fiscal advancement. Furthermore, moving to online instruction is daunting due to the high initial investment of resources, the large amount of time involved in learning and adapting online pedagogy, and the detraction from other academic pursuits.[6] Burnout and emotional exhaustion – especially

DOI: 10.4324/9781003258414-3

for female faculty – due to the large amount of effort exerted to create and maintain interpersonal relationships, all factor into the larger responsibilities and requirements of online classes.[7] Faculty may then believe that their time would be better spent on research or professional development, both of which an institution may reimburse.[8]

Additionally, history can be taught as a written discipline, which may make for more online writing-intensive assignments and more grading. Faculty worry that additional writing assignments will alienate some students from online history classes; furthermore, more writing assignments also create greater possibilities for plagiarism, giving the faculty member extra work and stress. Finally, some activities that do not translate well to a remote environment may require more effort to change.

Experience / Content Quality / Lack of Standards / IT Training and Support

Faculty's unfamiliarity with online learning management systems (LMS) such as Desire2Learn, Blackboard, or Canvas may also fuel resistance. For others who did not take online classes or use LMS software in graduate school, teaching online is utterly foreign. These faculty believe that online class training focuses more on technological understanding, or the "bells-and-whistles" associated with the online class technology, rather than properly applying the course material.[9]

Faculty may also feel that online content delivery lowers the quality of the class material. In asynchronous classes, this may lead to a lack of interaction and human connection. The perceived lack of "warmth" or "authenticity" in online classes can be considered by some as emotionless and impersonal, therefore leading to lower-quality education.[10] Faculty also assume that students will lack the motivation or effort to finish assignments.[11]

How to Overcome Reservations

With a bit of understanding and application, faculty can learn and successfully navigate LMS platforms by utilizing their institution's online resources and support, create and run an effective course, make meaningful connections with students, and foster productive interaction between students. Many faculty may have already used parts of their LMS in their face-to-face classes, which helps ease the transition to online.[12]

Discomfort and unfamiliarity with technology or online software can discourage many faculty. Coupled with limited knowledge of online delivery options, many faculty may refuse outright to teach online. This can be problematic when faculty have no choice, such as in spring 2020. Becoming more comfortable with the LMS platform and practicing helps to build confidence. When planning and teaching online courses, it is important to find out the

LMS training and support available at an institution, as well as each platform's troubleshooting guide and helpline. Additionally, many institutions offer or require faculty development courses for teaching online, which can help alleviate the initial cost of learning LMS functions and online pedagogical approaches.

Peer mentorship is another avenue for support and help. If there is no program or training course, ask a more experienced colleague. As one colleague commented, "[My colleague] helped me by typing up a list of instructions for putting exams online and also for unlocking special student access to exams… Typed instructions on how to do various procedures on [the LMS] would have helped many faculty members on campus."[13] Online peer mentorship programs can also benefit those who are already familiar with online learning, as there is always new information, or a "trick" to help facilitate aspects in the online classroom.

Setting up the Online Classroom

One of faculty's biggest concerns is the time involved in designing and implementing an online class. While one's first online class may be daunting and take hours to prep, the first class is usually the most time and labor intensive. However, most of the LMS software is intuitive and may help to lessen the necessary time, especially if faculty have practiced beforehand. Online or institutional tutorials can help new online instructors with software issues. After the initial setup, subsequent classes should only take a few hours at most to copy, update, and tweak.[14] Taking advantage of the above suggestions can help faculty learn these necessary skills.

Maintaining the Online Classroom

Good time management for online faculty (and students) is essential for successful online classes.[15] Good time management helps faculty to keep classes on track and to provide real-time help and support. One of the easiest ways to ensure this is to adjust the LMS settings so that the class receives regular notifications for important information and due dates. Setting up notifications only needs to be done once, and will help students keep up with the course load, ask questions, and tweak their studying/writing methods as necessary.[16] Also helpful is using automated messaging systems, which can be set at the beginning of the semester to automatically run at certain intervals throughout the semester.[17] Additionally, holding virtual office hours in an online classroom will help students who prefer face-to-face office hours by allowing them to have direct and immediate contact with their faculty.[18]

Equally helpful is having course materials readily available and keeping to a structured schedule while allowing for student flexibility. Due dates and times should be standardized for consistency: for example, every quiz should be due at 9:00am ideally on the same day(s), and every discussion should be due by

11:59pm on the same day(s) throughout the semester. Relaxed due dates such as opening all assignments on the first day of class or giving penalty-free grace periods lessens student anxiety and gives students autonomy to finish their work in a timely manner.[19] Finally, regularly log into the LMS classroom and spend 30 minutes to an hour a day in each online class. Respond to emails and questions in the faculty question forum in the online classroom, and make sure that email and response policies are included in the syllabus and online information sections.[20]

Some of the other main reservations are being approachable and visible in online classrooms, as online classrooms are usually perceived as producing less student–instructor and student–student contact. However, many faculty do not take into account that contemporary students have grown up in online communities with consistent online interactions. Many students are used to "faceless interaction," so, the idea that online classes are emotionless or disconnected is usually just the faculty's perception. There are many options for creating a welcome online environment, as many of these practices are similar to those used in physical classrooms. It is important to think about class goals: what skills and/or content do you want the students to learn? How will you present these skills? The answers do not necessarily have to be different from those for an in-person class, though the content presentation will likely change.[21]

During the 2020 transition online, many instructors typically lowered their expected contact with students or decreased their student interactions. This lessened involvement can be mitigated by faculty's efficacy and skills: those who have stronger online skills are able to maintain more class involvement.[22] Therefore, if faculty gain the knowledge and skills, they can maintain the same level of involvement and interaction as they do in their face-to-face instruction.[23]

Planning and Designing

Many faculty worry that online classes will be too much grading or that face-to-face activities will not translate well online. However, the design of online classrooms allows faculty to tweak their assignments to better help future students. There are two types of online activities: synchronous and asynchronous. There are benefits to each type of community building and online assignments. In a synchronous environment, it is easier for the instructor to convey meaning and personality through using facial and vocal expression. These methods also allow students to directly ask questions and immediately address concerns with the instructor. While it is more difficult in an asynchronous environment to convey this same meaning, it is still possible by posting videos and through thoughtful and deliberate written communication.[24] Additionally, asynchronous learning gives students time to think about their ideas before they share them with the class, leading to more meaningful discussion.[25]

For many faculty, synchronous instruction is a bit more familiar than asynchronous, simply because there are more "face-to-face" options and it is a closer approximation of the classroom environment.[26] Each institution's Center for Teaching and Learning or IT department can help to determine which face-to-face tools are supported. Additionally, preparing teaching materials – PowerPoints, videos, etc. – and practicing with them in advance will help to work out any potential problems during a lecture or discussion, whether synchronous or asynchronous.[27]

While there are many easy ways to build community in a synchronous learning environment, asynchronous learning seems colder and less genuine. However, this is not necessarily the case, though connecting with students asynchronously may take a little more work. Many synchronous tactics such as icebreakers can be adapted. Instead of having students introduce themselves during a class period, set up a discussion board with icebreakers. Remember to specify what mode of delivery students should use: a written introduction with a picture, a video introduction, or personal choice. Faculty should post their own introduction as an example and to put students at ease when they log into the discussion boards.[28] Most LMS platforms have very user-friendly procedures for making and posting videos and photos, helping faculty to create an inviting asynchronous learning environment.

If there is a deadline for an asynchronous icebreaker, remember to respond to students daily until the due date. It is wise to make this the only assignment due in class that week, as this first interaction will form the foundations for the class community. Next, students should be encouraged to ask the instructor and each other questions. Finally, to build rapport, it is important to personalize class discussions, and to participate with the students in a positive and friendly manner. Remember, these are not the only options for creating quality faculty–student and student–student interactions, and faculty will find a mixture of methods that works for them.

Responsibilities

Students need empathy, communication, and flexibility while learning how to navigate online classes. All students benefit from more personal connections such as using their name in discussions, icebreakers, and regular interactions with the instructor and classmates.[29] Thus, it is imperative to create a positive and welcoming online environment.

On the first day of class, it is vital to maintain a visible presence. The night before the class begins, send a welcome email to the students in the class, post an introduction on the announcements page, and post in the welcome/introduction discussion forum (which is helpful for student–instructor and student–student interaction throughout the rest of the semester).[30] Participating in asynchronous class discussions throughout the semester is also helpful in maintaining a visible presence in the online classroom. A good general rule is to respond to at least five people per discussion, as doing so helps students to feel that they are contributing, which will make them more likely to succeed.

Additionally, grading students in a constructive, detailed, and timely manner is necessary. Because students may not consistently see their faculty's face, it is helpful to use clear, encouraging, and motivational terminology when providing assignment feedback.[31] Regular announcements and automated messaging systems are useful communication tools, as well as using various media.[32] Quickly identifying high-risk and underperforming students and monitoring them is also necessary. It is imperative to reach out to offer help and compassion. Of equal importance is to encourage student progress, openness, and communication.[33] Engaging with students over various platforms such as email, LMS feedback tools, announcements, class chat rooms, or conferencing software such as Skype or Zoom will better help those who are struggling. It is important for faculty to remember that like in-person classes, online classes are constantly evolving and need tweaking. A first online class – or a 20th – does not have to be, nor will be, "perfect." As faculty grow and learn, so will their online classrooms.[34]

Conclusion

Overall, for historians who are unfamiliar with the online classroom, the transition to online instruction is fraught with doubt about the online learning environment. However, even the most stalwart champion of face-to-face instruction can implement a successful online learning environment for both students and professor by examining the reasons for their hesitation and how to overcome their resistance to teaching online as discussed in this chapter.

Any adaptation, whether by choice or force, provides an excellent opportunity for growth and improvement as an instructor. After the first semester of online pandemic instruction, a colleague and self-proclaimed Luddite said, "I actually don't want to go back to where I was before because I believe that what I have learned will better enable me to find ways to bridge the gap between medium and message that so shook and disturbed me decades ago."[35] Transitioning to online instruction allows all faculty to reconsider their instructional priorities and course materials, helping them focus on the best methods to achieve their goals in both face-to-face and online settings. Many history faculty's reservations regarding online teaching can be simply assuaged by becoming familiar with their LMS or by taking an institution's online teaching training course. Most importantly, keeping an open mind and asking for help are paramount. Another colleague stated, "[a] good piece of advice for others who are resistant to teaching online – be willing to do it, but make sure to ask for help."[36]

Notes

1 Ayers, Edward L. "The Pasts and Futures of Digital History." The University of Virginia, 1999. www.vcdh.virginia.edu/PastsFutures.html. Accessed May 31, 2018; Cohen, Daniel J., and Roy Rosenzweig. "No Computer Left Behind." *Chronicle of*

Higher Education, February 24, 2006. www.chronicle.com/article/no-computer-left-behind. Accessed November 22, 2022.
2. Bergstrand, Kelly, and Scott Savage. "The Chalkboard versus the Avatar: Comparing the Effectiveness of Online and In-Class Courses." *Teaching Sociology 41*, no. 3 (2013): 294–306; Ni, Anna Ya. "Comparing the Effectiveness of Classroom and Online Learning: Teaching Research Methods." *Journal of Public Affairs Education 19*, no. 2 (2013): 199–215; Perrotta, Katherine, and Chara Bohan. "A Reflective Study of Online Faculty Teaching Experiences in Higher Education." *Journal of Effective Teaching in Higher Education 3*, no. 1 (2020): 50–66; Stauss, Kimberly, Eun Koh, and Michael Collie. "Comparing the Effectiveness of an Online Human Diversity Course to Face-to-Face Instruction." *Journal of Social Work Education 54*, no. 3 (2018): 492–505.
3. Vivolo, John. "Understanding and Combating Resistance to Online Learning." *Science Progress 99*, no. 4 (2016): 399–412.
4. Lloyd, Steven, Michelle Byrne, and Tami McCoy. "Faculty-Perceived Barriers of Online Education." *MERLOT Journal of Online Learning and Teaching 8*, no. 1 (2012): 1–12.
5. Ibid., 8.
6. Bollinger, Doris, Fethi Inan, and Oksana Wasilik. "Development and Validation of the Online Instructor Satisfaction Measure." *Journal of Educational Technology & Society 17*, no. 2 (2014): 183–195.
7. Bennett, Liz. "Putting in More: Emotional Work in Adopting Online Tools in Teaching and Learning Practices." *Teaching in Higher Education 19*, no. 8 (2014): 919–930; Makarenko, Erica, and Jac Andrews. "An Empirical Review of the Mental Health and Well-Being of Online Instructors." *The Journal of Educational Thought (JET)/Revue De La Pensée Éducative 50*, no. 23 (2017): 182–199.
8. Ubell, John. "Advice for Faculty Members about Overcoming Resistance to Teaching Online." *Inside Higher Ed*, December 13, 2016. www.insidehighered.com/advice/2016/12/13/advice-faculty-members-about-overcoming-resistance-teaching-online-essay. Accessed June 20, 2022.
9. Conversation with Dr. David Janssen.
10. Ubell, "Advice."
11. Conversation with Dr. Jeremy Richards.
12. Because intellectual property, promotion/tenure, and compensation are institution-dependent, this section will cover time management, online responsibilities, content quality, perceived lack of standards, and institutional training/IT support. The author believes that there are few stigmas concerning how online teaching relates to and affects promotion and tenure, as online teaching is common today. For more information about intellectual property ownership and online classes, please see Chapter 6.
13. Conversation with Dr. Jeremy Richards.
14. The author's first new course online takes her, on average, up to half a day to build in the LMS (excluding creating new assignments or finding materials). As most LMSs allow instructors to copy previous courses and materials into new course shells, subsequent courses using similar material can be quickly updated, leading to repeated use and minimal work.
15. Olson, Joann, and Rita Kenahan. "An Overwhelming Cloud of Inertia: Evaluating the Impact of Course Design Changes Following the COVID-19 Pandemic." *Online Learning Journal 25*, no. 4 (2021): 346.
16. Many LMSs copy and update any important course dates when copying courses.
17. Automated messaging systems are internal LMS tools which will send emails based on certain criteria.
18. ECampus. "Faculty: Best Practices with ECampus." https://go.view.usg.edu/d2l/le/content/2451986/viewContent/45952082/View. Accessed November 22, 2022.

Most, if not all, online platforms include video software; however, Zoom, Microsoft Teams, or Google are also options.
19 Ensmann, Suzanne, Aimee Whiteside, Lina Gomez-Vasquez, and Ronda Sturgill. "Connections before Curriculum: The Role of Social Presence during COVID-19 Emergency Remote Learning for Students." *Online Learning Journal 25*, no. *3* (2021): 36–56; Olson and Kenahan, "An Overwhelming Cloud," 346–347; Weimer, Maryellen. 2013. *Learner-Centered Teaching: Five Key Changes to Practice*, 2nd ed. San Francisco, CA: Jossey-Bass. Olson and Kenahan agree with Weimer that more student control over online classrooms ensured student success in their graduate classes; however, they did not study these effects in undergraduate courses.
20 ECampus, "Faculty: Best Practices"
21 Schrum, Kelly, and Nate Sleeter. "Teaching History Online: Challenges and Opportunities." *Organization of American Historians Magazine of History 27*, no. *3* (2013): 35.
22 Rutherford, Teomara, Sarah Karamarkovich, Di Xu, Tamara Tate, Brian Sato, Rachel Baker, and Mark Warschauer. "Profiles of Instructor Responses to Emergency Distance Learning." *Online Learning Journal 25*, no. *1* (2021): 86–114.
23 Bollinger et al., "Development and Validation," 185.
24 Lyons, John. *Teaching History Online*. New York: Routledge, 2009, 15.
25 Lyons, *Teaching History Online*; Darby, Flower and James Lang. *Small Teaching Online*. San Francisco, CA: Jossey-Bass, 2019.
26 Some options are: Zoom, Blackboard Collaborate Ultra, Skype, Adobe Connect, Cisco Webex Meeting, Google Classroom, and Microsoft Teams. It is important to understand the software options and to ensure that everyone can access the software.
27 Darby and Lang, *Small Teaching*, Chapter 4.
28 Ensmann et al., "Connections Before Curriculum," 39 – note that video messages help personalize online teaching and help students become more comfortable in the online classroom.
29 Ibid., 51.
30 Infande, Al. "A Dozen Strategies for Improving Online Student Retention." *Higher Ed Teaching & Learning*, July 8, 2013. www.facultyfocus.com/articles/online-education/a-dozen-strategies-for-improving-online-student-retention. Accessed November 22, 2022.
31 Ibid.
32 Discussions, online chat, email, phone, text, video chat are all options to connect with students.
33 ECampus, "Faculty: Best Practices."
34 Schrum and Sleeter, "Teaching History Online," 38.
35 Conversation with David Janssen.
36 Conversation with Jeremy Richards.

Chapter 2

Teaching to the Whole Class
Accessibility and Inclusivity in Teaching Online History Classes

Christina Ghanbarpour

The Case for Creating Accessible[2] Online Classes

Faculty and institutions often interpret the term "accessible" as how we make physical classrooms available to students with disabilities. An example of this is by adding ramps and elevators to accommodate students who cannot walk or have difficulty walking. Another type of accommodation familiar to history faculty may be offering students time extensions or providing a quiet environment for exams, often in a separate room or building from the regular classroom. Regardless of the type of accommodation, however, all of these supports are understood as attempts to make classroom spaces more accommodating to students with disabilities, and thus, at a minimum, meet the standard for educational equity as outlined in the 1990 Americans with Disabilities Act (ADA)[3] and subsequent amendments.

The difference between the virtual and the physical classroom, however, is that, where institutions once provided most of the resources needed to create an accessible environment, that responsibility has now shifted more to faculty. That is not to say that faculty never had a role to play in creating an accessible classroom; rather, the choices that history faculty now make with regards to course content and delivery online—such as what documents we use, how we provide them, which websites, video, or other media we require students to view, and whether or not the class is asynchronous or synchronous—will have a profound effect on the students' learning environment, and thus require more faculty intervention and research to make sure the legal standard is met.

One mistake we may make as faculty is to assume that differences in ability are not very common, or that it is up to the student to choose a classroom that fits his/her/their needs. To the contrary, in a recent survey by the National Center for Education Statistics, 19% of undergraduates reported having a disability.[4] These figures are likely to be higher given that students with disabilities often avoid disclosing them.[5] As for the idea that students with disabilities would be better served in a traditional classroom rather than in an online one, given the barriers that can prevent students from attending an on-campus class, such as multiple disabilities, the growth in mental health concerns among adolescents,

DOI: 10.4324/9781003258414-4

and childcare and work obligations—particularly among low-income students—a student's best option, or indeed only path to degree attainment, may still be through online learning.[6] With the growth in online education, then, faculty will likely need to take the lead in making virtual classrooms truly accessible, rather than assuming that students with disabilities will somehow find their way.

Inclusive Education[7] and Universal Design[8] in the College Classroom

If the term "accessibility" often refers to how we address the needs of students with disabilities, then the term "inclusivity" may be best understood as a framework for addressing all students' needs, including—but not limited to—students with disabilities. Inclusive education is based on the principle of universal design first popularized in architectural circles in the 1970s. This idea shifted the paradigm of building for the "average person" to designing buildings for any person, regardless of whether the person fits the profile of presumptive normativity. Similarly, inclusive education strives for equitable access to education for all students, rather than only the "typical" or "traditional" student, through strategies such as providing multiple means to access course content and using real-time or simultaneous alternatives for accessing content, such as by providing subtitles, captioning, and/or transcripts of a lecture while it is being given. By providing multiple means to access learning opportunities, inclusive education focuses on increasing all students' ability to learn.

To clarify what I mean by "all students" rather than the "typical" or "traditional" student, it is worth noting that today's history classrooms often include a greater diversity of students than in the past. Students may be veterans, single parents, older (or otherwise fall outside of the 18–24 age range), minorities, low-income, first-generation, immigrant, international, refugee, LGBTQ, a resident of a rural area, and many others; and there is evidence to suggest that the number of non-traditional students is growing.[9] Once we recognize that this diversity exists, we can start to think about applying strategies that help more than one type of student, say, by making information on our website easier to find for a first-generation or ESL (English as a Second Language) student, or by using more affordable textbooks. Moreover, any changes should be done with the knowledge that students' needs can differ widely—even within, say, the same disability—and with a desire to avoid changes that have no real benefit for students, a practice often called "window dressing" or "retrofitting."[10] Faculty members should therefore focus on changes that are evidence-based, substantive, and that provide equal access in real time.

Why History Faculty?

Thus far, I have defined key concepts in the field of education that address how informed teaching methods can better meet the needs of today's virtual students and, thus, improve learning. But what is the historian's role in this? How can historians use theories such as universal design to build a better learning environment? I suggest three main courses of action: advocate, assess, and address.

Advocacy

History faculty at the administrative, chair, and tenured faculty levels can play key roles in advocating for institutional support. These efforts might include any of the following: training graduate students (a one-sheet list of best practices, with links to websites for further development, might be one way to get started); offering faculty paid time and training to make improvements; allowing inclusive course design to be included in a tenure-track portfolio; and assigning faculty the role of point person on inclusivity as a rotating position, or as an option for committee work. Faculty can also advocate for funding for resources, such as disability specialists, particularly specialists in online learning; promote accessibility and inclusivity as department goals; maintain and regularly update materials to support inclusivity, such as an e-library of annotated web resources; and adopt peer review of online classes, such as the POCR (Peer Online Course Review).[11] Finally, history faculty might consider collaborating with faculty in other fields, such as education, to develop research-based projects where students can test the inclusivity features of participating classes.

Faculty at all levels can advocate for some of these goals, such as training in online education; however, at most institutions, it will be incumbent on tenured faculty, chairs, and administrators to support part-time, contract, tenure-track, and other untenured/non-tenured faculty. A department or division-wide commitment to faculty training should include remuneration for part-time faculty, as paid training opportunities tend to increase participation. Flexibility and certification in inclusivity training—whether through peer evaluation workshops, one-on-one meetings with disability specialists, or a semester or summer training program—can further motivate faculty. Senior faculty can also advocate for classes to be tagged in course schedules as having inclusive materials, such as audiobooks, or highlight features such as an online class's asynchronous format.[12]

Beyond the institutional setting, faculty can be effective advocates for inclusive web design and textbooks. A starting point could be Web Content Accessibility Guidelines, a website that lists accessibility criteria for websites.[13] Faculty who use or make their own educational websites, or who create online textbooks or other free learning resources, can refer to this site to improve their web designs, and can urge the makers of educational content to do so as well. Another tool is the Voluntary Product Accessibility Template, or VPAT. VPATs help faculty identify which texts and websites are accessible by providing a list of the ways that a product conforms to accessibility standards; a simple online search for the publisher's name and "VPAT," or the publisher's name and "accessibility," is usually sufficient to find this resource.[14]

Faculty can also support inclusive online services and publishers. For example, faculty can request that their institutions subscribe to a web service, such as Bookshare, which supplies standard history textbooks in readable formats for students with dyslexia and other disabilities. They can ask publishers to offer their textbooks through electronic providers that have an audiobook or "read to me" formats, such as VitalSource and Cengage.[15] To make their students aware that these resources are available, faculty can list them under a "Resources" tab in an online class, provide a link to the resource, ask a disability-resource specialist to create a one-sheet for students that can be posted in the online classroom, and/or have a disability specialist talk to classes about resources via a pre-recorded video or a live-streamed visit to a Zoom classroom.

Assessment

A second way that faculty can build better learning environments is in our role in assessment. Senior faculty in the position of evaluating other faculty's work should include accessibility and inclusivity as a component of the evaluation, both for ensuring that faculty are meeting the legal requirement for accessibility and to inform them of best practices. Faculty may or may not have received training specific to accessibility before being hired, so including it in an evaluation can create uniformity across the department or division.

One way to improve assessment is to create a checklist of expectations and distribute it to faculty upon being hired or, at the latest, before an evaluation. The checklist could start with suggestions for simple fixes and then work up to more in-depth revisions. During the assessment, the evaluator should ask the instructor being evaluated to show how best practices were incorporated into the class. If additional changes are needed, faculty should be given the opportunity to complete them and be re-evaluated at a later date; or the evaluation could end with a note that further work needs to be done, and the instructor referred to a disability technology specialist for support. This will likely mean that evaluations will take longer and will increase the workload burden, particularly on disability specialists and chairs. Institutions will therefore need to adjust their expectations and resources to support faculty and compensate them accordingly.

Addressing Inclusivity in Our Own Work

The final way faculty can build better learning environments is by addressing inclusivity in our own work. Faculty can use software such as Wave Reader, a free browser extension,[16] to check their webpages for accessibility. Software such as accessibility checkers, which are now built-in to most office software, and guidance on topics such as model syllabi, are readily available. Below is a list of concrete steps that faculty members can take.

Practical Steps towards Creating Inclusive Classes

General Guidelines

Most historians will need to create electronic files for their classes. A few guidelines for making them inclusive are as follows:

- Use automated formatting features such as headings, bullet points, and numbered lists. These are available in most office software, webpage generators, and LMSs. They communicate the correct organization of a document or webpage to students who are using screen readers. Students can also use headers to jump backwards and forwards in a document to locate specific information or review information, which can be helpful for all students.
- Use an outline. To view the outline in Microsoft Office for Mac, from the ribbon, select View > Outline. The version you see here is how a screen reader will read the document to visually impaired students. Faculty can use the outline feature to edit, reorganize, or build a table of contents for a document quickly. Once the formatting is in place, no further work is needed to create an outline; it is generated automatically.
- Avoid serif fonts, all-caps, underlined text (except to indicate a hyperlink), excessive italics, hard-to-see color contrasts (such as light fonts on a light background), and color combinations known to be difficult for colorblind people, such as red/green and blue/yellow. When using a color font, use it in combination with another indicator of importance, such as bold text. When showing a map or other illustration that is not black and white, such as in a live stream or a video, be sure to explain the content for students who may have trouble seeing color. Guidance on color combinations can be found in the appendix.
- Avoid multiple blank spaces caused by pressing the Return button or the Space bar multiple times. Instead, use automated features such as Section Break and Page Break to create spacing. To do this, click on Insert > Break… and then select the appropriate break; or you can adjust line spacing using the Line Spacing icon on the Home tab; or, press the Shift +Return combination to add a soft return.
- When possible, replace long website URLs with descriptive hyperlinks along the lines of "View Map—Hyperlink" or "use this link," and avoid "click here." Screen readers read out web addresses letter by letter, resulting in much frustration for low-vision students, while "click here" lacks a clear referent.
- Make tables accessible by using header rows, adding alt text, and avoiding blank spaces and screenshots; or take them out and replace them with text. A link to Dallas College's detailed guide on this topic is provided at the end of this book.

- For images, use alt text. In newer versions of MS Office and in some templates, pictures will automatically prompt to insert alt text. If this does not happen, select the picture, then control-click, then Edit Alt Text.
- For slides, limit the amount of information per slide and use a larger font, such as 18-point or larger, with sufficient space between lines of text.
- For spreadsheets, avoid merged cells, split cells, and nested tables, and delete blank spreadsheets and spaces. Where possible, use automated features, such as borders, to create lines and spaces.[17]

Accessibility Checkers in Microsoft Office, Apple iWork Suite, and Google Workspace

In addition to the guidelines listed above, historians will find that all major applications now have accessibility checkers. Before you begin, check that your file is in the latest format. For example, for MS Office, this will most likely be a file in Word, Excel, or PowerPoint that ends in .docx, .xlsx, or .pptx. If you try the following and receive an error message that reads, "This tool is not available for this document," then you will need to update the file format. To do so, click on File > Save As... and then save the document in the most currently available format.

After verifying that the document is in the correct file format, run the Check Accessibility feature. For example, Microsoft Office for Mac users can run the Check Accessibility feature by doing the following:

1. In Word, Excel, and PowerPoint, locate the ribbon (Home, Insert, Draw, etc.) at the top of the application.
2. Select Review > Check Accessibility.
3. Review your results. You will see a list of errors, warnings, and tips with how-to-fix recommendations for each.
4. Select a specific issue to see why you should fix the issue and the steps to take to change the content.[18]

If you cannot find the Check Accessibility icon under "Review," try the following: at the very top of the window, you will see another ribbon. Select Tools > Check Accessibility. It will take you to the same location as the above.

Videos, Recordings, and Lectures

A best practice in universal design is to make classroom materials accessible in multiple formats simultaneously so that all students can access class materials at the same time.[19] To facilitate this, historians should use audio recordings and videos that are subtitled, have closed captions, or are accompanied by a transcription of the audio. Lectures can also be subtitled. To do this in Google Docs, open a new Google Doc, click on Tools > Voice Typing, and then click on the microphone. The text of the speech will appear as you talk. PowerPoint now has a subtitle feature that translates a lecture into text as it is being presented. To use this, in SlideShow mode, look for the circle with a text icon on the bottom left of the presentation, and click on it to activate.

PDFs / Adobe Acrobat

Although PDF software has undergone changes that have improved accessibility, PDF documents remain problematic for screen readers. Because of this, it is better to create a document in Word or something similar, or you can offer the document in both PDF and office formats. In addition, scanned documents—that is, documents that are copied and then saved as a PDF—are not readable by a screen reader; they have to be processed through an OCR reader first. To do that, you will need to use software such as Adobe Acrobat Pro, which can transform an image into readable text. However, the software is fairly expensive, the quality is often poor, and you will still need to run Adobe's accessibility tool to make sure that it works. Because of these limitations, it is best to use an office application when possible.

Other Approaches to Inclusive Education

In addition to making class content available to students in formats they can readily use, history faculty should consider ways to address differences in how students access online classes and how they interact with class materials. For example, a recent Pew Research Center study found that more adolescents own smartphones than computers and that, in low-income households, smartphone ownership is even more ubiquitous.[20] Likewise, a study by the Office of Policy and Development found that low-income households have greater access to smartphones than to other devices and that smartphones are often their main way to connect to the internet.[21] These findings suggest that low-income students may benefit more from online classes designed with smartphone use in mind than those designed for laptops and desktops.

One way to address smartphone use is to create a "liquid syllabus," a syllabus that can be accessed on a public website that does not require students to log in. Students can bookmark the website for quick access, and some website creation tools offer degrees of privacy, such as limiting who has access to the site or preventing the page from being found in a search. Several websites, such as Populr.me, Google Sites, and Smore, provide this service. Another way is to set image and document sizes as a percentage, rather than a fixed size, on course webpages. This allows images to re-size automatically depending on the size of the viewer's screen. At the HTML level, this would look like (bold font added for clarity):

wR_zgc&em=2" width=**"90%"**

Rather than this:

wR_zgc&em=2" width=**"288"**

Another way to address diversity in student learning is in how students use the syllabus. Syllabi can be used to support inclusive learning in many ways, such as by making the "hidden curriculum," or knowledge of how to navigate college that first-generation students often lack, an overt part of class content.[22] This might include clarifying the skills that students are presumed to have, such as the professor's expectations for work habits, attendance, and class participation, by writing them directly into the syllabus or other reference document. An example of a history syllabus that employs this strategy can be found in the "Syllabi" section of websites in the appendix.

Conclusions

History faculty can take many steps to promote student learning in online classes. The first is to recognize that today's diverse student bodies come with different needs. Those needs are best met by employing a framework of varied, accessible, and engaging strategies for learning. By offering students multiple ways to access and engage with the class material, historians can meet or exceed the legal and ethical imperatives of equitable access to education.

The second step is to leverage the many means that history faculty have at their disposal to influence policy and practice in the college or university setting. As advocates, assessors, administrators, and teachers, we can compel our institutions to support inclusive education by calling attention to the need for funding, training, and incorporating best practices. More broadly, as consumers and creators of educational content, we can promote inclusive content through publishers, web designers, and others with whom we regularly interact.

Finally, we can increase our knowledge of what works and use it to build better classrooms. This chapter has outlined some basic steps that faculty can take to make better classes.

Notes

1 Parts of this chapter were presented at the American Historical Association annual conference in January 2021. An attenuated list of some of the sources and techniques I discuss here can be found in my blog post, "Before You Do Anything, Start Here: Best Practices for Accessibility in Online Education," March 20, 2020. www.historians.org/publications-and-directories/perspectives-on-history/march-2020/before-you-do-anything-start-here-best-practices-for-accessibility-in-online-education.
2 Accessibility means the design of products, services, and environments such that they may be easily used by people with disabilities.

3   ADA is a 1990 law that builds on the Rehabilitation Act of 1973, both of which prohibit discrimination against people with disabilities. It was subsequently reinforced by amendments in 2008.
4   National Center for Education Statistics. "Fast Facts." 2020. https://nces.ed.gov/fastfacts/display.asp?id=60. Accessed June 20, 2022.
5   Lowenthal et al. "Creating Accessible and Inclusive Online Learning: Moving Beyond Compliance and Broadening the Discussion." *The Quarterly Review of Distance Education 21*, no. 2 (2020): 5.
6   Ibid., 6.
7   I follow Dalton et al.'s definition of inclusive education as the concept of designing "teaching and learning opportunities in ways that are varied, accessible and engaging for all students, including those with differing needs and/or disabilities." See Dalton, Elizabeth M., et al. "Inclusion, Universal Design and Universal Design for Learning in Higher Education: South Africa and the United States." *African Journal of Disability 8*: a519, 1.
8   Universal design is a term coined by Ronald L. Mace in 1972 that describes the concept of designing all products and the built environment to be aesthetic and usable to the greatest extent possible by everyone, regardless of their age, ability, or status in life. See California State University. "UDL-Universe: A Comprehensive Faculty Development Guide." https://enact.sonoma.edu/c.php?g=789377&p=5650608. Accessed June 20, 2022.
9   See, for example, Fry, Richard and Anthony Cilluffo. "A Rising Share of Undergraduates Are from Poor Families, Especially at Less Selective Colleges." www.pewresearch.org/social-trends/2019/05/22/a-rising-share-of-undergraduates-are-from-poor-families-especially-at-less-selective-colleges. Accessed May 22, 2019.
10 Dalton et al., "Inclusion, universal," 6.
11 California Virtual Campus-Online Education Initiative (CVC-OEI) Professional Development Workgroup. "Peer Online Course Review." https://onlinenetworkofeducators.org/course-design-academy/pocr-resources. Accessed June 20, 2022.
12 For a list of key terms that students with disabilities commonly seek out when looking for classes, see, for example, the "Folksonomy of Accessibility" section in Rodrigo, Covadonga, and Bernardo Tabuenca. "Learning Ecologies in Students with Disabilities." *Comunicar 62*, no. 28 (2020): 61; Crow, Kevin L. "Four Types of Disabilities: Their Impact on Online Learning." *Techtrends 52*, no. 1 (2008): 53.
13 Caldwell et al., eds. "Web Content Accessibility Guidelines." www.w3.org/TR/WCAG20. Accessed June 20, 2022.
14 An example of a VPAT can be found on the Lumen Learning website, which produces the Boundless World History textbook, "Lumen User Guide," https://courses.lumenlearning.com/userguide/chapter/accessibility-the-lumen-platform. Accessed June 20, 2022.
15 To see if your history textbook is listed, use this link, www.bookshare.org/cms/, to access the Bookshare website and enter the title or ISBN in the search field; for Vitalsource, use this www.vitalsource.com/.
16 A browser extension (or plugin) is a small software module used to customize a browser. These modules are typically downloaded from a website and installed to perform a specific task, such as ad blocking, grammar checking, or changing the style of webpages.
17 Other resources for making Microsoft Office (MS Office) documents accessible can be found by opening the program, choosing Help from the ribbon, and then typing "Make document accessible" into the "Search" field.

18 Selected text reprinted from the Word for Mac Help Guide. "Improve Accessibility with the Accessibility Checker." https://support.microsoft.com/en-us/office/improve-accessibility-with-the-accessibility-checker-a16f6de0-2f39-4a2b-8bd8-5ad801426c7f#PickTab=macOS. Accessed June 20, 2022.
19 Burgstahler, Sheryl. "What Higher Education Learned about the Accessibility of Online Opportunities during a Pandemic." *Journal of Higher Education Theory and Practice 21*, no. 7 (2021): 166.
20 Anderson, Monica and Jingjing Jiang. "Teens, Social Media, and Technology 2018." n.d. www.pewresearch.org/internet/2018/05/31/teens-social-media-technology-2018. Accessed May 31, 2018.
21 Office of Policy Development and Research. "Digital Inequality and Low-income Households." 2016. www.huduser.gov/portal/periodicals/em/fall16/highlight2.html. Accessed November 22, 2022.
22 The hidden curriculum is a term used to describe the unspoken norms and rules for navigating college life that first-generation students often lack.

Chapter 3

Balancing Act
Offering History Online from a Department Chair's Perspective

Kathleen A. Tobin

Context

Online postsecondary education has grown exponentially over the past two decades, and history instruction has played a notable role in that growth. While a face-to-face experience remains optimal in many ways and for many reasons, the learning of history does not require laboratories or team meetings in physical locations. History courses designed well and with meaningful virtual engagement in mind can serve many kinds of students. It also has become increasingly common for students to earn entire degrees through distance education from either an online institution or a brick-and-mortar university that offers online programs. Traditional, well-funded, residential schools serving students who matriculate and graduate in four years have resisted online options, as they seek to maintain the time-honored on-campus experience. However, most postsecondary students in the United States are served by other types of institutions, with many being categorized as "swirling," or taking courses from multiple colleges or universities before completing a bachelor's degree. Among those are students transferring credits while trying to find the right fit, and those credits might well include courses completed online. This is especially true when students want to prevent falling too far behind. Occasional online courses also serve students who are juggling work and family schedules. Department chairs must respond to these changing needs by working closely with faculty members and administrators in offering what is best for these new students. Data on student retention and improving time to graduation are commonly shared with department chairs, and incentive-based budget models (IBBMs) pose new challenges for chairs in insuring enrollment is high and sustainable. Department chairs are in a unique position as their responsibilities in running lean operations increase, while striving to schedule courses that attract students and lead to success.

As a department chair at a regional campus of a Tier 1 research university, I have found myself working to meet the demands of online instruction in ways that are complex and yet increasingly common. By detailing some of my experiences and challenges, there might be a greater opportunity for dialogue

DOI: 10.4324/9781003258414-5

and collaboration among faculty and chairs in similar situations. For example, it is often the department chair's responsibility to schedule classes "efficiently," to maximize enrollment so that we can "break even" in calculating instructional costs. Our recently adopted IBBM expects accountability at the college level; however, a department such as ours – History, Philosophy, Politics, and Economics – should be able to do our part to offset losses.[1] We are responsible for teaching a wide range of general education courses, with individual sections ranging in size from 30 to 35 students. In doing so, we have maintained a strong reputation for accessibility and meeting needs of first-generation college students who might otherwise find themselves lost in large lecture halls. Our salaries are lower in comparison to those in the colleges of technology, engineering, and business, which better allows us to balance costs and revenue; still, we are encouraged to take on as many students as we can.

From its inception, online delivery of courses became a budgetary matter. University leaders saw it as an opportunity to meet changing student expectations while increasing enrollment, and in the early years some imagined instructors serving seemingly infinite numbers of students in virtual classrooms unbounded by physical space and numbers of desks. However, comparatively few faculty members embraced the new trend without raising serious questions concerning their own workloads and apprehension about student success. They wanted to ensure authentic student learning was taking place under this model, and they did not want to lose students through alienation in a virtual world. Administrators, too, became increasingly conscious of the widespread effects of low student retention, but the responsibility for course and program completion remained largely on faculty. In the field of history, instructors shared digital materials and teaching tools and found faculty-to-faculty collaboration among peers who knew, understood, and loved history very beneficial. From a department chair's perspective, it became imperative to support this newfound passion, and assign online courses to those who could teach them well. Some faculty members would resist distance education altogether, and others might try and then decide it was not for them.[2] Adapting course assignments based on talents and strengths can work for the good of the department. Now that online options are embedded, it is important for department chairs to keep three key factors in mind when providing support for faculty and students: 1) optimum class size, 2) degrees of computer literacy, and 3) measures of student learning.

Research on Class Size

The number of students in an online class can influence teaching effectiveness and student success. In traditional classroom settings, course objectives vary, and the number of students enrolled may range from just a few individuals in a seminar to a few hundred in a lecture. The objectives of online classes vary as well, influencing the optimal number of students for each section. Researchers have studied the impact of online class size to determine what is best for both students and teachers. In face-to-face learning, the size of a class is ideally influenced by the instructor who determines what types of content delivery and activities are best suited for the course. If extensive group discussion is essential, a class might be capped at 15 to 18 students. If a course is lecture based, enrollment might be much higher. Some students prefer smaller classes and some prefer larger classes, which may be a factor in guiding their enrollment choices, but class size in a traditional setting may also relate to physical space. In trying to balance budgets and redirect resources, many institutions have attempted to use the IBBM as an incentive to increase the size of traditional classes. Many administrators embraced the advent of online classes, envisioning cost-effective increases to enrollment with little impact on resources. However, faculty worked to support realistic expectations in the size of online classes as they designed courses in ways that integrated with existing workloads and best facilitated learning for students. Research across institutions indicates the average online class section enrolls between 20 and 25 students. Instructors have taught as many as 60 to 70 students with sufficient course management techniques and organizational design; however, this practice is often supported more by administrators than by teachers. Department chairs are pulled in multiple directions in their efforts to reach a common ground. A good chair will support faculty in good teaching while demonstrating to upper administration that reasonably low class size can enhance student retention.

Research has shown that the demands of online teaching can be greater than those in traditional teaching and that faculty are justified in their requests for support in course development and in keeping enrollment to under 30 students. Studies such as Anymir Orellana's article "Class Size and Interaction in Online Courses" also show that online classes with high levels of interaction should be kept to an average of 16 students. Students in online classes can access material in a variety of ways – through readings, audio and visual media, lectures, and more. From this perspective, class size is not a factor. Where class size can play a significant role is in grading, discussion, and similar activities. Instructors often use discussion boards in online classes to stimulate student interaction and learning from one another.[3] Studies have shown that when classes are too large, students can be overwhelmed with the amount of information posted by classmates. When classes are too small, with fewer than ten students, discussions can be limited and lack diversity. If needed, instructors can divide larger numbers of students into smaller groups so that they may complete assignments and projects more effectively. Organizational strategies based on teaching experience or shared experiences of others can aid in determining optimal group size structured within larger classes. The creation of smaller groups within a larger class often results in greater in-depth learning. The American Association of University Professors (AAUP) has recommended that the size of a distance education class be determined based on pedagogical considerations. In addition, the AAUP suggests that faculty teaching large sections be compensated accordingly. Class size is not the only determining factor in the level of interaction among students and student success. Accreditation and quality assurance measures do take into consideration the relationship between class size and the value of the course.

It is often believed that teaching online courses is less demanding than teaching in a traditional classroom setting, but research shows that is not the case. It has been estimated that an online course may require anywhere from 15% to 45% more time in developing instructional content and teacher–student interaction. Much of this higher demand is related to class size. Assessment of online learning does not take place through observation in a physical classroom, so online courses generally require students to complete more assignments, exams, and discussion. Each of these requires grading, and each additional student requires the time devoted to grading. Even more critical is teacher–student interaction. To convey information to students, answer individual questions, respond to comments, and advise, instructors most often rely on email and discussion board threads. These generally require additional time and attention across a broader span of time during each week than a once-a-week or twice-a-week class would require of an instructor, and larger classes add significantly more time. Synchronous communication via group chats may save time but can only be achieved effectively with a comparatively small class. Asynchronous learning is more common, with students interacting and completing assignments on varying schedules. In these cases, the time spent teaching can be even greater, making class size a more critical factor. In considering instructor workload, it has been concluded that online classes should be smaller than traditional classes. At the same time, some recent research indicates that the pressures of online teaching may reflect instructors' inexperience and unfamiliarity with technology and online techniques in their early attempts. Once they master the technology and become more comfortable with teaching online, larger classes may be managed with less impact on workload.[4]

Computer Literacy

Over the last few decades, broader foundational literacy in the areas of technology, word processing programs, email, keyboarding, and internet surfing made it possible to communicate and share information online, increasing the number of online education courses and programs. In such courses and programs, basic computer skills are applied frequently, but students are also expected to engage by using more complex skills by adding to discussion boards, blogs, journals, and peer assessment activities. Their ability to learn these new applications is an indication of their computer literacy level, and ongoing use of these applications will in turn enhance their literacy. Computer literacy levels can affect a student's successful completion of online courses.

Literacy levels and perceived literacy levels can even influence enrollment, as students may resist online education and opt for traditional face-to-face courses where they have more experience. However, computer literacy is improving among students in ways that parallel the growing prevalence of online learning opportunities. In addition, many more students are entering online courses having been accustomed to computer use for their entire lives.

History department chairs should work to support faculty who experiment with enhanced technology in their courses. Many early online courses were developed by faculty in technology disciplines or in the instructional technology sectors of pedagogical studies. Within these areas, instructors were educated in the use of computers and applications in teaching, and as frontrunners, they were often more naturally inclined toward technology. Their computer literacy advanced easily as technology advanced. As online education grew, however, instructors in other disciplines – the humanities and social sciences, liberal arts, business, and nursing, for example – experimented with course development in their respective content areas. In the process, computer literacy improved among faculty in a wide variety of specialties. This literacy was followed by the digitization and digital supplementation of more traditional subjects. While many of these instructors had been comfortable in using computer technology to facilitate their own personal and professional lives, they often felt the need to improve their skills before creating online courses. Online courses can include applications that are unique to digital instruction delivery, and mastering those applications requires additional time and financial resources in faculty support and professional development. In addition, experienced faculty often spent years developing courses with detailed learning objectives, activities, assignments, and assessments designed for traditional classrooms, and adapting courses for online delivery requires a different approach.[5]

Workshops, online tools, release time, and monetary incentives should be put into place to support faculty in developing computer literacy when institutions see the value in expanding their offering of high-quality online courses. Courses often require the application of basic skills such as using email and search engines, and additional literacy needs can be discipline specific and dependent on instructors' creativity in course design. Importantly, instructors should be required to master online course delivery platforms to develop and teach their courses. As tools are added to new versions of the platforms, instructors must be comfortable in learning those adopted by their institutions. Choosing which tools to use and how to incorporate them into course designs – calendars, grading centers, blogs, journals, and discussion groups, for example – generally remains within the discretion of faculty members who are empowered to develop courses as they see fit. However, the decision to adopt a new version of an existing platform or an entirely different platform takes place at an institutional administration level. Faculty who feel most comfortable in navigating the systems and experimenting with tools available in an effort to enhance student learning will experience greater success and satisfaction. In this respect, computer literacy relates not only to a level of knowledge or ability to apply specific skills efficiently and effectively but also to the comfort level with which an instructor approaches online teaching while new technologies become available.

Increasingly, students begin an online course well prepared with digital knowledge because they were born into a world where computers are used on a daily basis. Researchers often refer to these students as "digital natives," versus those "digital immigrants" who were born into a non-digitized world and must take direct, practical steps to learn new skills. While newcomers to online learning may enroll in an online class with some trepidation regarding learning objectives, course design, or their own capacity for time management, digital natives often assume that they have the computer skills necessary to complete their classes successfully. However, their computer literacy has largely been acquired outside of formal education. Therefore, there may be unforeseen limits to their computer abilities – mastery of Snapchat does not guarantee comfort with Blackboard. Digital natives are accustomed to navigating the web quickly and easily, though often superficially, for content that interests them. They may not yet have utilized library databases to find information appropriate for university-level research. They may have created Word documents required for writing courses and printed them out for submission but may have not yet uploaded essays through a system used in online courses. They may have had the freedom to search online in efforts to gain answers to their own questions but are not yet familiar with an instructor's use of browser lockdown software, which prohibits students from searching for answers during an online exam. For digital immigrants, the acquisition of these and related new literacies may pose additional challenges.[6]

Keyboarding, or typing on a computer keyboard, may be basic, but it is also a component of computer literacy. Not only are students composing digitally; they are also expected to learn and understand the various special functions available on a computer keyboard. Students' keyboarding skills vary as well, just as their handwriting skills would vary in a traditional face-to-face class. In a traditional setting, instructors' expectations for writing quality, spelling, grammar, punctuation, and composition might be lower for an in-class, timed essay exam than they would be for a report completed at home with ample time for outlines, drafts, proofreading, and editing. The same may hold true for students' keyboarding skills in submitting discussion board responses versus a prepared composition. It is up to the instructor to determine what level of formatting is required for a submitted assignment, and quickly composed responses will demonstrate variations in students' capacities for using a computer keyboard. In addition, students are increasingly using voice to text technology to compose writing assignments, introducing an even greater chance for error. Instructors must remind students that there are differences between writing and speaking when conveying information articulately, and using voice to text can hinder this.

Faculty members who have been teaching for some time in traditional classroom settings before entering the world of online education often assume all students are computer literate and will engage easily in their classes free of technical obstacles and with little frustration. This is not always the case. Students must be introduced to the computer tools necessary for successful learning in online courses, and they must be given clear instructions to perform well. In early attempts at creating online courses and programs, developers considered the benefits of requiring successful completion of a computer skills course before enrolling in any other online course. In recent years, however, this seems a more outdated approach, as students enter higher education programs with an array of past experience in using computers.

There continues to be a significant degree of disparity in computer literacy based on economic class, location, and age, a phenomenon often referred to as the digital divide. Much of the disparity parallels that of access related to hardware, infrastructure, and internet availability. Because technology is scarce in less developed regions of the world and among the poor in some developed nations, computer access has been limited and, as a result, so has computer literacy. This can cause added hardship, as students living in remote geographical areas or with inadequate financial resources for traditional education can benefit significantly from online courses. Improving access, and subsequently literacy, can have a critical impact on their ability to attain individual educational success and expand a region's overall educational level. Disparity in literacy related to age is less likely to depend on economic class or access to hardware, infrastructure, or internet availability. Rather, it is usually based on generational differences in experience and attitudes. These affect not only computer literacy but also the larger classification of digital literacy, which includes the efficient and effective use of smartphones. Older learners are considered digital immigrants and might be more hesitant to enroll in online courses if they lack confidence in their ability to navigate and utilize a system in ways that will support success.

History department chairs recognize that the greater demand for online courses is at the survey level. These courses fulfill general education and college core requirements and are often taken by non-majors and those returning to university studies after some time. As a result, chairs should focus on scheduling classes with optimum size and supporting computer literacy with an eye toward success whenever possible. Students across the history survey courses – face-to-face and online – deserve greater attention to some of these basic concepts and strategies if they can aid in their success. The greater onus is on online instructors, as the medium presents some obstacles to interpersonal communication when conveying these. In subsequent semesters, implementation, data collection, reflection, and revisitation can change the way we teach. Sharing findings with faculty in other disciplines across the college and university to see a greater impact may have long-term effects on an institution. Department chairs can support faculty through these processes and in fostering collaborations by compensating with money and/or time.

In addition, department chairs can benefit greatly from data collected through offices of institutional research to determine student success among courses delivered online. However, much depends on the size of the institution and the commitment to collecting data at a department level. Department chairs and other administrators must keep in mind extenuating costs of preparing students to succeed through assuring digital literacy and support of faculty in effective course design. Adding an inordinate number of sections can transform the nature of a college or university into something more comparable to an online institution. For "brick and mortar" schools it can be difficult to determine where that tipping point might be if not regulated by a credentialling body. The presence of Covid and pressures in transitioning to remote learning suggested to many that institutions of higher learning might never be the same. As historians, we understand consistently that there are many factors which contribute to change, and scholars of the future should be able to make greater sense of our times than we can. However, it is unlikely that young people from the ages of 18 to 20, or more non-traditional students for that matter, will forsake face-to-face classroom experiences altogether.

Notes

1 Budget-mindedness has driven department restructuring and consolidation in many cases. This is true in our case, where over the past decade the department has transitioned from History and Political Science, to History, Political Science, and Economics, to History and Philosophy, to History, Philosophy, Politics, and Economics.
2 This was the standard until the pandemic of 2020 forced all instruction online.
3 Orellana, Anymir. "Class Size and Interaction in Online Courses," *Quarterly Review of Distance Education 7*, no. *3* (2006): 236–242.
4 See Tomei, Lawrence A. "Impact of Online Teaching on Faculty Load: Computing the Ideal Class Size for Online Courses," *Journal of Technology and Teacher Education 14*, no. *3* (2006): 531–541; and Taft, Susan H., Tracy Perkowski, and Lorene S. Martin. "A Framework for Evaluating Class Size In Online Education," *Quarterly Review of Distance Education 12*, no. *3* (2011): 181–197.
5 See Ting, Yu-Liang. "Tapping Into Students' Digital Literacy and Designing Negotiated Learning to Promote Learner Autonomy," *The Internet and Higher Education 26* (2015): 25–32.
6 Jacobs, Gloria E., et al. "Production and Consumption: A Closer Look at Adult Digital Literacy Acquisition," *Journal of Adolescent and Adult Literacy 57*, no. *8* (2014): 624–627.

Chapter 4

Advising Online History Majors

Chrystal Goudsouzian and Amanda Lee Savage

Unlike history professors, who guide students through a particular period or theme in the past, history advisors are the stewards of each student's learning experiences throughout their collegiate journey. History advisors introduce their advisees not only to the practices, expectations, and resources of higher education but also to the study of history and the culture of their academic departments. They maintain open lines of communication with their advisees to facilitate continuous engagement and community building. History advisors help to situate students in their departmental home base and show them that it is the place to question, develop, and thrive.

But what happens when that departmental home base is virtual? Online history majors may never set foot on the physical campus of the university. They cannot visit the brick-and-mortar library, hang out in the student union, or grab a coffee with a classmate. They cannot visit their professors in their offices or drop by to see their advisors. Online students are more likely to feel disconnected from and underserved by their institutions of higher learning. How can history advisors meet the needs of their online majors in a virtual environment? Online teaching, as we know, should not replicate the classroom environment. Online advising, likewise, should not mirror on-the-ground practices. Rather, it should adapt an existing departmental advising model that serves to address the unique needs of remote students.

The developmental advising model is a natural fit for history advisors and their students, and it is relatively easily tailored to the online advising environment.[1] First introduced in the early 1970s by B. Crookston, developmental advising is focused on the process of developing the whole student.[2] Under this model, advisors move away from a "prescriptive" relationship where "the advisor is the doctor and the advisee the patient."[3] Prescriptive advising positions the advisor as the authority figure and problem solver; developmental advising, conversely, positions the advisor as a guide for both the advisee's higher education journey and for their path of self-discovery.[4] Developmental advisors encourage advisees to ask open-ended questions, use university resources to find answers, and plan courses of study and schedules around the outcomes of their explorations."[5] Like study in the humanities, a developmental advising

DOI: 10.4324/9781003258414-6

experience pushes the student not to plan for a particular career, but to develop their educational interests so they may better place themselves in society and achieve a fulfilling life.[6]

The developmental advising model recognizes that students need to have positive interactions in the campus environment to engender a sense of educational belonging, confidence, and satisfaction.[7] When the campus environment is virtual, the developmental model must be adapted to suit the specific needs of online students. As online history majors embark on an educational journey similar to, but unique from, their on-campus peers, academic advisors must work to understand this particular student group to help close the distance felt by "distance learners."

Your Online Advisees: Knowing the Profile, Opening Pathways to Success

Online learning options have made higher education more accessible, and more students are completing four-year degrees as a result.[8] Online history majors are very rarely first-time freshmen; they are often adult students, or what we now call "post-traditional students."[9] To be classified as post-traditional, students meet one or more of the following requirements: entry to college delayed by at least one year; having dependents; being a single parent; being employed full-time; being financially independent; attending college or university part-time; or not having a high-school diploma.[10] It also seems prudent to add active military members and student veterans to this list. In addition to being "post-traditional," often these learners are also transfer students, many of whom have completed previous coursework face-to-face at an on-the-ground institution. Transitioning not just to a new university, but also to an entirely online environment is a daunting task for even the most digitally savvy students.[11] Advising literature is thick with studies and recommendations for how academic advisors can best serve these students, but little attention has been paid to the ways that overlapping identities affect students in the online environment.

Schlossberg's 4-S model for assessing transitions is particularly helpful when talking to potential or new online history majors. Advisors can work with students to evaluate the "4-S's"—situation, self, support, and strategies—before they ever enter the virtual classroom. This self-assessment helps advisees set realistic goals and manage expectations. Through this evaluation, advisors are given the opportunity to provide information on campus and departmental resources while identifying barriers that they can help the student break down. More important, advisors can make clear those barriers that the student will need to overcome on their own.[12] This means of assessment not only pushes the student to introspection and self-management, but also provides the advisor an opportunity to lay out appropriate boundaries in the advisor–advisee relationship. Post-traditional students often "prefer self-direction" and often "bring a vast reservoir of experience"[13] to their studies. When advisors play an early, active role in planning for their educational success, these students meet it with interest and action. The process also builds student confidence and competence, while establishing a relationship of trust between advisor and advisee early in the advising process.

Advisors of online history majors also need to clearly articulate the types of obstacles and potential misunderstandings presented by both the online environment itself and the time requirements of virtual historical study. For example, an adult transfer student with a family might struggle to assess their actual availability for learning if they do not know how much time an online upper-division history class will take. Asynchronous learning can be deceptive in that regard for all students, but fully online programs often market themselves as flexible degrees that work around a remote student's schedule and life. But there is a difference between having a scheduling conflict for a class and having no time in your schedule for a class.[14] Online students are rarely told, or taught, to adequately plan for the work that accompanies learning. The reading requirements and writing-intensive nature of history and other humanities courses often act as a multiplier for existing time management issues. Helping prospective or newly matriculated online history majors understand how the online environment works, and the time different types of online classes require, is essential for their success.

Orienting Online History Majors

When your online students "arrive" for their virtual degree program, they rarely encounter any fanfare. Unlike the centrally organized, on-campus programming that is put on to orient first-year students or new transfer students, the orientation of online majors is often left to individual academic departments. While this lack of attention to online students creates additional labor for academic advisors, it also provides an opportunity to introduce your advisees not just to your institution, but also to your department and to their new community of peer and mentor historians. Scheduled meetings, accessible information, frequent communication, and assorted opportunities for engagement with other majors and faculty all help to situate students within their virtual departmental home base.

An online history major's first advising appointment should be scheduled shortly after admission to your program. Quick contact is preferable since online students often feel adrift until they meet with their departmental advisor. Once you receive a new student's contact information, reach out with a friendly welcome email. This email should provide a list of helpful links for students to peruse, including the undergraduate section of your department website and your department's social media accounts. Ask students to consult the resources and produce a list of questions about the university and the department. Finally, be sure to ask the student to nail down a particular time for an orientation advising meeting via phone, Zoom, or Skype. If the student is unable to meet in real time, and instead prefers to do advising via email exchange, make sure that this digital exchange is scheduled for a specific day and time. Scheduled meetings, even if for email advising, allow online students to anticipate when they will get the information they need. Having the student prepare questions in advance of the meeting or email exchange pushes them learn the digital resources at their disposal and helps to minimize the volume of clarification emails needed after the appointment.

During the first meeting with a new online advisee, communicate your advising model and set realistic expectations for the advisor–advisee relationship. Since advisors do not have the asynchrony to their workdays that online students have to their schooldays, be clear about departmental advising schedules and advisor availability. Respond to students within 24–48 hours, but do not feel compelled to respond when away from work or on vacation. Respecting your own personal time, and training students to do so as well, reinforces healthy attitudes regarding work/life boundaries and eliminates the expectation of instant communication. Scheduling hours to respond to advising emails and/or hosting virtual office hours will help minimize some of the communication traffic that occurs when advising entirely online students. These scheduled points of interaction also show advisees that you carve out specific time to address their needs and concerns.

Crafting the Virtual Home Base and a Sense of Community

Once online history majors are oriented to the department, and expectations are clear for the advisor–advisee relationship, advisors should plan to meet with online advisees at least once a semester, if not more, to discuss degree progress, class choices, personal and professional interests, and opportunities for growth, support, and development. Outside of these one-on-one appointments, history advisors should communicate with their advisees as a group in a variety of ways. Departments with online degree students need to have a strong online presence. This presence includes a well-organized and up-to-date website, engaging emails, and active social media accounts. You should make efforts to get all undergraduate programming—such as lectures, info sessions, and student organization meetings—live-streamed or posted after the events in video format with closed captioning. The appearance, organization, and accessibility of your digital department are critical to communicating with your students and crafting their virtual departmental home base.

Your website is the window to your department; it should look clean, modern, and organized. All links should be checked periodically to ensure they are up-to-date. The undergraduate portion of your departmental page is particularly important for online majors and should include your undergraduate mission and vision, a link to faculty profiles, your upcoming classes and community events, your full course catalog, contact information for academic advisor(s), career center and career pathways information, and history major enrichment opportunities such as internships, study abroad, honors programs, directed research, and departmental tutoring. Links to your history student groups, honors societies, and social media accounts are also vital. Advisors should make frequent use of the website during advising; driving online majors to the website makes students active seekers and retrievers of information. This helps them better navigate the university's websites overall and increases their information independence.

All pages on your website should be ADA compliant—this is non-negotiable. (See Chapter 2 for more on this topic.) Not only is it the law, but students with disabilities are one of the fastest-growing populations served by online learning, and a population for whom the digital environment has the potential to provide significant benefits. Likewise, the materials you use to advise should also be compliant for students with disabilities. Everything should be accessible: videos should have captions, images should have appropriate descriptions, and written content should use headings. Accessibility and compliance demonstrate your department's commitment to inclusivity and eliminate barriers for students of all learning types.

Engaging history students frequently via an "all majors" email with information for both on-campus and online students fosters a sense of connection, while keeping students up-to-date with university and department deadlines, opportunities, and events. While email is often a one-way form of communication, a weekly or bi-weekly email practice serves as a consistent point of communication on which all majors can come to rely. It is also an expression of advisor care that strengthens the developmental relationship between advisor and advisee. Students appreciate being prompted, pushed, and supported so they can make the best decisions based on their individual needs and interests. Reminding majors that deadlines for class changes, financial aid, or scholarships are approaching reinforces the idea that advisors have students' broader educational success at the center of their advising practice. Sharing opportunities from potential employers, internship hosts, and study abroad partners displays the advisor's commitment to encouraging students' self-discovery and professional development. Creating and promoting undergraduate events that are both on-campus and virtual shows students that the department is committed to building intellectual community in both settings for all its majors. The weekly email also often serves as a catalyst for continued dialogue; it provides an opening for students who may not have reached out otherwise. Particularly for online students, who can feel isolated or adrift, the weekly email not only serves as a needed departmental check-in, but also reminds the student that the advisor is open and available for engagement within the virtual setting.

Student-centered departmental social media accounts are another integral part of advisor–student digital communication. Social media platforms provide visually stimulating and socially dynamic settings for advisors to craft a virtual home base for their advisees. While social media posts often communicate the same information as the weekly emails, they do so in a less formal and more interactive format. Links, images, and videos allow students to engage with the department and advisors in shorter, more frequent bursts; these posts meet the student in their own preferred virtual social setting. Since students can quickly "like," comment on, and share posts, the platforms allow them to both observe and shape their department's culture. These points of engagement and conversation can help breed feelings of belonging for students and increase their comfort with their department and its members.[15]

While connection via social media is an important part of any department's advising practice, these platforms are essential to building community for online history majors. Not only can online students get information and access to events on social media, but social media posts also provide an opportunity for low-stakes interactions with peers, advisors, and faculty that online majors would not be able to access otherwise. An online student might not be able to joke around with peers after class, but they can comment on a historical meme! They might not be able to chat with their professor after class, but they can attend their professor's streamed event and ask questions in the chat. Because online majors come from various backgrounds, age groups, and abilities, it is particularly important to post on a wide range of social platforms for broad access and engagement opportunities for this student group.

If your history department does not already have departmental and/or student group accounts on Facebook, Instagram, YouTube, and TikTok, starting some, or all, of these accounts is highly recommended. Facebook is an excellent platform for sharing discipline-specific news and departmental events; it also offers a means to live-stream events for online students or students who cannot be on campus at the time of the event. Instagram is well-suited for sharing marketing images for departmental talks, student and faculty profiles, and advertising upcoming courses. YouTube provides a great repository for lectures and information sessions that your department hosts for students; online students especially benefit from being able to view these programs on their own schedule. TikTok is a student favorite for micro-interactions. The quick nature and levity of TikTok videos brings students inside the virtual home base. The videos play into already existing trends and soundbites, which helps students relate to the department and gives them a shared language, set of jokes, and experiences that make the majors feel connected to their educational community.

A history-focused student group is another excellent way to foster undergraduate community and engage majors of all types. If your department does not currently have a student history group, we strongly encourage you to rally your students to start one. Student-driven programs and social events help strengthen student bonds and give majors a place to engage in talk about history. If your student group does not already include online majors in its membership, it is essential to encourage the group to think carefully about how online majors can contribute to the organization. Isolate a few roles that can be done by entirely online students and reserve those positions for them.[16] Have the group stream their meetings and events so online majors can attend. Encourage the group to communicate through texting apps such as GroupMe, which allows all majors to engage in banter with one another from anywhere and everywhere!

Also, be sure to connect your virtual advisees to additional registered student organizations (RSOs) that are within their interest areas. If it turns out that an RSO does not have online roles or streamed events, see if the group might consider adding them for your online majors. Your college or university's Office of Multicultural Affairs, Veterans Affairs, Disability Resource Office, and Counseling Center are additional places of connection and support that you may want to recommend to your online majors. If the events and services of those offices do not seem accessible to your online students, be sure to reach out and prompt those offices to offer virtual access. It is important to remember that history majors do not cease to have identities and interests, simply because they are online.

Professionalizing Online History Majors

Developmental advisors help advisees to identify their personal and professional interests and guide them towards educational opportunities, experiences, and programming that prepare them to find their place in society and pursue career paths that bring them joy and satisfaction. History advisors who follow this model, then, point students to internships, individual research projects, and professional workshops and events. These points of participation may originate within the department, or they may be found outside its bounds. While these experiences and events are widely accessible for on-campus/local students, advisors of online history majors must commit themselves to offering equitable and accessible pathways for participation in these growth opportunities for their online students.

Internships are an excellent way for history majors to try out different careers and to cultivate their historical thinking, writing, and oral communication skills. Whether working in an archive, museum, or nonprofit, these internship experiences help students decide what they may want (or not want) to do for professional work upon graduation. If your college or university or department has an internship office or coordinator, it is important to work with this office or individual to identify digital history internships and other virtual internship positions open to online history or humanities majors.[17] It is also essential to remember that online students do not have to experience all their learning in an exclusively virtual environment. Advisors should encourage their online majors to seek out local internship opportunities and help them find appropriate locations, institutions, and professionals with whom they might work. Training students to make these professional contacts is a practical way to impart soft skills while working towards a concrete goal. Wide-ranging student internship placements also allow your department to broaden its regional, or even national, reach.

History advisors should also work to match advisees with faculty members who teach a period or theme in the student's main area of historical interest. Ideally, each history major will then follow a particular professor through their upper-level classes and have an additional mentor in the department on whom they can rely. This professional relationship is essential for majors who would like to author senior theses and/or pursue graduate school in the discipline of history. Facilitating these relationships for online students, especially those who would like to take directed research courses, is especially important.[18] Often, online students are told that it is impossible to do independent research projects with faculty, and some faculty have been conditioned to believe that directing research online is too difficult. Both perceptions discredit the online environment and remote history majors. Online history majors can use online databases for primary source material, check out digital copies of monographs through the university library, and use their student status to conduct research at their local institutions.[19] Advocating for research opportunities for your online majors helps show faculty that this student group is able to conduct and complete sophisticated research projects, while helping students prepare for graduate work.

Departmental advisors should create personal development workshops for history majors and stay abreast of relevant information sessions and workshops in the broader campus that fit the interests of their advisees. Departmentally sponsored events that allow current majors to interface with recent program alumni are particularly helpful for investigating post-graduate pathways. History majors also benefit from co-sponsored sessions that focus on topics such as teaching careers, law school, or graduate school in the humanities. Making these departmental and co-hosted events accessible to online majors through live-streaming and session recording/posting is easy and essential. Larger university-sponsored events such as career and graduate school fairs are just as relevant to remote students as to campus students. When advisors become aware of these events, they should reach out to the program host to inquire about online accessibility and ensure the university provides equitable attendance options to its on-the-ground and online student groups. Being an active opportunity advocate for your department's online student major population is a necessary part of being an effective developmental advisor.

Notes

1 For an overview of definitions of the developmental advising model, see Bloom, J. "Developmental Advising Definitions." NACADA Clearinghouse of Academic Advising Resources, March 20, 2014. https://nacada.ksu.edu/Resources/Clearinghouse/View-Articles/Developmental-advising-definitions.aspx. Accessed July 23, 2022

2 Crookston, B.B. "A Developmental View of Academic Advising as Teaching." *NACADA Journal 14*, no. 2 (1994): 5. Article reprinted from *Journal of College Student Personnel 13* (1972): 12–17.
3 Ibid.
4 The prescriptive advising model is particularly unhelpful in a virtual setting. Establishing a one-way line of engagement between advisor and student inhibits relationship building, especially when facilitated over email and phone. Online students are even less likely than their on-campus peers to reach out and/or question prescriptive advisors. The prescriptive relationship hinders student growth opportunity and hampers student proactivity.
5 Frost, S.H. "Advising Alliances: Sharing Responsibility for Student Success." *NACADA Journal 14*, no. 2 (1994): 56.
6 Ibid., 55.
7 King, M. "Developmental Academic Advising." *NACADA Clearinghouse of Academic Advising Resources*. November 5, 2012. https://nacada.ksu.edu/Resources/Clearinghouse/View-Articles/Developmental-Academic-Advising.aspx. Accessed November 22, 2022.
8 Wavle, S. and G. Ozogul. "Investigating the Impact of Online Classes on Undergraduate Degree Completion." *Online Learning Journal 23*, no. 4 (2019): 281–295.
9 In a 2020 report of online college students, A.J. Magada, D. Capranos, and C.B. Aslanian reported that 87% of students came to online undergraduate programs with transfer credit and roughly half of those students had been out of school for five or more years. The credits transferred often came from one to two institutions and were generally from on-the-ground programs. For more see Magada, A.J., D. Capranos, and C.B. Aslanian. *Online College Students 2020: Comprehensive Data on Demands and Preferences.* Louisville, KY: Wiley Education Services, 2020. https://universityservices.wiley.com/wp-content/uploads/2020/06/OCS2020Report-ONLINE-FINAL.pdf.
10 Ross-Gordon, J.M. "Research on Adult Learners: Supporting the Needs of a Student Population that Is No Longer Nontraditional." *Peer Review 13*, no. 1 (2011): 26–29.
11 Advising to avoid "transfer shock" is important for those students transitioning from on-the-ground to online learning. Studies recommend that advisors share information about transfer shock with advisees early in the advising process. In certain cases, they recommend that these students take a lower course load their first term. For more, see Karmelita, C. "Advising Adult Learners during the Transition to College." *NACADA Journal 40*, no. 1 (2020): 64–77.
12 Anderson, M., J. Goodman, and N. Schlossberg. *Counseling Adults in Transition: Linking Schlossberg's Theory with Practice in a Diverse World*, 4th ed. New York: Springer, 2012.
13 Ross-Gordon, "Research on Adult Learners."
14 Be prepared to support your students' needs when they choose to make decisions that are best for their unique learning situation, even when those choices are not best for your institution's bottom line. Many colleges and universities, for example, are pressured to graduate students in four-year cohorts and insist that students take a minimum of 15–18 credit hours per semester. Suggesting that an online student progress towards their degree more slowly might be best for the advisee, even if it is not best for your institution's statistics.
15 It is also important to note that social media platforms not only help advisors craft departmental identity and foster virtual community, but also help advisors better understand their students. Social media creates a more democratic space for students to engage in discourse about their department and the discipline of history.

Student engagement on departmental posts helps advisors see what interests and excites students. These comments can help with future programming and often inform advisors about student concerns and issues. Since students tend to feel more comfortable and empowered on these platforms, being able to absorb this multiplicity of voices can be helpful not just to advocate for students, but also to use their input to spark change and encourage inclusion in your department.

16 A student-driven social media account with multiple authors is one easy way to bring online students into your student organization.

17 If this support is not offered at your institution, finding these opportunities might fall to you as the online advisor.

18 It is worth noting that this is difficult to facilitate for online students in history departments that do not adhere to a regular and predictable schedule of online courses taught by full-time faculty.

19 Learn what borrowing privileges your majors can enjoy at your home institution and help them navigate their local options for obtaining historical research materials. Some school libraries allow online students to have interlibrary loan materials sent to their homes for use. In many cases, a university ID can grant remote students access to a library at a local institution of higher learning. Students may also be able to use interlibrary loan services through their local library.

Chapter 5

Working with Publisher-Produced Material

David L. Toye

College instructors typically design history survey courses that organize class lectures, activities such as class discussions, and assignments around their own intellectual interests and research. The assigned textbooks for these courses align with these interests, include primary sources, and provide supplementary resources such as maps and images. In online courses, instructors can still personalize their survey course through recorded PowerPoint presentations or video lectures, but the informal interaction and engagement with students of the traditional classroom is absent. The assigned textbook in online courses can be a tool to provide some of this missing interaction and engagement. Textbook book publishers such as Pearson and Cengage have created digital textbooks and programs (Revel and MindTap),[1] which include assessments that do engage students with the course material. In what follows, we will be examining these publisher-produced materials and discussing how instructors can incorporate these materials into their online courses. We will also evaluate their pedagogical benefits and explore an alternative to such publisher-produced materials, open educational resources (OER).

Publishers of digital textbooks break down the material one would typically find in a traditional, hard copy textbook chapter into small segments and then assess students' understanding of each segment with a brief quiz. Students can click on these segments in these digital texts on their computer or mobile device and navigate through the text, which may include maps, images, and excerpts from primary sources. The quizzes are computer graded automatically, and students can see their scores immediately. Students can have the option of completing these quizzes multiple times to improve their scores. These assessments may include multiple choice, matching, and true/false questions. Publishers also include open-ended questions, requiring students to write a response, which instructors can review. These digital texts also provide students with instant feedback regarding their performance on these quizzes. In Cengage's MindTap digital text, *The Enduring Vision, A History of the American People*, for example, a textbox pops up and accompanies each quiz question after it is answered, which provides an explanation for the correct answer to that question.

DOI: 10.4324/9781003258414-7

In the traditional classroom, the instructor can stress key points in the course material that students should note as they prepare for assessments. In an online course, these opportunities for the instructor to highlight this content are not as extensive. The quizzes in these digital texts can therefore serve to fill this void and underline certain key concepts. In choosing a digital textbook for a course, instructors should ensure that the quizzes in these texts review and highlight material that is consistent with their course design.

Publishers of digital textbooks also provide instructors with tools to measure student performance on these quizzes as well as their engagement with the textbook content. Instructors can access students' scores on the quizzes and discover how much time each student spent reading each chapter and completing the quizzes. These digital textbooks also offer data to instructors concerning the average scores of the entire class on each quiz as well as the dates when individual students accessed the digital text and whether their scores on these quizzes are trending higher or lower. In the traditional class, an instructor can measure student engagement simply by monitoring which students are regularly attending class and participating in class activities and discussions. In the case of online courses without any synchronous online class meetings, instructors cannot measure student engagement through this simple process. This data provided by these digital texts, however, informs the instructor which students are accessing the course material and whether they comprehend this content based on their quiz scores.

Instructors can use this data to measure students' interest and engagement with course content as well as their understanding of this material, so that instructors can take corrective action. In a traditional face-to-face classroom, instructors can deduce that students are losing focus through observation. Under such circumstances, instructors take action on the spot to redirect the students' focus onto the course content. They may recount some strange, exotic historical tale, associated with course content, which may spark students' interest, or ask the students in group discussions to relate the course content to some contemporary issue that is relevant to the students. In online courses, such strategies to retain student engagement are not available. Instructors, however, can analyze the data on the quizzes in the digital text and determine if students are completing and performing well on these assessments. Instructors can then direct students' attention to that course material, which students are ignoring or not understanding based on the outcomes of these assessments. For example, instructors could observe that a number of students in an online United States history survey course were either not completing or doing poorly on the chapter quizzes concerning westward expansion and the Mexican War. In response, instructors could post articles on this subject in the announcements page of the online course or send these articles by email to students to direct attention to this topic. The intent of this action would be to pique student interest in the topic through these articles and remind students that they would encounter this subject matter on a future exam.

Navigating through and interpreting the quiz data provided by these digital texts may be more challenging to some history instructors. Fortunately, the publishers of digital texts do provide resources and personnel to facilitate instructors' use of these programs. Instructors may contact the publishers' designated representatives by phone or email to request assistance. These representatives on occasion meet in person with faculty on their college campuses to demonstrate how to set up and utilize their digital texts for college courses. Publishers also host webinars to provide instructors with tips and suggestions on how to make the most effective use of these programs.

After becoming familiar with how these programs operate, instructors can integrate these programs easily into their own courses. Instructors are able also to arrange the content of these textbooks to align with their courses' particular design. For example, in Cengage's *The Enduring Vision, A History of the American People*, instructors could move the section on the French and Indian Wars, "Triumph and Tensions: The British Empire, 1750–1763" from the chapter on the Revolutionary War to the chapter on Colonial America. The instructors' focus is thus on how this conflict reflects Colonial America's place in the British Empire.

Another instructor, however, may desire to retain this section in the chapter on the Revolutionary War, emphasizing instead this conflict's role in creating the political and economic conditions prior to the outbreak of the Revolutionary War. Instructors in this same textbook may also rearrange the order of entire chapters. This is an option with most publisher-produced material, however, it is a good idea to check with your publisher's representative about these options prior to adopting their material. Instructors also have the option of setting due dates for the completion of the assessments associated with the textbook chapters. Consequently, instructors prompt their students to read the textbook chapters and to complete the assessments synchronously with the instructors' own online course lectures and lessons, which complement this material and supplement it. After aligning the textbook content with a course's particular design, instructors can create links for their personalized textbook and insert these links into their online courses through their colleges' learning management system.

Using publisher-created digital texts may alleviate certain recurring problems concerning students and textbooks in general: the failure of students to read or even "crack open" the textbook and the unproductive student tradition of "cramming" for an exam by rapidly completing all the assigned textbook readings just prior to taking that exam. Historically, students who do not read the assigned textbook material or hurriedly do so generally do not perform as well academically, whether in online or traditional face-to-face classes, as students who do complete these reading assignments at a reasonable pace. Instructors must first make clear to students that they will lose points toward their final grade by not completing the quizzes in the digital text and not earning a passing score (as defined by the instructor) by a specific due date.

Students usually will only complete class assignments if the failure to do so will have a substantial negative impact on their final grade in a course or if completing the assignments will substantially improve this final grade. Instructors can also space out the due dates for these quizzes in the weeks and months prior to a major exam, so that students are engaging with course content effectively and regularly in a piecemeal fashion rather than inefficiently engorging large chunks of this material just before the exam.

Digital texts also address another problem that students often have with textbooks: reading comprehension. Students often fail to distinguish between reading for entertainment purposes such as reading a romance novel or a comic book and reading for study purposes. Consequently, students often read textbooks passively without engaging intellectually with the material. The quizzes in digital texts immediately follow a brief section of the chapter and include questions which measure students' comprehension of that reading material. Since these assessments are computer graded automatically, students who do poorly on these assessments can go back, reread that section, and take the assessment again to see if they can improve their score. These programs therefore enable students to gauge and improve their reading comprehension.

Students usually find textbooks boring and tiresome to read, unless they possess some pre-existing interest in the subject matter. Very rarely do instructors find in perusing their students' course evaluations after the academic term is over some expression of affection for the assigned textbook. In the traditional face-to-face courses, instructors have offset tiresome textbooks with course lectures interspersed with spontaneous, humorous puns and silly, inoffensive "dad" jokes or through lively class discussion, touching on relevant, contemporary issues. In an online course, such entertaining and engaging spontaneity is not an option. Consequently, textbooks in an online course must play a larger role in engaging and retaining students' interest in the course material. Digital texts include interactive maps as well as historical images and brief videos that provide a visual context for the historical developments discussed. Textbook chapters also include links, which briefly define key terms, or open primary sources, which the textbook narrative discusses.

For example, in Pearson's Revel text, *Connections: A World History*, students first encounter a brief video outlining the chapter content and describing the port of Lisbon in the sixteenth century, when they begin to navigate through the chapter, "Global Exploration and Global Empires, 1400-1700." This chapter then weaves together maps, images, and text, providing a series of interactive maps that illustrates the voyages of major Iberian explorers together with embedded links that define terms such as "Council of the Indies." In addition, the chapter incorporates excerpts from primary sources, such as Columbus' description of his first encounter with Native Americans as well as a variety of historical images including paintings and maps from this era. With these digital texts, students also have the option of listening to an audio recording of the textbook narrative, which can be available through a smartphone app as well. All such features together may improve engagement with the subject matter, especially among the current, social media savvy generation of students, who may not retain interest in plain text.

These chapter quizzes in these digital textbooks may be especially beneficial to first-generation college students who are taking history survey courses. History instructors in these courses often include a writing component, which requires students in exams and assignments to compose essays in response to interpretive questions, which assess students' critical thinking skills. First-generation college students often lack the academic background of their peers and often struggle with course work that requires such compositions.[2] These students often have less experience in note-taking as they prepare for writing assignments. Quizzes in these digital texts reinforce key concepts and ideas for these students, which they can then incorporate into their written compositions. All students, regardless of their background, vary in their writing abilities. Quizzes in these digital texts offer students the opportunity to improve their overall grade in the course, if they are struggling with this writing component. Since students have multiple opportunities to improve their scores on these quizzes, their final score on these quizzes ultimately assesses their persistence and effort while over time improving their reading comprehension.

Digital texts also provide data regarding how much time students have spent accessing the text online. This data combined with the students' performance on the embedded quizzes can serve to document student contact hours. College accreditors still require online, asynchronous courses to have the same number of contact hours as traditional face-to-face courses. Instructors can also provide students with estimates regarding how long assigned readings should take to complete each week. For example, an instructor could report that the reading of a chapter of the digital text associated with quizzes should take x amount of time and the quizzes, y amount of time, as a guide for the average reader.

The main drawback to using this publisher-produced material, however, is their cost, especially for first-generation students, whose financial resources are often limited. Instructors may therefore choose instead to assign a free OER. An OER is a literary work available online that is in the public domain or made accessible for use by educators and students without cost since its author has licensed that work through Creative Commons (https://creativecommons.org/). Instructors have numerous OER options for survey courses, especially in United States history.[3] All these OER online textbooks include maps, images, and primary sources, just like publisher-produced materials. Instructors can insert links to these OER resources directly into their online courses. Some of these OER textbooks also present to their readers review and discussion questions, but none offer computer-graded assessments as do the Revel and MindTap textbooks or analytical tools that provide data to instructors regarding the extent to which students have accessed these textbooks. Since OER resources are free for students to use, instructors may want to include an OER textbook in their online courses as an option for those students with limited financial resources, even if requiring students to purchase publisher-produced materials. OSCQR – the SUNY online course quality rubric – recommends instructors employ OER in their courses if they are available and appropriate.[4]

Reading a textbook is often a laborious task for students, but necessary, as textbooks provide a storehouse of content, which students must consult to complete college course requirements. The textbook in online courses is especially important for students to acquire course content since these students do not have regular access to instructors as in the traditional classroom setting. Publisher-produced materials such as Revel and MindTap through their assessments and analytical tools enable the instructor to establish some presence in an online course and thus stimulate student engagement with the course content.

Notes

1 The author has used Cengage and Pearson publications for survey courses for a number of years and received monetary honorariums from these companies on occasion for reviewing their textbook materials.
2 Concerning academic obstacles facing first-generation college students, see White, J. W., A. Pascale, and S. Aragon. "Collegiate Cultural Capital and Integration into the College Community." *College Student Affairs Journal 38*, no. *1* (2020): 34–52.
3 See Stanford University's The American YAWP (www.americanyawp.com), Lumen Learning's Boundless US History (https://courses.lumenlearning.com/boundless-ushistory), Rice University's OpenStax (https://openstax.org/details/books/us-history), and Georgia State University's United States History to 1877 (https://human.libretexts.org/Bookshelves/History/National_History/Book%3A_United_States_History_to_1877_(Locks_et_al.)).
4 See this website: https://oscqr.suny.edu/standard32.

Chapter 6

Instructor, University, and Other Contributors
Balancing Copyright Protections for Online Learning

Elizabeth F. Buchanan and Stephen K. Stein

Over the past couple of decades, many university history departments have added online courses to their offerings, attracting new students, and this process has accelerated over time as more universities required departments to offer online courses. This transition to online teaching provoked a host of questions ranging from technical support to payment for online course development, and added urgency to unresolved questions over the ownership of online course materials and the fair use of course materials created by others. Could universities take instructors' online courses and assign adjunct faculty to teach them? Could instructors profit from their online course materials or take them with them if they obtained a position at a different university? Could instructors show movies, assign journal articles, and provide students with other class materials in an online course the same way they did in classroom courses? What materials could they incorporate into their online courses?

This chapter addresses two substantive issues: 1) who owns and can thereby control and profit from online course materials, and 2) the responsibilities of online course developers for obtaining permission when incorporating other people's work into their courses. It reviews important issues in online course development but is not a legal opinion. Copyright law, which works to balance the rights of the author(s) and the rights of the user(s), is complex and evolving. Anyone with specific questions should seek legal advice.

Who Owns the Course Materials for an Online Class?

This section discusses the relationship between instructors who develop courses and the university for which they create and teach courses. As Carol Twigg points out, a course has several aspects, including the content (subject matter), course materials used to explain that content, a structure to lead students through the course, and student interaction (planned and spontaneous), as well as aspects managed by universities, including offering and assigning credit for courses and hosting them on a learning management system (LMS), generally subject to a contract between the provider and the university. Only some course aspects are subject to copyright protection. The general subject

DOI: 10.4324/9781003258414-8

matter and interactions with students are not subject to copyright by instructors or their universities. Course materials, which Twigg defines as "the fixed expression of ideas and resources" used to explain and convey the subject matter, and include the syllabus, lecture notes, multimedia presentations, exercises, simulations, group projects, and assessments, may be copyrightable by their authors. These generally include a mix of the instructor's original materials and materials created by others, such as textbooks, journal articles, or multimedia.[1]

While this section asks who owns the course materials, the real issue is who controls them – who decides how and when they are used and licensed for others to use. It is most useful to think of ownership as a collection of rights, which can be shared. United States copyright laws protect authorship original works, including literary, musical, dramatic, and artistic works, such as poetry, novels, movies, songs, computer software, and architecture. The law does not protect facts, ideas, systems, or methods of operation, though it may protect the ways these are expressed.[2] Copyright owners generally have the exclusive right to copy their creation; prepare derivative works; sell, lease, or lend the creation to the public; and perform or display it publicly.[3]

The creator of a work, who has translated an idea into a fixed, tangible expression, is entitled to copyright protection.[4] An important exception is work prepared within the scope of one's employment or works specially commissioned. In these cases, the employer or commissioning party, not the creator, is considered the author for purposes of copyright protection "unless the parties have expressly agreed otherwise in a written instrument signed by them."[5] Courts use several factors to determine who is an employee, including employer control over the manner, means, and time of work, the duration of employment, assignment of additional duties, and method of payment. Most full-time university instructors fit the definition of employees because they are on indefinite contracts, may be assigned additional duties, are paid salaries, and receive benefits.

How then do instructors maintain copyright protection over the articles and books they author? What about lectures and course materials they create for their courses? Traditionally, universities deemed all of these as the instructor's property.[6] Several cases decided under the 1909 Copyright Law upheld this position, including *Williams* v. *Weisser* (1969) in which a company paid a student to take detailed notes of an archaeology professor's lectures and then sold the notes. The professor sued, and the Court ruled in his favor. He, not his university, owned the copyright for lectures, because, as the Court said, "[A]s far as the teacher is concerned, neither the record in this case nor any custom known to us suggests that the university can prescribe his way of expressing the ideas he puts before his students."[7]

One of the reasons for giving copyright protection to the instructor is academic freedom. Courts have upheld principles of academic freedom defined by the American Association of University Professors and the Association of

American Colleges and Universities. Instructors have the right to freely research and publish their results, subject to the adequate performance of their other academic duties, and discuss their subject in classrooms, providing they avoid controversial matters with no relation to their subject.[8] The United States Supreme Court held, "[t]he college classroom, with its surrounding environs, is peculiarly the 'marketplace of ideas,' and we break no new constitutional ground in reaffirming this Nation's dedication to safeguarding academic freedom."[9] University ownership of faculty copyrights could potentially silence instructors and destroy the principle of academic freedom.

Congress amended copyright laws in 1976, and the 1976 Copyright Act and its amendments remain unclear as to traditional exceptions to employer copyright ownership for instructors and scholars. The few cases directly addressing the issue are split.[10] Nevertheless, most universities continue to respect faculty ownership of "scholarly and aesthetic copyrighted works." This reflects both principles of academic freedom and the lack of potential profit for most scholarly articles, books, and lecture materials. In most cases, universities have neither contributed substantial resources to faculty-produced articles and books, nor specifically commissioned particular works. Their assertion of control could also irretrievably damage their relationship with instructors.

Yet, online courses often require assistance from university technology and education specialists who help instructors develop their courses, create quizzes, polls, and other learning elements, and load courses onto university LMSs. This support strengthens universities' argument that they own the copyright to online course materials.

Since the introduction of online teaching, university deference to instructors' copyright ownership has diminished for two related reasons. First, universities are under increasing financial pressure as state funding decreases.[11] Second, there are potential profits from online classes, which can support larger class sizes, reach non-traditional students, and may be taught by low-cost or part-time instructors.[12] Even free massive open online courses (MOOCs) benefit universities by attracting students to traditional, profitable courses of study. Universities can also obtain profits from MOOCs by charging for certificates of completion.[13]

So how do course material creators determine copyright ownership of those materials? The place to start is the copyright policy of one's university. These usually assign copyright of scholarly products to the instructor-author. If the materials involved significant resources from the university, other than usual library and clerical resources, or the university specifically commissioned them, the instructor should discuss copyright ownership with the appropriate university administrators. If the university will claim an interest in the work, the course instructor should ask the university for a written agreement covering the instructor-author's use of the materials outside of the university, and how to divide any proceeds over and above normal course allocations for which the instructor is already paid. These agreements should be in writing to meet the requirements of the 1976 Copyright Act.[14]

A recent examination of copyright issues by instructors, university administrators, lawyers, copyright experts, and technology experts reached several important conclusions.[15] First, there are many ambiguous areas in determining copyright entitlements between the author and the author's employing university. The author is presumed to be the copyright owner, except when a work is a work by hire. Professors are employees of the university and so their work may fall within the work by hire exception, except that there has historically been an academic exception. Second, the 1976 Copyright Act revision may have weakened the academic exception, but it might also persist depending upon the level of university oversight of the teaching materials.[16]

The study recommended leaving copyright ownership with the instructor unless there were substantial contributions by the university and providing for standard agreements to permit the instructor to use the materials for teaching, scholarship, and research plus publication with notice. This does not directly answer the question of copyright ownership, but the focus on the authority to use and publish does provide a process for analyzing and negotiating mutually acceptable answers to the question.

What Are the Rules for Using Materials Prepared by Others in an Online Class?

One must also consider the rights of the creators of any additional materials used in a course. Instructors often assign additional articles and other materials. Fair use exceptions allow their use in the traditional classroom, but these exceptions may not apply to online courses. The fair use exception permits limited, or fair, use of a copyrighted work without receiving permission from the owner for the purposes of criticism, news reporting, teaching (including multiple copies for classroom use), scholarship, and research. Courts balance four factors to determine fair use and copyright infringement: 1) the purpose and nature of the use and whether it is for commercial or nonprofit education, 2) the nature of the copyrighted work, 3) the portion used in relation to the copyrighted work as a whole, and 4) the effect of the use on the copyrighted work's potential market or value.[17] An example of the balancing can be seen in *Harper & Row Publishers, Inc. v. Nation Enterprises* (1985). In this case, the United States Supreme Court held Nation Enterprises liable for infringement when it published excerpts of an unauthorized copy of former President Gerald Ford's autobiography in *The Nation* Magazine, causing *Time* Magazine to cancel a contract with the book's author for publishing similar excerpts.[18] *Nation* Magazine's use was commercial and supplanted *Harper & Row*'s valuable right of first publication.

Where instructors post course materials affects the fair use exception. Posting copyrighted materials on a public website requires permission from copyright holders, though courts have permitted the display of short excerpts, as the Google Book Search Project does.[19] Larger excerpts or commercial use risk copyright infringement.[20] Posting materials on a closed university LMS, limited to students taking a particular course, poses less risk.[21] Nevertheless, instructors should carefully evaluate their use of copyright-protected materials. Proper attribution of posted materials is only the first step. "While certainly ethical and satisfying the requisites necessary to avoid a charge of plagiarism," attribution is "no substitute" for obtaining the copyright owner's permission.[22]

One cannot upload entire articles, books, or movies to one's students, even if the material is confined to a university LMS. Their use is covered by the Technology, Education, and Copyright Harmonization (TEACH) Act. Advised by professors, publishers, and authors, Congress passed the TEACH Act to facilitate the performance and display of copyrighted materials for distance education by accredited, nonprofit educational institutions and governmental entities.[23]

The TEACH Act permits the display of works in a classroom, in person, or transmitted through digital means provided the performance or display is directly related to class objectives, is limited (to the extent technologically feasible) to students enrolled in the class, and the university has instituted copyright protection policies. Universities must provide information to faculty, students, and relevant staff members that accurately describes and promotes compliance with copyright laws and notifies students that course materials may be subject to copyright protection. They must also implement technological measures to reasonably prevent unauthorized dissemination and retention of copyrighted materials after course completion.[24]

There are many conditions to this complex statute, which leaves room for uncertainty. In the case of dramatic works, only reasonable and limited portions may be shown. An instructor may use clips, but not entire songs or plays. Similarly, instructors can include excerpts from articles or books, but not entire books or multiple book chapters. Reproduction, derivative works, and distribution are prohibited. The instructor may not transmit textbooks or course materials "typically purchased or acquired by students" or works developed specifically for mediated instructional activities. Commercially available educational materials must be used according to their instructions.

The use of pirated media is not protected. As a result, it may be impossible to show some films in an online class. Screening your old VHS copy of a movie no longer for sale in a traditional class is probably fine, but you may not digitize it for display to your online students. When movies are available for sale, it is best for students to rent them themselves through Amazon, Apple, Netflix, or similar services. Many university libraries subscribe to movie databases, such as Kanopy, which provide another option because use has been authorized by the provider.[25]

As Kristine Hutchinson notes, the TEACH Act leaves educational institutions three choices: 1) they can continue to rely on traditional fair use and licensing principles, 2) they can enact the requirements of the TEACH Act and rely upon it, or 3) they can use some combination of the two, implementing the requirements of the TEACH Act where possible while relying on traditional fair use practices in other cases.[26] While essentially an anti-piracy law, the Digital Millennium Copyright Act (DMCA) of 1998 is also important.[27] It increased penalties for copyright infringement on the internet and provided protections for online service providers who, having received an infringement claim, remove offending items.[28] It is relevant for online teaching because it permits the United States Librarian of Congress to issue exemptions from the law's provisions for nonprofit archival, preservation, and educational purposes, including research and scholarship.[29] Current exemptions allow college instructors to add captions and audio descriptions to address accessibility issues when accessible versions are not available and to circumvent some anti-piracy measures in order to display motion pictures (including television shows) to enrolled students for nonprofit educational purposes.[30]

The fair use doctrine balances interests between copyright owners and the nonprofit educational community. Minor uses of copyrighted materials for nonprofit educational purposes which do not significantly impact the market for the copyrighted materials should not present a problem. Unfortunately, what exactly constitutes "significant" remains unclear. Cases are subject to interpretation and decided in court. Therefore, course developers should err on the side of caution.

More significant uses must be carefully weighed, and a license obtained if possible. Textbooks and their commercial equivalents, such as course packs and films, should be obtained from authorized sources. Works in the public domain can be used according to any licenses, such as the Creative Commons license, as can most government documents and films. External links, including links to university library resources, should be provided to students for online materials, when available. These links allow course developers to clearly indicate content owned by and hosted by someone else and to use existing permissions. If the university has implemented the requirements of the TEACH Act, instructors can use copyrighted materials online consistent with its requirements. If not, instructors must rely on the fair use doctrine.

Finally, the relationship between the instructor and the LMS contractor and staff must be considered. Courseware, which includes the LMS and any other software used in the course, are also subject to copyright.[31] The university signed a license with the LMS provider, and this license describes who owns what in the system. Instructors should not assume they can move their entire course to another university. Portions of the course will be managed differently. Syllabi, lecture notes, and comparable items will probably migrate easily. However, some materials, such as quizzes and similar learning elements, may be so entwined with the previous university's LMS that separation and migration prove impossible. Instructors should plan accordingly and keep copies of all course materials separate from the university's LMS.

Conclusion

The laws governing the mutual rights of instructors and universities are unclear and evolving, as are those governing online instructors' use of materials created by others. Historically, instructors owned course materials, but some universities have recently sought online course and course material control. Most, though, continue to respect course developers' intellectual property rights. Furthermore, the TEACH Act encourages universities to exert control over the arbitration of copyright issues between instructors and outside copyright holders. A dialogue on these issues between university administration and faculty is essential.

Ideally, instructors should obtain permission from copyright owners before using their works. When this proves difficult, instructors have relied on fair use doctrine, but its application to online courses is more restricted than for traditional classroom courses. Instructors must evaluate the types of materials that they want to use. We recommend putting them into four categories: 1) commercial; 2) publicly available or under common use licenses; 3) materials that involve very minor use clearly within the scope of fair use doctrine; and 4) those that are broader in scope and use.

Commercial materials must be paid for, either by students, the university, or instructors. Materials that are in the public domain or which come with common use licenses can be used in compliance with any license restrictions. Instructors may continue to rely on fair use doctrine for materials that are minor in scope and use, such as short excerpts of articles, books, and other media, especially when hosted on a university LMS and restricted to enrolled students.

The fourth category is the most difficult. These are materials in which course developers must spend the most effort to determine the legal and ethical propriety of their anticipated use in online classes. Examples include full movies or television shows, more substantial use of written or other materials, and more expansive sites for retention – such as websites, social media, and open Google Drives. These require thought and the assistance of knowledgeable people, such as the librarian staff and university legal counsel.

Copyright is a balancing of the rights of the author(s) and the rights of the user(s). It is inherently complex. Doing the right thing for ethical reasons is helpful on many levels but a general understanding of the law, which represents a negotiation of interests, is also important. Fortunately, most of us will never have to deal with litigation involving our classes. They are too small to affect most copyright owners in economically meaningful ways. However, we should be careful with larger applications because they may become sufficiently visible and meaningful to result in litigation.

Notes

1 Twigg, Carol. *Who Owns Online Courses and Course Materials? Intellectual Property Policies for a New Learning Environment.* Troy, NY: Center for Academic Transformation at Rensselaer Polytechnic Institute, 2000, 1–27, 15–16; and Latourette, Audrey,

1 "Copyright Implications for Online Distance Learning," *Journal of College and University Law 32* (2006): 613–654, 616–617.
2 Library of Congress, US Copyright Office, *Circular 1, Copyright Basics*, revised December 2019, 1–2.
3 Ibid., also 17 USC 106.
4 *Community for Creative Non-Violence* v. *Reid*, 490 US 730 (1989), 737, citing 17 USC 102.
5 17 USC 201(b); Library of Congress, US Copyright Office, *Circular 9, Works Made for Hire*, revised September 2012.
6 Latourette, "Copyright Implications," 629.
7 *Williams* v. *Weisser*, 273 Cal. App. 2nd 726, 734, 78 Cal. Rptr. 542 (1969).
8 *1940 Statement of Principles on Academic Freedom and Tenure*. www.aaup.org/file/1940% 20Statement.pdf. Accessed December 24, 2020.
9 *Healy* v. *James*, 408 US 169 (1972), 180–181 [internal cites removed].
10 See *Hays* v. *Sony Corp of America*, 847 F. 2d 412 (7th Cir. 1988) versus *Shaul* v. *Cherry Valley–Springfield Central School Dist.*, 363 F.3d 177, 185–86 (2d Cir. 2004) and *Pittsburg State University/Kansas Nat'l Edu. Ass'n* v. *Kansas Board of Regents/Pittsburg State University*, 280 Kan. 408, 421–24, 122 P.3d 336 (2005).
11 Whitaker, Jonathan, J. Randolph New, and R. Duane Ireland, "MOOCs and the Online Delivery of Business Education What's New? What's not? What now?" *Academy of Management learning & Education 15*, no. 2 (2016): 345–365, 353.
12 Jordan, Katy, "Initial Trends in Enrolment and Completion of Massive Open Online Courses," *International Review of Research in Open and Distance Learning 15*, no. 1 (2014): 133–160.
13 Ospina-Delgado, Julieth, Ana Zorio-Grima, and María García-Benau. "Massive Open Online Courses in Higher Education: A Data Analysis of the MOOC Supply," *OmniaScience 12*, no. 5 (2016): 1401–1451; Schaffhauser, Dian, "How MOOCs Make Money?" *Campus Technology*, March 20, 2019. https://campustechnology.com/Articles/2019/03/20/How-MOOCs-Make-Money.aspx?p=1Accessed May 1, 2022; and Whitaker et al. "MOOCs and the Online Delivery."
14 Please see the sample course development contract in the appendix.
15 Twigg, *Who Owns Online Courses*.
16 Twigg, *Who Owns Online Courses*, 21–24.
17 17 USC 107.
18 *Harper & Row Publishers, Inc.* v. *Nation Enterprises*, 471 US 539 (1985).
19 Garon, Jon, "Ownership of University Intellectual Property," *Cardoza Arts and Entertainment Law Journal 36*, no. 3 (2018): 635–674, 648–9, citing 17 USC 106; and *Authors Guild* v. *Google, Inc.*, 804 F. 3rd 202 (2nd Cir. 2015), cert. denied, 136 S.Ct. 1658 (2016).
20 The posting of clip art without a copyright license by a commercial organization has been found to be infringement. See *Marobie-Florida, Inc.* v. *National Association of Fire Equipment Distributors*, 983 F. Supp. 1167 (N.D.Ill. 1997), 1176. The reproduction of articles for academic use by a printing shop for profit was infringement when the prevailing practice was for the print shops to obtain and pay for permission to use the articles. See *Princeton University Press* v. *Michigan Document Services, Inc.*, 99 F.3d 1381 (6th Cir. 1996).
21 Garon "Ownership of University Intellectual Property," 650.
22 Latourette, "Copyright Implications," 619.
23 17 USC 101, 110 (2), 112(f). Performance includes not only physically performing the work, but also playing a recording of it, showing its images in any sequence, or making sounds accompanying it audible.
24 17 USC 110 (2) D.

25 Hutchinson, Kristine H. "The Teach Act: Copyright Law and Online Education," *New York University Law Review 78*, no. *6* (2003): 2204–2240; Delaney, Kevin, "Balancing in Light of the Purposes of Copyright: Whether Video Music Lessons Constitute Copyright Infringement," *Communication Law and Policy 20*, no. *3* (2015): 261–285; and 17 USC 110(2).
26 Hutchinson, "The Teach Act," 2016, 2035.
27 17 USC 512, 1201, and 1202.
28 17 USC 512.
29 17 USC 1201(a).
30 37 CFR section 201.40(b)(2)(i) and 201.40(b)(1)(ii).
31 Latourette, "Copyright Implications," 618.

Part 2

Innovative Pedagogy for the Online Class

Stephen K. Stein and Maureen MacLeod

Over the last few decades, instructors developed a host of innovative approaches to online teaching. The online environment provides many new ways to engage and teach students, which various new technologies and software applications facilitate. Story mapping, short videos, and role-playing games enliven classes and encourage students to seek new information and think beyond course texts. This is not to say online teaching is all about new technologies and the latest app for your iPhone. As the authors of this part's chapters emphasize, new technologies enhance, rather than replace, tried and true methods for engaging students and encouraging and facilitating their learning.

Emphasizing the benefits of reading, writing, and critical thinking skills in the online classroom over the traditional classroom, Elizabeth F. Buchanan's chapter "More than a Mode of Delivery: Benefits and Challenges of Teaching History Online" argues that the online instructor needs to look beyond the challenges and embrace the benefits of the online classroom. While Buchanan lauds the advantages of the online classroom, her chapter also emphasizes that students need to be taught how to succeed in an online learning environment. Students' understanding of subject material increases when they understand how to learn in a new environment and the purpose behind specific assignments and course requirements. In addition, when students are more engaged in their learning, they become better learners and more active in the classroom.

The ability of students to be engaged in the online classroom and offer their unique perspectives is the focus of Molly J. Giblin's chapter, "Intercultural Learning Online: Using Students' Diverse Perspectives to Build Connections to History." Giblin addresses the idea that students can feel more comfortable in an online setting to bring their perspectives and experiences to the classroom. There is no hiding in an online class, and thus that allows students to engage in critical inquiry through creative curriculum design. Through prior knowledge and critical inquiry, students can process history uniquely, allowing them to connect to history differently than in a traditional classroom.

Maureen MacLeod discusses several exciting software tools that allow instructors to move away from the traditional classroom experience and to connect to history differently in her chapter "Using Technology in Pedagogy and

DOI: 10.4324/9781003258414-9

Assessment: Timelines, Story Mapping, and Edpuzzles." These tools help make the online classroom an exciting place to learn. Online classrooms offer a unique learning environment with its own advantages and opportunities. MacLeod encourages online instructors to embrace these opportunities. Software tools that allow students to create interactive timelines and chart historical events engage students and immerse them in history. Rather than a barrier to learning, new technologies help us engage students in innovative ways that enhance learning.

Incorporating movies and other videos into one's teaching is hardly new, but instructors creating their own video content to enhance online learning can be intimidating. However, Courtney Luckhardt explains in her chapter, "Dynamic Video Content in the Online History Classroom," that creating videos and incorporating them into online courses should not be a daunting process. A variety of tools can help instructors. They can start with short videos and slowly add them to courses. Making engaging video content relies on the same expertise and skills instructors apply in their in-person classes. Of course, the important thing is ensuring these videos enhance a course's learning goals rather than becoming an entertaining distraction.

In "Assessment and Feedback as Instruction in the Online History Classroom," Cassandra L. Clark explains how assessment and feedback can become core elements of online history courses. Without the personal interaction common in face-to-face instruction, instructor feedback to students is critical for student improvement in reading, writing, critical thinking, and related skills, as well as for mastering historical content and analysis. Moreover, privately and on discussion boards, continuing instructor feedback is an effective—even essential—instruction tool.

In "Games and Gamification in Online History Classes," Mary A. Valante demonstrates that games and gamification, increasingly popular in traditional classrooms, also work online. Online classes may be the ideal environment for some games. Other games, such as the increasingly popular Reacting to the Past series, which have students play the roles of historical figures in important events, such as the trial of Socrates, the French Revolution, and the US Constitutional Convention, are readily adapted to online environments. Regardless of the game, Valante explains, it is critical to explain the technology and game rules to the students so that these fade into the background, allowing students to immerse themselves in the game. More importantly, however much fun students have in these games, they are a means to an end. They enhance course learning objectives but cannot be allowed to supplant them.

These chapters offer important details and compelling examples of how instructors can enhance their online history classroom using engaging new methods and technology. Yet, as each author notes, technology enhances teaching. It cannot replace the work of active, engaged instructors who prioritize student success in their courses. Instructors must apply these technologies in ways that reinforce the learning outcomes and purposes of their courses.

Chapter 7

More than a Mode of Delivery
Benefits and Challenges of Teaching History Online

Elizabeth F. Buchanan

It is frequently said that teaching history online is merely a change in the mode of delivery from traditional teaching in-person. For example, Stephanie Budhai and Maureen Williams stated that:

> As faculty move their courses to an online environment, it is important to develop the pedagogical skills, practices and methodologies that mirror the quality and substance of teaching in traditional face-to-face courses.[1]

Carolyn Lawes similarly pointed out that the online course has more in common with a traditional course than may at first appear. It differs most in its mode of delivery – online rather than in-person.[2] As a third example, Courtney Luckhardt noted:

> it is also important to remember that teaching online is just a mode of delivery – it is the habits of mind that the study of history can bring that are key. For students in our introductory survey courses, we should emphasize the process of questioning received wisdom about the past, connecting the past to the present, and thinking and writing critically about these ideas.[3]

In making these statements, these scholars are trying to reassure instructors who hesitate to teach online that the move from teaching in-person to online is not difficult and the instructors can obtain the same results of historical thinking and critical engagement, using most of the same methods.

It is certainly true that most of the methods of teaching in-person can be transferred to teaching online with relatively minor change. A lecture given to an in-person course can be recorded or recreated in PowerPoint or another media and embedded into the learning management system for online students. Even more interactive teaching techniques, such as lectures punctuated with questions, class discussions and various interactive teaching methods, can be easily transferred to the online environment.[4] This essay, however, takes a different perspective – that the difference between teaching online and in-person is more significant and potentially more valuable.

DOI: 10.4324/9781003258414-10

Benefits of Online Instruction

Teaching in-person is traditionally an oral process – lectures and group activities, punctuated by written quizzes, tests, and papers. Although courses normally require the reading of a textbook or other written source(s), some students today try to minimize reading and rely on taking notes from the lecture and discussion, if they can. Online teaching is much more dependent upon reading and writing. Online instructors can and do use video-recorded lectures, as well as movies, photographs, and podcasts as sources, but there is a much heavier dependence upon the written word as a framework for learning. This has its drawbacks – some students find it difficult to complete an online course, partially because they may not have the desire or self-discipline without the enforced discipline of an in-person classroom and partially because online courses are so dependent upon reading. As Lawes noted, a certain percentage of students do very poorly in an online course because they cannot learn enough to get by through merely listening to an in-person class lecture and discussion.[5] Even with great efforts to create regular interaction, some students forget about the course requirements or perhaps even that they are in the course and fail to thrive in this environment.

There are also students who expect that an online course will involve less time than an in-person course, and dislike the time required to complete the online requirements. A student in one of my online courses wrote in the instructor review that she was a nursing student with much more important educational requirements and thought that the time required for the weekly assignments was excessive. From her perspective, that the course required about the same number of total hours as an in-person course did not matter. She had developed habits of minimizing work in courses that she felt were not directly useful for her. Minimizing work in an online course is possible, but not always very easy, and much more obvious to the instructor.

Thus, one benefit of an online course is that it forces the student to read and follow instructions carefully, and to read the required texts and to respond more frequently with a considered response to questions. The study of history traditionally has relied on the close reading of written sources, yet we often introduce students to history through oral lectures. Online history instruction provides the opportunity to teach students from the beginning how to critically analyze written sources and develop a narrative from them. Another benefit is that the students can be required to engage with peers and instructors. In a 2011 article, Lisa Lane wrote that while some students want distance from instructors – that is, they want to do the reading, take the tests, and be done with it – this is not necessarily a good thing because:

> [the study of] humanities demands social interaction, the sharing of ideals, the collective interaction with people, past and present. Today's technologies allow instructors to create rich experiences in their online classes

and ameliorate the isolation inherent in taking a class in a distancing environment.[6]

Other instructors have argued that online discussion boards can be more effective than in-person class discussions because everyone must participate, there is time for reflection and the more outgoing students do not overwhelm shyer students.[7] Requiring students to appropriately attribute their sources is also very helpful both for teaching them how to do it (necessary to avoid plagiarism allegations) and for giving them the opportunity to explore the credibility of their sources.[8] Online courses provide a regular and recurring opportunity for students to read, consider what they have read, respond to their peers, and practice attribution, and then to receive near-immediate feedback.

As you can see, teaching online offers several benefits over the traditional classroom. These benefits include the emphasis on reading and writing, critical skills for budding historians, and the opportunity to engage regularly with the materials or other people. But there are other benefits. Online courses can also encourage problem-based learning in more collaborative and student-centered ways than are available in traditional courses. There are many inspirational examples published in recent articles. One example comes from the articles by Kelly Schrum, Nate Sleeter and their colleagues that describe the *Hidden in Plain Sight* modules developed for Virginia teachers. These modules ask students to observe what they can about an object, and then to hypothesize about how the object was used historically and about its social meaning. Students then research the time period and finally write an essay re-thinking their original hypothesis and putting the object into historical and social context.[9] This program uses asynchronous discussion boards to encourage productive discussion among students and regular feedback to instructors using the modules to give them additional research resources. The modules could be used in all levels of education from K-12 through graduate courses, with commensurately difficult research requirements.

Kristyn Harman offers another example. She described a course done by the University of Tasmania, Australia, which involved teaching students baseline computer and research skills, and then assisting them through a search of public records concerning their ancestors who were brought to Australia as convicts.[10] The modules had three learning objectives for the students: to be familiar with a wide range of historical records to locate convicts transported to Australia and trace their life experiences, to be able to read and understand key materials in these records and to situate the experience of individual convicts within a wide context, and to convey this information clearly and succinctly.[11] Biggs and Tang write that "e-learning... offers possibilities of engaging learners that are not possible in the classroom," by opening up a whole new domain for student learning that does not rely upon lengthy lecture recordings and taking part in mandated discussion groups.[12] This type of engagement was possible to do because of the vast expansion in primary sources now available online. Teaching online also provides an opportunity to move instructor time from preparing and giving lectures into personal feedback on student-centered projects.

Helping Online Students Thrive

Making the argument that online courses can provide significant benefits to students is a first step in the process of using courses online more successfully, but to obtain the benefits from this form of learning, students must first learn techniques for being successful in this environment. As discussed above, a certain percentage of students fail to thrive. This is not acceptable. Most students have spent the majority, or all, of their previous educational experience sitting in classrooms. While students in traditional classroom education also profit when they have learned how to manage their own learning, this is even more important in an online environment because the student is potentially more isolated, especially in asynchronous courses.

One of the important learning techniques for online classes is self-regulated learning. This was defined by Barry J. Zimmerman in his 2008 article as "the degree to which students are metacognitively, motivationally, and behaviorally active participants in their own learning process."[13] Self-regulated learning involves being able to establish achievable learning goals, and then to apply strategies that work for them to allow them to complete their goals, and finally to use self-reflection to consider what worked and what did not to improve their performance.[14] This type of learning is important because it allows the student to motivate themselves, plan an appropriate strategy for learning and modify their strategy when it does not work as well as anticipated. The instructor's clear explanation and periodic repetition of the learning outcomes anticipated for the course are key because if the students see the learning outcomes as important, they will be more motivated to accomplish them. They can then develop their own strategies – deciding when and where they will do the work, and what will constitute success for them. The instructor can encourage the development of a strategic plan for accomplishing the required tasks and self-reflection by building self-regulated learning into the curriculum. For example, the instructor can ask for a work plan, and then provide detailed feedback, or provide a detailed rubric and then ask the student to do the initial assessment of their work, subject to feedback from the instructor. Either approach can help the student learn to assess the quality of their own work and thus more accurately decide how much work to expend in return for meeting their own goals. Zimmerman and Tsikalas conducted a very interesting survey of various online learning environments to gauge their ability to teach self-regulatory learning skills and found that the best of these systems could provide not only forethought, performance, and self-reflection phase processes, but also multilevel instructional processes, which assist in motivation and perseverance, such as modeling, tutoring, and feedback.[15] Universities should consider providing training in self-regulated learning skills in their academic preparedness classes before they place new students in online courses. If this is not possible, entry-level courses could provide this training.

Second, instructors can plan both their programmatic curriculum and their individual courses to develop incremental knowledge and skills. This is standard curricular guidance but it is sometimes ignored. The push to offer survey courses to engage general education students can overwhelm the desire to develop the historical research and writing skills necessary for graduate-level or professional work. The instructor should explain the utility of these skills in other types of employment. Research over the past 20 or 30 years has clearly shown that businesses need high levels of transferrable skills from their employees, and that although hard skills (technical knowledge) remain important, most will hire an applicant with fewer hard skills if their transferrable skills are strong.[16] Transferrable skills, also called soft skills, include written and oral communication skills, integrity, teamwork, flexibility, responsibility, and work ethic. Students teach themselves using the materials provided by the online course and can benefit from a carefully planned process of incremental skill development. When they see that their skills are increasing, many students will continue to put work and time into the process.

Third, instructors must develop learning activities and assessments to accomplish their learning objectives in ways that maximize the effectiveness and attraction of their courses. This also is part of traditional curricular training, but it is even more important in online courses.[17] Learning activities must be matched to the purpose and level of the course. There are many tools to assist in this – from short, taped lectures followed by individual or group activities to gamification to assessments that include both written products and use of other media. In this regard, modeling is an important principle. Research has shown that complex skills can be learned through modeling. Students learn more when they both see an expert perform a task and receive an explanation of how the expert is approaching their task.[18] The observation then should be followed with an opportunity for the student to practice the behaviors, and to receive constructive advice on how to improve their practice.[19] The point is that online courses, even asynchronous courses, do not have to be boring. They can use a variety of techniques to engage and excite students, leading them on a learning adventure with the help of the instructor and other experts.

Finally, and this is also not new by any means, engagement among the student, material, and instructor is critical. Students learn when they want to learn. Research shows that students must understand the reasons why they are doing the required activities and assessment.[20] They must understand what useful knowledge and skills they will gain from their effort. They perform better if they think that the instructor cares and is willing to invest in them personally. All this must be incorporated into the online experience and continually re-affirmed through communication between student and instructor.

Conclusion

Online history courses can teach historical knowledge and skills as effectively as in-person courses. They may not provide the pleasure of watching an expert explain a difficult aspect of history in-person, but they can permit a more incremental and personalized development of knowledge and skills, with direct supervision by instructors. As students move from sitting in a traditional lecture hall listening to an expert historian wax eloquent to working through a series of problems, they are making a major and potentially valuable move forward. One is fun but vicarious; the other is riskier, more self-directed but ultimately a more robust learning experience. As T. Mills Kelley said:

> By structuring our teaching and their learning about the past around ways that digital technology now promotes active engagement with, rather than passive acquisition (and reading) of historical content, we will be creating learning opportunities for our students that have a higher likelihood of producing the learning gains that we hope for when we teach. Instead of asking them to sit, listen and record what we say – a teaching strategy that cognitive science has demonstrated quite conclusively to be unproductive – we can now ask our students to do what we do: make history out of the raw material of the past.[21]

Historical sources, both primary and secondary, are increasingly available online. Teaching students how to use the material permits a more creative and interactive relationship between the past and present. This is what online history teaching can and should aspire to become.

Notes

1 Budhai, Stephanie, and Williams, Maureen, "Teaching Presence in Online Courses: Practical Applications, Co-Facilitation and Technology Integration," *The Journal of Effective Teaching 16*, no. 3 (2016): 76–84, 76.
2 Lawes, Carolyn J. "Talking Less but Saying More: Teaching US History Online." *Journal of American History 101*, no. 4 (2015): 1204–1214, 1209.
3 Luckhardt, Courtney. "Teaching Historical Legacy and Making World History Relevant in the Online Discussion Board," *The History Teacher 47*, no. 2 (2014): 187–196, 194.
4 See Miller, Khadijah, "Before We Begin, Preparing to Teach Online," in *Teaching the Humanities Online: A Practical Guide to the Virtual Classroom*, ed. Steven Hoffman. London and New York: Routledge, 2011, 3–12.
5 Lawes, "Talking Less but Saying More," 1213.
6 Lane, Lisa. "Reducing Distance in Online Classes," in *Teaching the Humanities Online: A Practical Guide to the Virtual Classroom*, ed. Steven Hoffman, 13–25. London and New York: Routledge, 2011, 24.
7 See for example, Minielli, Maureen and Ferris, Sharmila, "Using Electronic Courseware," in *Teaching the Humanities Online: A Practical Guide to the Virtual Classroom*, ed. Steven Hoffman, 26–45. London and New York: Routledge, 2011, 37; Ter-

Stepanian, Anahit. "Online or Face to Face?: Instructional Strategies for Improving Learning Outcomes in e-Learning." *International Journal of Technology, Knowledge & Society 8*, no. 2 (2012): 41–50, 43–44; Lawes, "Talking Less but Saying More," 1208.
8 Lane, "Reducing Distance," 200–202.
9 Schrum, Kelly, and Nate Sleeter. "Teaching History Online: Challenges and Opportunities." *Organization of American Historians Magazine of History 27*, no. 3 (2013): 35–38; Schrum, Kelly, Nate Sleeter, et al., "Teaching Hidden History: Student Outcomes from a Distributed, Collaborative, Hybrid Course," *The History Teacher 51*, no. 4 (2018): 574–596.
10 Harman, Kristyn, "The Transformative Power of Digital Humanities in Teaching Family History Online," *Journal of University Teaching and Learning Practice 15*, no. 3 (2018). https://doi.org/10.53761/1.15.3.7.
11 Ibid., 3.
12 Ibid., 4, quoting from Biggs, J. and Tang, C., *Teaching for Quality Learning: What the Student Does*, 4th ed. Berkshire: Open University Press, 2011, 78.
13 Zimmerman, B.J. "Investigating Self-Regulation and Motivation: Historical Background, Methodological Developments, and Future Prospects," *American Educational Journal 45*, no. 1 (2008): 166–183, 167, referring to the definition developed in a 1986 symposium of the American Educational Research Association.
14 Ebner, Rachel, "Tips for Fostering Students' Self-Regulated Learning in Asynchronous Learning Environments," *Online Education*, September 2, 2020. www.facultyfocus.com/articles/online-education/tips-for-fostering-students-self-regulated-learning-in-asynchronous-online-learning-environments. Accessed November 22, 2022; Zimmerman, B.J. "Attaining Self-Regulation: A Social Cognitive Perspective," in *Handbook of Self-Regulation*, ed. M. Boekaerts, P.R. Pintrich, and M. Zeidner, 13–39. San Diego, CA: Academic Press, 2000; Zimmerman, "Investigating Self-Regulation," 166–183.
15 Zimmerman, B.J., and Kallen Tsikalas. "Can Computer-Based Learning Environments (CBLEs) Be Used as Self-Regulatory Tools to Enhance Learning?" *Educational Psychologist 40*, no. 4 (2005): 267–271. For a more recent literature review, see Garcia, Rita, Katrina Faulkner and Rebecca Vivian. "Systematic Literature Review: Self-Regulated Learning Strategies Using E-Learning Tools for Computer Science," *Computers & Education 123* (2018): 150–163.
16 See for example, Robles, Marcel, "Executive Perceptions of the Top 10 Soft Skills Needed in Today's Workplace," *Business Communication Quarterly 75*, no. 4 (2012): 453–465; McGunagle, Doreen, and Laura Zizka. "Meeting Real World Demands of the Global Economy: An Employer's Perspective," *Journal of Aviation/Aerospace Education and Research 27*, no. 2 (2018): 58–76; Kim, Yuna, "Developing a Work Ready Social Media Marketing Analytics Course: A Model to Cultivate Data-Driven and Multiperspective Strategy Development Skills," *Decision Sciences Journal of Innovative Education 17*, no. 2 (2019): 163–188; and research cited within.
17 Steed, Marlo, "New Media Design for Learning, An Argument for Curriculum Change," *The International Journal of Learning 17*, no. 3 (2010): 291–301; Biggs and Tang, *Teaching for Quality Learning*; McKeachie, W., and M. Svinicki, *McKeachie's Teaching Tips: Strategies, Research, and Theory for College and University Teachers*. Boston, MA: Houghton-Mifflin, 2006; Smith, Gregory, and Cynthia Brame. "Active Learning Cheat Sheet." https://cdn.vanderbilt.edu/vu-wp0/wp-content/uploads/sites/59/2019/04/22143029/Active-Learning-Cheat-Sheet.pdf. Accessed November 22, 2022.
18 Zimmerman, B.J. "From Cognitive Modeling to Self-Regulation: A Social Cognitive Path," *Educational Psychologist 48*, no. 3 (2013): 135–147, 136.
19 Ibid., 140–142.

20 Boud, D. and Falchikov, N., "Aligning Assessment with Long-Term Learning," *Assessment and Evaluation in Higher Education 31*, no. *4* (2006): 399–413; Martin, F., A. Ritzhaupt, S. Kumar, and K. Budhrani, "Award-Winning Faculty Online Teaching Practices: Course Design, Assessment and Evaluation, and Facilitation," *The Internet and Higher Education 42* (2019): 34–43.
21 Kelly, T. Mills. *Teaching History in the Digital Age*. Ann Arbor, MI: The University of Michigan Press, 2016, 12, also 8–9.

Chapter 8

Intercultural Learning Online
Using Students' Diverse Perspectives to Build Connections to History

Molly J. Giblin

While the COIL (Collaborative Online Intercultural Learning) model is perhaps best known in the field of virtual teaching, there are many ways to engage history students in intercultural pedagogy beyond connecting with overseas counterparts. Using students' lived experiences, communities, and diverse perspectives in historical inquiry connects existing knowledge to course material and expands our collective knowledge. Including intercultural pedagogy in our online teaching offers the potential to engage students more deeply, as they see themselves and learn to understand others in the histories we teach.

What Is Intercultural Learning?

Intercultural learning encourages students to learn from and across difference. Although historians often examine cultural alterity, intercultural pedagogy is still relatively uncommon in history classrooms due to a healthy skepticism of its early theoretical underpinnings. Intercultural communication theory is rooted in Cold War-era attempts to develop American soft power, training American agents in cultural adaptation drawing on colonialist Western anthropological theories of culture that emphasized static customs and reified racist linear models of cultural evolution.[1] Developmental theories of intercultural competence prevalent in study abroad orientations and global workforce training posit that individuals who encounter difference move from a monocultural state, which denies or minimizes cultural difference, toward cultural competence, or active acceptance and cultural bridging.[2] These models grow out of the desire to help students acknowledge and respect difference, but they do not intentionally grapple with power, privilege, local particularities, or historical legacies. Like many aspects of higher education, intercultural competence models designed for a narrow segment of the population can fail to serve the diverse students in our programs.[3]

Critical intercultural pedagogy – my focus here – is a more complex practice designed to decenter traditional structures of power and value the diverse forms of knowledge we encounter in our classrooms.[4] Amy Lee's germinal

DOI: 10.4324/9781003258414-11

text, *Teaching Interculturally*, emphasizes that we already teach in intercultural spaces. "Human diversity… is present in every classroom, regardless of whether it is visible and whether it is solicited."[5] Yet we know that numerical diversity does not magically foster better cultural awareness or equity and inclusion.[6] The key ingredient is teachers' willingness to "commit to continuously reflecting on for whom and to what extent course design, activities, and instruction are achieving these outcomes."[7] Another critical approach to intercultural learning comes from Kathryn Sorrells, whose work emphasizes the dynamic intricacies of global culture.[8] Both Lee and Sorrells insist that we acknowledge the workings of power and privilege in our ways of knowing, seeing, and doing.

Global learning, a related pedagogy, can also help students seek and parse diverse viewpoints as they address the legacies of historical problems. The Association of American Colleges and Universities, or AAC&U, describes global learning as "the critical analysis of and an engagement with complex, interdependent global systems and legacies."[9] It offers students opportunities "to work collaboratively, to examine the world's human and natural systems from multiple perspectives, and to integrate learning across the curriculum by following the threads in an increasingly complex reality."[10] Put differently, it encourages students to understand that we need many minds to solve complex global problems.[11] I think of intercultural praxis as developing a mindset that we can apply through global learning.

Global and intercultural learning are not just value-added elements. For historians, embedding critical intercultural pedagogies is a step toward unlearning the received knowledge, historical myths, and harmful white supremacist ideologies that still pervade historical practice and teaching.[12]

Intercultural Learning in Online History Courses

Intercultural pedagogy was not developed for online learning, but its focus on marshaling diverse perspectives to better understand local and global issues make it a natural fit for engaging the diverse students who enter online classrooms. Moreover, pedagogies proven to enhance student learning in face-to-face settings are often effective in online contexts.[13] Intercultural pedagogy is possible in any learning context and can easily align with online pedagogies.

Because intercultural pedagogy defies universalizing impulses, there is no singular approach to implementing it in online history teaching.[14] Instead, I want to share some theoretical frameworks that might inform intercultural history teaching online, and then outline some examples of what this has looked like in my own online courses. I hope this will serve as a starting point for instructors who are new to intercultural pedagogy or online teaching. As more of us share our processes, we can help to build a community of practice around virtual intercultural pedagogy for history.

When I began teaching fully online courses, I realized that there was no way for anyone to hide in the back of the classroom. Every student had to participate in every discussion, and generally maintain a higher level of engagement than they might in a traditional classroom. This meant that I also had to be very mindful of how I interacted with each student; without the opportunity to "read the room," I could not always be sure when someone left an activity feeling alienated or unheard. How could I better frame questions to encourage engagement with difficult ideas without harming some learners? How could I help students understand that what they were saying and seeing – or missing – had real consequences for the people's lives?

Nanda Dimitrov and Aisha Haque propose that educators mobilize a tripartite intercultural pedagogy to engage students and facilitate learning in diverse spaces:

- Foundational skills.
- Facilitation skills.
- Curriculum design.[15]

Dimitrov and Haque's three skillsets are interwoven and, for the purposes of online teaching, somewhat mutually constituting. Because the virtual setting can limit the kinds of in-the-moment adjustments that we might make in a face-to-face classroom, student engagement depends largely on advance planning (curriculum design), while how we frame issues, the kind of language we use to refer to historical figures and events, and how we embrace – or diminish – the importance of students' existing knowledge are all based on what we might think of as foundational and facilitation skills.

As a starting point, being conscious of our foundational skills asks that we interrogate how our own assumptions and intellectual orientations inform the choices we make in assembling each piece of a course. In "The Past Is Another Country," Tony Judt wrote that identifying and unraveling historical myths involves interrogating the differences between collective memory and the myriad, contingent ways that people experienced historical events.[16] Although we are trained to discern these myths, we are not immune to them. We cannot escape our identities and relationships to power, either in the university or in our broader lives. Yet we *can* examine our intellectual assumptions and identify areas that we need to develop. What do we know, and how did we come to this knowledge? How are we, and our discipline, entwined in – or responsible for – the systems and structures that affect our historical subjects and contemporary students? How can we work within and move beyond our personal viewpoints and disciplinary constraints to better understand our students and our subjects?

Next, we might focus on facilitation skills. In other words, we need to mindfully engage all of the students in our classrooms. How we respond to discussion posts, the feedback we offer on assignments, and even our facility with the technology we use to deliver our courses contribute to students' experiences. How do we respond when students raise sticky subjects or hot moments arise? How can we make sure that we are not teaching some at the expense of others? Are we replicating methods like long lectures, which many students find challenging even in face-to-face environments, or considering how we can make the most of the virtual spaces that we share?[17]

Finally, curriculum design works at several levels to scaffold and assess student learning. Curriculum design is the umbrella under which we gather foundational and facilitation skills, from the reading and other resources we assign (whose voices are we including?) to how we encourage intellectual growth to how we ask students to demonstrate their learning. If, for example, the purpose of an activity or assignment is to encourage critical thinking, it must be set up in a way that does not merely reward students who arrive in our classrooms with this skill and punish those who have not gained proficiency in it. Scaffolding learning to allow students to see the purpose of each activity, learn and practice skills, and apply them in novel ways, is crucial if we are serious about moving away from a "finishing school" model of higher education.

I have also found Sorrells's Intercultural Praxis model useful in connecting theory to historical legacies and lived realities. Moving clockwise around a wheel, students might begin at the Inquiry phase (wanting to know more about a subject), consider their framing (how their backgrounds and existing knowledge inform their understanding or limit their knowledge) and positioning (how they are connected to the subject, and what relative power and privilege people who share some of their identities might experience in relation to the subject), engage in Dialogue and Reflection (seeking out diverse perspectives on the topic, and understanding how and why they diverge), and move toward Action (ethically responding to problems while continuously striving to improve one's understanding of the issue and others' relationship to it).[18] The model does not have an endpoint, and its cyclical nature suggests that intercultural praxis is a lifelong process. Historically speaking, it reminds us that the practice of deepening our understanding is never complete.

How Can I Do This in My Own Courses?

Intercultural pedagogy can work at many registers, from the assembly of course materials to discussion to assignments to experiential opportunities. There is no terminus: at its core, intercultural pedagogy is a process of reflection and critique to challenge what has been handed down to us, in our societies, institutions, and practices.[19]

In my own classes, intercultural pedagogy tends to manifest in three stages:

1   *Prior knowledge*: Students identify their existing knowledge, relationship to an event or issue, initial thoughts or feelings, and any areas of curiosity or uncertainty. This also applies to me, as I examine my own ideological investments while I revise my syllabus.

2 *Critical inquiry*: As students encounter assigned materials, they consider who is involved in a historical period, event, or issue, contemplate historical and contemporary hierarchies and social categories, and think through the implications of different interpretations.
3 *Processing*: Students apply their critical inquiry skills and connect their theoretical and conceptual learning to historical and contemporary issues.

All three are present in weekly activities; they also inform collaborative and individual projects in the second half of the semester.

Activating Prior Knowledge

We know that students learn best when they can connect new ideas with previous knowledge.[20] Asking students to record some initial impressions allows all of us to see variations in thinking. This reinforces a few key ideas: that preconceptions are not necessarily truths; that limited knowledge does not equal limited intelligence; and that new perspectives help us to improve our own understanding of a topic or issue. Activating prior knowledge is instrumental to individual and collective learning.

I typically use a preparation activity to allow students to identify their existing knowledge, and to help me discern learners' varying levels of exposure to a historical event or topic. This could be a set of pre-reading questions about the topic, a quick true/false exercise that aggregates student answers before and after they complete reading and engage in discussion, or an exercise that asks students to reply "agree" or "disagree" to a set of statements framed as truths. Then, using the Intercultural Praxis model, we might consider where students' responses diverge, and look for patterns in background, social position, or previous education that might explain the divergence (Framing and Positioning). Students then have a structured opportunity to talk through and reflect on the implications of different understandings (Reflection and Dialogue). Depending on the course format, this could be a one-minute essay, a live discussion, or a blog post.

Activating prior knowledge is an important way to begin to move beyond preconception, help students see how issues pertain to them, model critical thinking, and show students that we trust their ability to grow.[21] Grappling with different perspectives in a pre-reading phase primes students to do the same with sources, supporting critical analytical skills and awareness of the implications of real-world historical narratives. These activities also build community as students learn more about one another.

Critical Inquiry

I use reading and other resources that include expertise beyond traditional intellectual sources, or examples from perspectives students may not have encountered before. Re-situating authority can itself be important, but the critical point is that it is not enough to show that people disagree on an issue, whether historically or historiographically. It is essential to include guiding questions, an introductory video, or opportunities to construct narratives to help learners contemplate what informed the emergence of different viewpoints, and how wielding them has affected different constituencies. Who held different views? Why? What were the consequences of believing or acting upon them? These are some of the critical thinking elements you would build into any documentary analysis in a traditional face-to-face course. Using them in an online course requires planning to walk students through the analytical process, but it can extend into every activity and conversation, and consistently encourage every student to examine their own viewpoints and how they intersect with identity, social positioning, and power.

In discussion, give students opportunities to ask their own questions, and respond to others' questions. If responses appear to be flattening or universalizing (some common threads I have seen are "this society didn't care about women," or "this is the same as America today"), asking open-ended questions can help to foster deeper inquiry that adds complexity to the initial contribution rather than shutting it down. In asynchronous classes, students might miss follow-up questions, so it is important to come back to ideas in future, building complex questioning into prompts or problems.

Processing

Projects – some individual, some team-based – encourage students to connect theoretical or conceptual knowledge to historical and contemporary issues. For instance, in a course on Pacific histories, students watched TEDx talks focused on oral histories of family and social formation. Students then created short videos exploring how stories within their own families testify to past events or ways of being. An ensuing virtual discussion led them to realizations not only about the promises and limitations of oral history, but also to the ways in which their personal stories were connected to historical events – and how narratives might shift according to the narrators' social position. In a final project, teams of students evaluated professional historians' work on Pacific histories prior to contact with Europeans, noting built-in assumptions, contemplating the reliability of written and oral sources, and unpacking how discourses reflected community knowledge or colonialist primordialism.

Global and intercultural pedagogy that is attentive to power equips students to understand and grapple with historical legacies. Likewise, historicizing analyses of how identity and privilege exist within local, regional, and global matrices denaturalizes the hierarchies that our students have inherited, offering opportunities for richer engagement with both the course content and with the legacies of historical issues in the world around them.[22]

Critiques and Why We Should Do This Anyway

In my experience, historians' resistance to global and intercultural learning is grounded in the belief that examining lived experience limits students' understanding of the past and its alterity.[23] For me, this critique smacks more of academic gatekeeping than of serious methodological deficiency.[24] Students' identities inform how they are likely to engage with course material. Students from socially dominant backgrounds might see some hierarchies as natural or even desirable, and miss past injustices or ignore their complicity in current systems of inequity. Students from minoritized backgrounds, whose identities reflect how they have borne the brunt of historical and contemporary inequality, tend not to encounter historical issues as abstract ideas, but as ongoing violence in their daily lives.[25] If we are to provide both equitable and rigorous training in historical inquiry, we must elicit, unpack, and reframe how students connect to history and live within historical legacies – and help learners (ourselves included) understand that knowledge and experiences are embedded within systems of power and privilege.

Joy Castro argues that, "[i]n the face of… intense and varied pressures, the academy must find ways to preserve itself as a place for thought to flourish – yet *everyone* needs to be invited to think. The discussion has to matter to everyone, and everyone's voice must be heard."[26] This is critically important in the online classroom, where a preponderance of low-income, first-generation, minoritized students who are also parents, veterans, and working adults have perspectives that need to matter in both discussion and in curriculum design. Teaching interculturally is a process by which we can show students that their cultural and social backgrounds are assets, not liabilities. As Amy Lee notes, pedagogies that "more fully utilize and honor human difference… maximize learning in our classrooms."[27]

Intercultural pedagogy is a process, not an outcome. Coupled with constant re-evaluation of best practices in online teaching, we can set up spaces and opportunities for intercultural learning, and adapt as we reflect on changing conditions and student needs. I hope that this will serve as a catalyst for further conversation with diverse colleagues, students, and communities about how intercultural online pedagogy helps generate better histories and historians.

Notes

1 McAllister-Grande, Bryan. "Changing the Foundations of International Education: Fixing a Broken System and Working for Social Justice." *The Global Impact Exchange, Diversity Abroad* (2018): 16–19: 16.
2 Bennett, Milton J. "A Developmental Approach to Training for Intercultural Sensitivity." *International Journal of Intercultural Relations 10*, no. 2 (1986): 179–196; Hammer, Mitchell R., Milton J. Bennett, and Richard Wiseman. "Measuring

Intercultural Sensitivity: The Intercultural Development Inventory." *International Journal of Intercultural Relations 27*, no. *4* (2003): 421–443.

3 Deardorff, Darla K. "Identification and Assessment of Intercultural Competence as a Student Outcome of Internationalization." *Journal of Studies in International Education 10*, no. *3* (2006): 241–266 Greenholtz, Joe F. "Does Intercultural Sensitivity Cross Cultures? Validity Issues in Porting Instruments across Languages and Cultures." *International Journal of Intercultural Relations 29*, no. *1* (2005): 73–89; Punti, Gemma, and Molly Dingel. "Rethinking Race, Ethnicity, and the Assessment of Intercultural Competence in Higher Education." *Education Sciences 11*, no. *3* (2021): 110.

4 I am indebted to Stephanie Doscher at Florida International University for introducing me to these concepts, and Ellen McManus, Director of the Borra Center for Teaching and Learning Excellence at Dominican University, for guidance in applying these methods in online courses. I am also grateful to Northeastern University colleagues from the Global Experience Office, Center for the Advancement of Teaching and Learning Through Research, Community-Engaged Teaching and Research, and Center for Intercultural Engagement-Social Justice Resource Center for helping to shape these thoughts.

5 Lee, Amy, Robert Poch, Mary Katherine O'Brien, and Catherine Solheim. *Teaching Interculturally: A Framework for Integrating Disciplinary Knowledge and Intercultural Development*. Sterling, VA: Stylus Publishing, 2017, 15.

6 Tienda, Marta. "Diversity ≠ Inclusion: Promoting Integration in Higher Education." *Educational Researcher 42*, no. *9* (2013): 467–475.

7 Lee et al., *Teaching Interculturally*, 15.

8 Sorrells, Kathryn. *Intercultural Communication: Globalization and Social Justice*. Los Angeles, CA: Sage, 2016.

9 Association of American Colleges & Universities. "Global Learning VALUE Rubric." n.d. www.aacu.org/initiatives/value-initiative/value-rubrics/value-rubrics-global-learning. Accessed October 23, 2021.

10 Hovland, Kevin. *Shared Futures: Global Learning and Liberal Education*. New York: Association of American Colleges and Universities, 2006.

11 Landorf, Hilary, Stephanie Doscher, and Jaffus Hardrick. *Making Global Learning Universal: Promoting Success and Inclusion for All Students*. Sterling, VA: Stylus Publishing, 2018, 5.

12 Lee et al., *Teaching Interculturally*, 17. See also Chapdelaine, Robin, and Megan Toomer, "Experiential Learning in Ghana: Decentering the White Voice." *Radical Teacher 121* (2021): 5–14.

13 Mehanna, Wassila Naamani. "E-Pedagogy: The Pedagogies of E-Learning." *Research in Learning Technology 12*, no. *3* (2004): 279–293.

14 Lee et al., *Teaching Interculturally*, 3.

15 Dimitrov, Nanda, and Aisha Haque. "Intercultural Teaching Competence: A Multi-Disciplinary Model for Instructor Reflection." *Intercultural Education 27*, no. *5* (2016): 437–456.

16 Judt, Tony. "The Past Is Another Country: Myth and Memory in Postwar Europe." *Daedalus 121*, no. *4* (1992): 83–118.

17 Expecting instructors to have great facility with constantly-changing technology can be both daunting and highly inequitable. However, in my work with faculty and in my own teaching, I recognize that we do not always need to be the experts. Co-creation with students – allowing them to help design activities, assignments, and even outcomes – can bridge this gap. It is important that this feature does not reinstate other forms of equality, so remember to assess students based on the outcomes you (all) agree upon – not on their technological proficiency, unless that is a core component of your course.

18 Sorrells, *Intercultural Communication*, 16–22.
19 Lee et al., *Teaching Interculturally*, 16–27.
20 Angelo, Thomas A., and K. Patricia Cross. *Classroom Assessment Techniques: A Handbook for College Teachers*. San Francisco, CA: Jossey-Bass, Wiley, 1993 and 2012; National Research Council. *How People Learn: Brain, Mind, Experience, and School*, Expanded Edition. Washington, DC: National Academies Press, 2000.
21 Canning, Elizabeth A., Katherine Muenks, Dorainne J. Green, and Mary C. Murphy. "STEM Faculty Who Believe Ability Is Fixed Have Larger Racial Achievement Gaps and Inspire Less Student Motivation in Their Classes." *Science Advances 5*, no. 2 (2019). www.science.org/doi/full/10.1126/sciadv.aau4734.
22 Ahmed, Amer. "'Glocal' Justice: Toward an Equity Imperative in International Education." Keynote Address at WISE Connect Symposium, Winston-Salem, NC, February 11, 2022.
23 Generations of scholars learned to distrust personal testimonies of lived experience due to a (perhaps misguided) reading of Joan Wallach Scott's essay, "The Evidence of Experience." *Critical Inquiry 17*, no. 4 (1991): 773–797. However, Indigenous scholars have noted the colonialist nature of privileging testimony from cultural outsiders. See Simpson, Audra. "On Ethnographic Refusal: Indigeneity, 'Voice' and Colonial Citizenship." *Junctures 9* (2007). https://junctures.org/index.php/junctures/article/view/66; Sium, Aman, and Eric Ritskes. "Speaking Truth to Power: Indigenous Storytelling as an Act of Living Resistance." *Decolonization: Indigeneity, Education & Society 2*, no. *1* (2013): I–X.
24 After all, we not only accept but routinely admire other types of lived experience, like familiarity with academic theory, jargon, and genealogies. See Castro, Joy. "On Becoming Educated." *The Scholar and Feminist Online 8*, no. 3 (2010). https://sfonline.barnard.edu/polyphonic/castro_01.htm.
25 Chapdelaine and Toomer, "Experiential Learning in Ghana," 6.
26 Castro, "On Becoming Educated," 4.
27 Lee et al., *Teaching Interculturally*, 3.

Chapter 9

Using Technology in Pedagogy and Assessment

Timelines, Story Mapping, and Edpuzzles

Maureen MacLeod

There is no way to exactly replicate the in-person classroom to distance learning. I start with this statement because instructors need to realize that while exact replication is not possible, this does not mean that distance learning is inferior or "bad." When an instructor who has only taught in-person teaches an online course for the first time, much of their worry is regarding how they will translate their teaching methods from in-person to online.[1] Usually, instructors fall into one of two groups, the lecturer or the interactive instructor. The lecturer is typical in a history course, the content is delivered from the front of the room, and students furiously take notes. Assessment in a lecture-based course is usually through papers and exams. The interactive instructor gives mini-lectures, but much classroom time is spent on group discussions or activities. Typical assessment is through projects, engagement in discussions, papers, or exams.

Both methods of instruction, lecturer and interactive, provide challenges when transitioning to an online course. Recording a 50-minute lecture will not keep students engaged, and it is unlikely they will watch it. The questions that a lecturer may pepper throughout a lecture may seem impossible through an asynchronous online course. Additionally, traditional assessment methods of exams and papers make the course feel more like a correspondence course rather than an online one. The interactive instructor is usually more panicked regarding an online course as they feed off student interaction. They do not have lengthy lectures ready to record and often feel that discussion boards do not mimic the robust in-person discussions they are used to having in the classroom. Both these types of instructors and those who fall in-between need to use technology to align their pedagogy and assessment when teaching history online.

This chapter explores how one can use different technology and techniques to develop their pedagogy and assessment to engage students in examining history in an asynchronous online course. While the online class cannot be the same as the in-person experience it can be just as rigorous and interesting by using technology. Through the use of timelines, story mapping, Edpuzzles, and online exhibits instructors can provide an engaging manner to have students participate in historical thinking, analytical skills, and learning outcomes.

DOI: 10.4324/9781003258414-12

Types of Technology

Numerous types of software and websites assist students with engaging in history in an online course. This section is not a comprehensive review of everything available; instead, it highlights some of the more popular and user-friendly technology for the history online classroom.

Timeline Software

Some of the essential learning outcomes that instructors attempt to impress upon their students are change over time, causality, and significance. Students can read about these ideas in a textbook or monograph, but do they understand the content, primarily if they cannot interact in real-time with their instructor or classmates? One way to accomplish this is using timeline software that allows students to present their understanding of change of time and causality. The instructor can incorporate research into the use of timelines or ask students to use material they were already presented with throughout the course.

Timeline software has come a long way in the past few years. Most timeline software requires no downloads, is free, and is shareable.[2] Before asking students to use the software, it is highly recommended you use it yourself. This allows instructors to write better assignment instructions, understand the time involved in creating a timeline, and help students troubleshoot if needed.[3] While most of the websites for the timeline software have instructional videos, it is a good idea to record a few of your own as the students are familiar with you and prefer to hear your voice and expectations when using the software.

Creating a timeline allows students to interact with the course material and allows them to present it in a new way. The instructor may require the student to use only readings from the course or research further, which is possible with this type of assignment. If asking the student to complete research, the instructor will need to go over best research practices and require a bibliography. For this assignment, the instructor and student should agree on an appropriate timeframe; this can be accomplished in a short one-paragraph project proposal. It is essential to have an agreed-upon timeframe as this will focus the student's timeline.[4] They will need to compile each slide's[5] images and videos and develop a description and analysis for each slide. The instructor should have a required minimum number of slides for the timeline. Having a reflection or process paper to complete the project is also good pedagogical practice. This can be a 1–2-page requirement asking students to assess their work.[6]

To provide a better understanding of the type of assignment and the benefits, here is an example from one of my courses. I have assigned timeline projects in numerous classes, from broad surveys to more focused upper-level courses. Students, overall, really enjoy creating the timelines. They get to use technology, do research, and present information creatively. As a sample, a student decides to create a timeline on the history of midwifery in the course "Problems in Women and Gender History." What does this entail? Throughout the semester, we read about childbirth, birth control, abortion, witchcraft, and women's medicine in the United States and Europe. The student must use readings from the course and two outside scholarly sources. The timeline must include 15 slides and a specific period and location agreed upon with the instructor. The student decided to examine midwifery in the United States, 1716–1914, and divided the timeline into three parts: traditional midwifery (1716–1799), new midwifery and the rise of the hospital (1799–1864), and the decreasing role of the midwife (1864–1914). While there is no formal thesis statement, the timeline begins with the purpose "to examine the shift from the active central role of midwives delivering babies to the professionalization of obstetrics and the decreasing role of midwives in deliveries and maternal care." The student uses images from the Library of Congress and other academic sources to highlight the information on each slide in the timeline. Each slide has a citation under the image or video and at the end of the text. The text varies in length but is never shorter than four sentences. When the student submits the timeline, they also submit a two-page reflection paper where they highlight what they learned and what was new to them. The student reflected on why midwifery diminished in the United States over the last three centuries but remained prominent in many European countries. Hopefully, this example can show you the possibilities of a timeline project. It can be as detailed or as minimal as the instructor desires while easily meeting course learning outcomes.

Story Mapping

Geography is a central component for all students of history. All history instructors use maps at some point in their teaching to give students a spatial understanding of where and when the history they are learning is located. In an online course, it is easy to post maps and instruct students to examine them. A student may give a cursory look at the map or maybe even a little further examination if there is a map quiz, but how do they engage with maps and geography as a whole? One way to do this is to have a project in your online course using story mapping. There is different free user-friendly software available for students to create story maps.[7]

In addition to geography, story maps incorporate central historical thinking and analysis skills with the concepts of continuity and change and make connections between people, places, and time. Story maps allow for the use of interactive maps, multimedia, and text to demonstrate the concepts described above. Some story map software allows for the use of geographic information system (GIS) mapping. GIS, as one of its features, allows for map layering, which allows students to look at how a place changes over time and provides spatial perspectives. To give you an example of a type of project a student can create, I will put on my hat as a French historian. A student could create a story map examining King

Louis XVI's flight to Varennes, a famous event that shifted the tone of the French Revolution. The options of how a student could interpret this event through a story map are endless. The student should use the map to display the path taken by Louis XVI from Paris to Varennes. They could use the stopping points on the map to give a timeline of the flight to Varennes, but they also could use points on the map to discuss the situation that led to the king's flight. Essentially, the student must use research to create this story map; they also need to make connections between the king's flight and the impact on the people.[8] A story map project can be as straightforward or as complicated as you wish to make the assignment. Having some form of an assessment at the end is essential, such as a reflection or process paper. Having detailed instructions and requirements is also very helpful as this will save the instructor time when responding to emails.

Edpuzzle

Many history instructors find showing films or documentaries useful in classes. The videos provide visual evidence to support ideas and concepts from readings or classroom discussions. In online courses, it is easy to assign these videos to correspond with readings and hope students watch them. Often, instructors will have a cumulative assessment tied to such videos asking for reflections or thoughts on what students watched. This can be an effective mode of assessment, but many times students tend to "wing" this type of assessment without watching the entire video. So, how do instructors ensure students are watching the videos, and is there a better way to assess these types of assignments?

One of the better tools available is Edpuzzle,[9] which allows instructors to conduct assessments while students are watching the videos. Edpuzzle and similar software allow instructors to upload videos to Edpuzzle and then place questions at specific points in the video for students to answer. Students cannot fast forward to the questions and cannot proceed with the video without inserting an answer. The questions can be in different formats throughout the video, such as multiple choice or open-ended. Edpuzzle also integrates with most learning management systems (LMSs)[10] and allows for scoring inserted directly into the LMS grade book. The videos can be uploaded directly to Edpuzzle or accessed through a YouTube tool in Edpuzzle. If using your own recorded lecture, uploading it to YouTube first allows for Edpuzzle to process it faster. While instructors can use different types of questions to assess comprehension, know that this is a basic level of assessment only asking for remembering and understanding. If the instructor wishes students to demonstrate higher level skills a different assignment outside of Edpuzzle is more appropriate.

Online Exhibits

It is expected in online courses that all material is available to students while they are at home using their computers. Asking students to leave their homes to engage with museums or performances is not usually viable in an online course. However, instructors know that sometimes students need to interact with material culture to gain further knowledge of the topic. One way to do this is to have students engage with online exhibits. The digital world is constantly expanding, and many museums, historical societies, and other historical entities are creating ways for people to engage with their materials from home. To find these exhibits, you can navigate directly to a museum website or use other search engines to find online exhibits. Google Arts & Culture[11] is a good search engine for finding such exhibits.

Online exhibits can enhance readings and learning outcomes of your course through active engagement and assessment. In a course on the history of the Middle East, one of the learning outcomes is for students to compare and contrast the region's three major religions. Almost everyone can agree that this is a difficult task, and while students are assigned readings that explain the differences between Judaism, Christianity, and Islam, it is usually still tricky for some to grasp how they overlap; students tend to understand the differences well but not the similarities.

One way to assist students in getting the similarities and differences is through an online exhibit created by the J. Paul Getty Museum called "The Art of Three Faiths: Torah, Bible, Qur'an."[12] This exhibit looks at the illumination of these holy books detailing the artwork. Students can read the exhibit's descriptions and move through the artwork. The assessment associated with this online exhibit asks students to think about the reading and the online exhibit and explain how the three faiths are interconnected. These types of online exhibits allow for student exposure to material culture and a different kind of historical source; it also engages them to contextualize the other faiths and engage them in historical reasoning by asking them to make connections between the different materials within the exhibit. The use of online exhibits within online courses can enhance the type of material students engage with and assist students in meeting learning outcomes through a different medium.

Rubrics

Throughout the above discussion on the types of technology, there is a consistent emphasis on the importance of assessment and learning outcomes. These terms make everyone roll their eyes, but they have a place of significance in all courses; however, there is an enhanced need for assessment and learning outcomes in asynchronous online courses. As instructors do not interact "live" with students, expectations and requirements must be extra precise. Placing learning outcomes in every assignment and having a detailed rubric will eliminate many headaches for the instructor. It also sets a shared understanding of expectations when using technology that students may not be familiar with. While instructors use rubrics to grade, they also should think of the rubrics as student checklists. A useful tip is to have students submit a rubric they complete with their final assignment. It allows them to treat the rubric as a checklist but also allows you to gauge how the student measures their success on the assignment and to see if there was any disconnect in the instructions or comprehension.

There should be a clear connection between the set learning outcomes for the assignment and the rubric. For example, when a student completes a timeline assignment, one of the learning outcomes could be: students will be able to display a historical understanding of change over time and how events contributed to the historical causation. How can this be assessed within a rubric? A scale of five is usually the most effective and easiest to calculate. You could label the rubric with excellent, above average, average, below average, and did not complete. Each section needs clear definitions and expectations of what these ratings mean. For a timeline that requires a minimum of 15 slides for the entire project, the rubric could state that an excellent rating is:

> Across at least seven slides, the timeline visually displays and has a written discussion regarding how the topic changed over time. The timeline also explains the historical causation of this change for each of these seven slides with supporting evidence.[13]

Tying learning outcomes to assignment rubrics should be commonplace for all assignments. However, it is imperative to do so when teaching online, as expectations often get blurred. Instructors should incorporate their rubrics into the LMS as this will make grading easier for instructors.

Conclusion

No matter what camp you fall into in a traditional classroom, lecturer or interactive instructor, you can transition to teaching online. Teaching online can be a daunting task your first time, if you believe it needs to be exactly like a traditional in-person course. Using technology such as the material highlighted in this chapter, timelines, story mapping, Edpuzzle, online exhibits, as well as other tools, allows for a different and more effective online teaching experience. If instructors are willing to use the technology available, it can make your online course more engaging and student-centric while meeting learning outcomes and having worthwhile assessment.

Notes

1 See Chapter 1.
2 Two examples of timeline software are Knightlab Timeline JS (https://timeline.knightlab.com) and Tiki-Toki Timeline Maker (www.tiki-toki.com).
3 When using Knightlab it was found that many universities' G-suite products did not provide authorization as you have to use Google Sheets. You can ask your

university to grant permission to use with G-suite or you can have students use their personal accounts to produce the timelines.
4 In survey courses, it may be better to have an established list of topics from which students select, particularly for courses covering broad subject matter, since it will allow instructors to better monitor project topics.
5 The term slide refers to each year or period in the timeline.
6 A note of experience: It is a good idea to have students submit 1–2 slides about two weeks before the assignment is due so you can see that they understand how to use the software. This will save the instructor a lot of time and students are less likely to be emailing last minute with technical questions. Make this check-in a small part of the overall final grade.
7 Two examples of story map software are: StoryMap JS (https://storymap.knightlab.com) and ArcGIS Storymaps (https://storymaps.arcgis.com).
8 Another option that does not require independent research would be to have a common text such as Timothy Tackett's *When the King Took Flight* (Cambridge: Harvard University Press, 2004) and have students interpret the Flight to Varennes through this source and additional primary documents provided by the instructor, and then create a story map.
9 Edpuzzle (https://edpuzzle.com).
10 You may need to check with your institution's online department to make sure the building block is in your LMS. It is a simple thing for them to do but sometimes it needs to be activated for the entire LMS before you can use it.
11 "Google Arts and Culture" (https://artsandculture.google.com).
12 J. Paul Getty Museum, "The Art of Three Faiths: Torah, Bible, Qur'an," Google Arts and Culture. June 15, 2022. https://artsandculture.google.com/story/aAVRFg2-TKDIKQ. Accessed November 22, 2022.
13 Please note this is just a sample, the author wants to convey that the rubric needs to be detailed and comprehensive for students. This is a best practice and while quite a bit of work on the front end, will make grading easier for the instructor.

Chapter 10

Dynamic Video Content in the Online History Classroom

Courtney Luckhardt

We are all experienced online educators now, as new global challenges in education have brought even those who were not particularly interested in teaching virtually into the world of online teaching. Many people felt thrown into the deep end without the technological skills to transition to online learning from teaching and learning face-to-face. An evergreen problem in education is that instructors and administrators alike can be attracted to the shiny new software or hardware that purports to solve problems ranging from student engagement in a course to student persistence at a university. Creating video content for online courses that is dynamic is not merely about using technology, but about serving student learning goals.

As with teaching in a face-to-face classroom, online teaching mastery is gained one step at a time.[1] Instead of being overwhelmed by the amount of technology to learn, instructors should take small steps to improve student learning rather than making large-scale changes. Indeed, the thesis of the recent book *Small Teaching Online* argues that "paying attention to the small, everyday decisions we make in teaching represents our best route for successful learning for our students, in almost any learning environment we can imagine."[2]

In the case of the creation of video content for online courses, video recording and editing technologies are tools that are best used to enhance learning goals of the course, rather than as an end in and of themselves. Developing dynamic and engaging video content is not the ultimate objective; student mastery of the learning goals is. As historians, we have the skills to create content for online and hybrid courses that will enable student learning because it's the exact same expertise we have for our fully in-person classes. While technological skills are needed to translate this to the screen rather than the lecture hall or seminar room, focusing on content and course design rather than video recording and editing technology shows why courses taught by experts in their field are so valuable for student success.

DOI: 10.4324/9781003258414-13

Media Richness and Video Content

To explore the importance of marrying course design and content with video technologies, I will use my own introductory world history survey course as an example. When designing the online delivery for the course History 101, "World History to 1500 CE," I kept the learning goals of the course firmly in mind. The course is part of the general education curriculum and is a required course for the majority of the student body. Good course design is not so much about gaining a few new technical skills as it is about learning to be more thoughtful and specific about our purposes and what they imply.[3] My central principle of course design is balancing both student success and intellectual rigor, which is as difficult to achieve online as it is in a traditional face-to-face classroom.

When selecting a medium to convey information that in face-to-face courses is normally given in classroom lectures, it is helpful to think about the relative "richness" of the medium. The richest media have the ability to accomplish four goals: sending both verbal and non-verbal cues, supporting language variety, including oral and written, providing synchronous feedback, and allowing for personalization.[4] Along a spectrum then, an asynchronous "wall of text" would be the leanest element in an online course, while a synchronous Zoom class would be the richest medium. Recent work acknowledges that media richness is not a simple objective measure. Changing technology as well as the use of mobile devices means that text-based media like text-messaging or social media DMs are perceived as rich because of their immediacy and the asynchronous ability for participants to control their presentation by filtering messages, images, or videos.[5]

In an educational context, an online course composed of richer media elements generally yields higher rates of student–instructor and student–peer interaction, as well as higher rates of student satisfaction.[6] However, another important aspect of media richness theory includes matching the communication medium with the equivocality of a task, or the extent to which a student might be confused or uncertain. Simple tasks are not enhanced by rich media; instead, they detract from it. This is exemplified by the modern employee complaint: "this meeting could've been an email."

Not every element of a course needs to be in the richest environment; basic reminders are best as text-based emails or announcements, while discussions of primary sources may be best in Zoom or another video conferencing software. For material that instructors would normally deliver in lecture format in face-to-face courses, the medium-rich media environment of asynchronous video is an ideal format, with the only missing element of richness being the ability to provide synchronous feedback; that is, students cannot raise their hands (as they can in an in-person lecture) to ask questions. However, video is an excellent online medium for conveying both verbal and non-verbal cues (using tone and body language), language variety (with both aural and written elements, such as chyrons), and instructor personalization of the material.

Segmenting Video Material

Not all video serves the needs of students equally. In our survey course's original online format, students watched 50–75-minute video lectures recorded live by the professors teaching the course. However, it was a struggle to get students to watch these long videos; the view numbers of the posted videos indicated that only about a quarter of the 300 students enrolled in the class were watching a given lecture. To create effective online video content, it's necessary to think about the way that people interact with online media.[7] Good instructional design involves thinking about the rhythm of online engagement, meaning that it is common to read some text, watch a video, comment on that video, then read or watch again. In order make students more engaged with course content and have a more active online lecture experience, mimicking this online rhythm is essential.

Shorter video lectures made students more engaged with course content and have a more active online lecture experience. In recent research on the efficacy of different types of instructional videos, one element had the most impact on students achieving the learning outcomes of the course: segmenting.[8] Segmenting in this context involves breaking a presentation into meaningful chunks with the student controlling when the system moves on to the next segment (e.g. by clicking a "Next" button). This technique helps learners manage the "intrinsic cognitive load," or the inherent difficulty of the lesson. When the material is complex, presented at a fast pace, or unfamiliar to the learner (and world civilizations courses are generally all three), segmenting is a particularly useful way of allowing students to adjust the pace of a lecture or lesson themselves.

When redesigning the video content, I focused on creating shorter videos that would engage students with the content and enhance the student acquisition of the learning goals of the course. I edited video lecture content into manageable 5–20-minute chunks (the size of a standard YouTube video) inside Apple's Final Cut Pro X video editing software, hosted locally on the university's subscription video platform, Yuja. This involved teaching myself how to use a complex set of software tools (everything from learning how to make transitions to creating chyrons, etc.) All told, I created and edited 86 videos with a total of about 20 hours of running time. This is around 90 minutes per week of video content (about the same as they would get in a face-to-face lecture), broken up into manageable chunks averaging about 13 minutes each. I used this new content in dynamic lessons created in an eLearning authoring tool called Softchalk. This software incorporates text, image, and video all together, as well as allows quizzing and activity functions to be embedded into a lesson, with assessments automatically integrated into learning management systems.

Accessibility for students with disabilities is a key feature of making online education work well. Making our history courses fully ADA-compliant is legally required, but videos are often a place where accessibility fails disabled students by not providing transcripts or relying on auto-captioning inside software programs. Auto-captioning is generally very poor for academic videos on historical topics, as there are many specialized terms and names. In my case, a graduate student worker in the history department transcribed the videos created for the course, which ended up being a total of 188 pages of single-spaced text. The student worker also used these transcriptions to closed-caption the videos, ensuring that names (of ancient Chinese emperors, for instance) were spelled correctly in both the PDF transcription and the closed captioning. Non-disabled students also benefit from accurate closed-captioning; many students turn it on to aid in note-taking.

Some instructors may have the expertise of instructional designers or other technical support professionals at their university to help them with video creation and accessibility. Some might have an aptitude for computer software and be able to teach themselves key skills or hire student workers for additional support. Whatever the level of support or expertise might be behind the creation of video content for an online course, it is important to remember that "these are powerful educational tools – powerfully beneficial or powerfully distracting."[9] We should use them purposefully, especially in choosing what technology to use and why.

Learning Outcomes and Video Content

To be active and dynamic, video content must apply directly to student mastery of learning outcomes. Video length and creation was only one part of the solution to this problem in my introductory world history course. The shorter videos also needed to focus specifically on ideas and skills that applied directly to the course learning outcomes. One learning goal for the course was for students to be able to identify concrete examples of the themes of world history in different historical civilizations and discuss their significance. The four themes chosen are: religious development and syncretism, elite power and political organization, trade and economic development, and technological innovations and development. I developed this thematic approach to the introductory history course because of the challenges of both covering the required content of the course (10,000 years of the history of the entire world) and engaging students. The chronological "coverage" model for the first half of the world history survey course is fundamentally flawed.[10] Instead, I structure my survey course around four themes to demonstrate continuities between very disparate cultures across a vast timespan.

In a long face-to-face lecture, professors have the opportunity build a narrative structure that tells a story or advances a clear argument. Short videos must stand independently of one another, even if they are part of the same module or lesson, as they are designed to give students the ability to leave a lesson and return to it later. Since the course learning goals were focused on thematic connections and their significance, long, narrative lectures were discarded, which were a barrier to student success because of their length in any case. This allowed the new style of short video to combine with original content that demonstrated relevance of each world civilization studied to the chosen themes of the course. Every short video addresses one or more of the four themes; in this way, the lecture doesn't need to have a clear narrative structure (in the manner of a face-to-face lecture) but can stand alone while still advancing learning goals.

A second learning goal for the course is for students to be able to understand the ways in which historians use primary sources to gather information, identify biases, and reconstruct the ideals and assumptions of a distant past. Introductory students often struggle with understanding historical primary sources; this is often their first (and perhaps only) encounter with the type of close reading that requires not just attention to the text, but also applying historical context to reading. For the online course, there is an important short scaffolding video in the first week, "What Is Historical Context?" that lays out this key definition and skill set for students. After learning that historical context is the circumstances that form the setting for an event or idea that help them understand or analyze the past, subsequent videos model primary source analysis for students using the weekly readings.

These dynamic short videos are an ideal place for an instructor to model the skill set of primary source analysis by having one to three of the short videos analyze the required primary source weekly reading. Being explicit in how historians and history students should use primary sources to both gather information and reconstruct the ideals of the people of the past is key. In these short "historical thinking" videos, I discuss and model how to connect close reading (interesting observations and analysis of the primary text) with historical context (what was happening at the time), consistently and clearly asking and answering the same two questions on historical context for students: What was happening at the time and place this source was written that sheds light on the significance of the source? And what does this source contribute to our knowledge of world history in this specific time and place? Another important part of the puzzle is connecting these videos for student learning goals to other assignments (and their associated learning goals) in the course. For instance, the video lesson modeling of critical thinking and historical contextualization skill set always relates directly to active discussion and/or written assignments of the course, i.e. discussion boards, reading annotation assignments, paragraph writing assignments, exams, and/or longer papers.[11]

Evaluating Student Success

There has been much excellent research done on the role that discussion and other active learning techniques play in student success. However, in history survey courses, there is a certain amount of content that is most easily conveyed via the lecture format. It is also true that students like lectures and often self-report that they are a key component of their learning gains. Students' self-evaluation skills are not an especially reliable measure of their learning and development, despite the widespread use of student self-reporting on how much they have gained during college.[12] However, using both qualitative and quantitative measures of student learning can be instructive.

For instance, for student self-evaluation I deploy a mid-semester survey for students in which they are asked seven questions that seek qualitative feedback, including: "What aspects of this course and your instructor's teaching help you learn best?" During my online course in fall 2017, before the redesign of the videos away from recorded live lectures of 50–75 minutes, nearly 58% of students chose lectures as the most helpful element of the course (despite the view numbers on a given lecture showing only about a quarter of the students were watching the lectures).[13] Asked the same question in a course taught two years after the redesign in spring 2021, an even higher number (72%) reported that the video lessons helped them learn best. Showing quite a bit of self-awareness, one student put in their final course evaluation that semester, "I personal[ly] prefer video lectures or reading lectures to help me learn best. I also prefer the video lectures to be broken down into very small segments, because when they are long and lengthy, I find myself losing focus after 15 mins or so."

In terms of quantitative measures of student learning gains, the average grade in the class for the content quizzes for the video lessons was 80.1%. Even more dramatically, the rate at which students did not pass or dropped the course (DFW rate, an acronym that combines D and F grades with students who withdraw, earning a W, from a course) fell from 40% in fall 2017 to 25% in spring 2021 (see Survey Results at the end of this chapter).[14]

Recently, a new study among students in introductory history courses in the California State University system shed light on the precise ways that professors who make the practice of historical interpretation transparent and understandable for their students make a difference in "student success" in the way that *we as historians* care about (improving students' historical thinking skills) *and* the new metrics of student success that administrators are concerned with (DFW and retention rates).

As the authors put it: "In the era of big data, we [in the Humanities] still insist on broader and harder-to-quantify measures of success, even (or especially) in lower-division introductory courses enrolling introductory students. For us, success in these classes involves more than a passing grade. Success also means ensuring that all our students understand history as interpretation supported by evidence, that they develop stronger academic skills, and that they go forward with a sense of how the past informs their lives as active participants in a larger political community."[15]

Many other things have changed in my World History courses in the two years since I created and deployed the new video content, including new short quizzes after the videos to incentivize watching the lectures and active learning primary source discussions using reading annotation software.[16] However, the use of short video lessons was an integral part of increasing student success in the course both quantitatively with measurements of DFW rates, and qualitatively, helping improving students' historical thinking skills. As one student said in their end of semester evaluation for spring 2021, "I always hated history because I had to remember dates and names but this class was nothing like that, thank goodness! I loved learning the material and found it interesting and engaging. I really liked that the class videos were short and weren't just reviewing what the chapter said, but actually adding information that wasn't covered in the book."

Video Content Going Forward

Once content has been created for an online environment, it can be redeployed in hybrid and face-to-face classes as well. The barrier to the "flipped classroom" model is often the creation of online lecture content.[17] However, with many instructors having created video lecture material during the pivot to online learning during the pandemic, this barrier has been significantly reduced. For instance, in fall 2021, I taught a hybrid version of the course that has students viewing these video lectures during the week, and then meeting on Fridays for active-learning discussion classes of 50 minutes, led by the instructor and supported by graduate teaching assistants and undergraduate learning assistants.[18] The course was targeted at students who often underperform in huge lecture-style or online courses, defined as students who have previously failed the course or who scored 19 or below on the English and/or Reading sections of the ACT standardized test.

Online education is not reinventing the wheel; we should use our expertise in our field (both research and teaching) in teaching online, including in creating and curating our video and multimedia content. Resources are available from many institutions and for-profit educational entities. I have used the Arizona State University "Teaching Online" website[19] as well as the "Quality Matters" rubrics.[20] Some programs have more value than others depending on one's discipline and previous skill sets. Part of learning to teach well is absorbing some of this pedagogy, just as we did when we were learning to teach face-to-face. But the expertise we bring from our PhD training is key; the rest, whether it is online pedagogy or video editing software, are just new tools we can bring to bear on our teaching.

Survey Results: Fall 2017

Q: What aspects of this course and your instructor's teaching helps you learn best?
Numerical results: 202 total responses
Lectures (50–75 minute recorded lectures) – 116 students (57.5%)

Discussion (discussion boards) – 54 students (26.5%)
Textbook (online publisher-produced content) – 15 students (7.5%)
All aspects – 8 students (4%)
None – 6 students (3%)
Other – 5 students (2.5%)
DFW – 115/287 (40%)

Survey Results: Spring 2021

Q: What aspects of this course and your instructor's teaching helps you learn best?
Numerical results: 160 responses
Video lectures (shorter video lessons) – 115 students (72%)
Discussion (primary source annotation discussions) – 12 students (7.5%)
Textbook (online publisher-produced content) – 25 students (15.5%)
All aspects – 0 students
None – 3 students (2%)
Other – 6 students (3.5%)
DFW – 46/186 (24.7%)
Video lesson quiz average grade – 80.1%

Notes

1. For an excellent overview of the scholarship on teaching and learning in the discipline of history, see Hughes, Richard. "New Guidelines for SoTL in History: A Discipline Considers the SoTL Turn?" *Teaching History: A Journal of Methods 44*, no. 2 (2019): 34–43. https://openjournals.bsu.edu/teachinghistory/article/view/2371.
2. Darby, Flower and James Lang. *Small Teaching Online*. San Francisco, CA: Jossey-Bass, 2019, xxii.
3. Wiggins, Grant and Jay McTighe, *Understanding by Design*. Alexandria, VA: Association for Supervision and Curriculum Development, 2005, 14.
4. Shiefelbein, Jill. "Media Richness and Communication in Online Education," Blog entry for Magna Publications, April 10, 2012. www.facultyfocus.com/articles/online-education/media-richness-and-communication-in-online-education. Accessed November 22, 2022.
5. Ishii, Kumi, Mary Madison Lyons, and Sabrina A. Carr. "Revisiting Media Richness Theory for Today and the Future," *Human Behavior and Emerging Technologies 1*, no. 2 (2019): 124–131, 127. https://doi.org/10.1002/hbe2.138.
6. Shepherd, Morgan M. and William Benjamin Martz, Jr., "Media Richness Theory and the Distance Education Environment," *The Journal of Computer Information Systems 47* (2006): 114–112.
7. Ou, Chaohua, David A. Joyner, and Ashok K. Goel, "Designing and Developing Video Lessons for Online Learning: A Seven Principle Model," *Online Learning 23*, no. 2 (2019): 82–104.
8. Fiorella, Logan and Richard E. Mayer, "What Works and What Doesn't Work with Instructional Video," *Computers in Human Behavior 89* (2018): 465–470; Berg, Richard, et al. "Leveraging Recorded Mini-Lectures to Increase Student Learning," *Online Classroom 14*, no. 2 (2014): 5–6. www.csusb.edu/sites/default/files/upload/file/Leveraging_Recorded_Mini-Lectures_to_Inc.pdf.

9 Darby and Lang, *Small Teaching Online*, 42.
10 See Calder, Lendol. "Uncoverage: Toward a Signature Pedagogy for the History Survey," *The Journal of American History 92*, no. 4 (2006): 1358–1370; and Sipress, Joel M., and David J. Voelker. "The End of the History Survey Course: The Rise and Fall of the Coverage Model." *Journal of American History 97*, no. 4 (2011): 1050–1066.
11 Carter, Genesea and David Korostyshevsky, "Valuing Process Over Product: Using Writing to Teach History in the Undergraduate History Classroom," *Teaching History: A Journal of Methods 46*, no. 1 (2021): 10–22. https://openjournals.bsu.edu/teachinghistory/article/view/3204.
12 Bowman, Nicholas A. "Can 1st-Year College Students Accurately Report Their Learning and Development?" *American Educational Research Journal 47*, no. 2 (2010): 466–496. https://doi.org/10.3102/0002831209353595.
13 Deslauriers, Louis, Logan S. McCarty, Kelly Miller, Kristina Callaghan, and Greg Kestin, "Measuring actual learning versus feeling of learning in response to being actively engaged in the classroom," *Proceedings of the National Academy of Sciences, 116*, no. 39 (2019): 19251–19257.
14 The redesign of this History 101 "World Civilizations to 1500" course was a part of a five-year Quality Enhancement Plan (QEP) required for University of Southern Mississippi's renewed accreditation with the Southern Association of Colleges and Schools Commission on Colleges (SACSCOC). The QEP, *Eagles Engaged: Enhancing Gateway and Pathway Experiences*, sought to improve student success at "gateways," that is, historically difficult, high-enrollment courses foundational to the general education curriculum or to a major: BSC 110 (Principles of Biological Science I), BSC 250 (Anatomy and Physiology I), CHE 106 (General Chemistry I), HIS 101 (World Civilization I), and MAT 99 (Intermediate Algebra). https://sacscoc.org/app/uploads/2020/12/University_of_Southern_Mississippi_QEP_Executive_Summary.pdf
15 Ford, Bridget, Katherine Chilton, Christopher Endy, Michael Henderson, Brad A. Jones, and Ji Y. Son, "Beyond Big Data: Teaching US History in the Age of Student Success," *Journal of American History 106*, no. 4 (2020): 989–1011.
16 The online reading annotation software I used is Hypothes.is, which is a social annotation tool. This application improved my students' discussion interactions – instead of traditional discussion boards inside an LMS, Hypothes.is asks students to highlight key quotations and write in the virtual margins of a document (in this case, a primary source text) provided by the instructor. https://web.hypothes.is.
17 Murphree, Daniel, and Kevin Mercer, "Flipping the University Classroom: A Three-Year Analysis of Methods and Impacts," *Teaching History: A Journal of Methods 43*, no. 2 (2019): 17–41.
18 Learning assistants (LAs) are undergraduate students who, through the guidance of weekly preparation sessions and a pedagogy course, facilitate discussions and active learning among groups of students both online and F2F. The use of LAs is also part of the QEP at the University of Southern Mississippi (see note 14 above). www.learningassistantalliance.org.
19 The ASU instructional design community created a set of vetted resources as a toolkit for quality online course development and delivery. https://teachonline.asu.edu.
20 Quality Matters is a company that provides training and online course quality assurance. www.qualitymatters.org.

Chapter 11

Assessment and Feedback as Instruction in the Online History Classroom

Cassandra L. Clark

Assessment and feedback are key components of effective online teaching. Online learning assignments present opportunities for instructors to expand their reach by introducing historical information using a variety of mediums. Yet, the online environment can disorient students. Instruction can become overwhelming when instructors carelessly adapt traditional methods to online classes. One way to enhance online learning is to use assessment and feedback to break down and clarify instructions. Practical assessment and informative feedback assist students' absorption of historical content and the development of practical skills that benefit their personal, professional, and civic lives.

How do we design assignments and write feedback to encourage student engagement with history and develop critical thinking and communication skills? What types of assessment and feedback enhance student learning but are also efficient for instructors?

The digital classroom can produce a disconnect between students and instructors. Inundating students with text or video lectures can overwhelm them. Yet, studying history requires students to absorb large amounts of information to explore historical topics and themes. The physical classroom offers a space for instructors to evaluate how each student engages with historical material and adjust their teaching style in real time to fit particular student needs. Online course materials, whether text, video, or other media, lack this adaptability and may hinder student engagement. One can alleviate this problem by weaving instruction and historical information into course assignments and feedback.

Well-designed assignments and clear and positive feedback are key components of online learning. Instructors can teach their students methods for investigating the past by developing assignments that speak directly to historians in training and create feedback that encourages and educates learners. Historians are often trained to speak to one another, which is problematic for students beginning their academic careers.[1] Additionally, students from underprivileged backgrounds often are systemically unprepared to succeed in an academic environment.[2] Instructors should create assignments that teach all students how to understand the past and communicate their knowledge to

DOI: 10.4324/9781003258414-14

others. Assignments, such as discussion posts and reading analysis worksheets, assist students to identify historical trends, develop a timeline of events, and enhance critical thinking and writing.

Students come from different socioeconomic and educational backgrounds, which influence their approach to college courses. A 2017 study revealed that over their lifetime college graduates earn more than $1 million more than those with just high school diplomas. Unfortunately, only 23% of first-generation college students (who constitute almost a third of enrolled students across the nation) earn an undergraduate or graduate degree.[3] Additionally, marginalized students struggle for numerous reasons in the college environment. For example, a third of first-generation LGBTQ+ students reported they did not complete their degree because of on campus harassment.[4] For many students, though, online classrooms offer accessible and safe spaces to learn.[5] Further, students who feel humanized by their instructors are better equipped to learn.

Assessment is a fluid term. Assignments that work well for some disciplines and instructor personalities might fail for others. In history, assignments help students gain the background and skills to learn about the past from multiple perspectives. Assessment is less effective when it punishes students for lack of perfection or demands "conformity or obedience only."[6] Some effective assignments for teaching history online include discussion and engagement prompts, analytical tasks such as guided worksheets, short writing prompts, essays, and readings that encourage students to continue to develop their understanding of history and reading, writing, and critical thinking skills.

One of the biggest challenges to teaching history online is to encourage students to interact with all forms of instruction. A well-designed assignment is only effective if a student reads or studies the prompt. Additionally, learning continues when students study instructor feedback.[7] Weekly instructor feedback furthers the development of historical skills and context by highlighting student work and including applicable skill development and historical detail.

One obstacle history instructors face is the preconceived notions about the definition of "history" as a discipline. In short, students often assume the study of history involves the presentation and memorization of dates, names, and details. Teachers can explain and demonstrate how history is taught in the physical classroom in real time by discussing the difference between memorization, contextualization, and the differences between heritage and history. In my physical classrooms, I demonstrate history is more than memorizing and regurgitating one-sided views of the past. I explain the importance of perspective, and we participate in activities that consider historical events from the perspectives of different actors.

In contrast, my online instruction regarding history practice takes place in a ten-minute video during the first week of class. I balance that instruction with a short writing prompt asking students to explain what they learned about the practice of history. So, my instruction balances the video, the assignment prompt, and their practice. By keeping the response short (150 to 200 words),

I encourage students to focus on sentence and paragraph structure, grammar, and use of detail. Longer assignments tend to produce mixed results because students often feel overwhelmed by longer writing assignments. Shorter assignments allow students more time to proofread, edit, and seek writing help from the university writing center or me. They also help students find and articulate their voice during the course's first week.

I design each assignment to teach my students the skills I demonstrate in my physical classes. I begin the prompt by summarizing the historical topic(s) we are studying that week. I then give a few lines about the skills students gained from previous assignments. I then identify the skill they will practice and connect it to their previous work. By designing my prompts with brief overviews of weekly content, prior skills, and the next objective, students see how each assignment builds on another. My strategy also provides students with the steps needed to write a well-argued and organized essay.

Students are assigned a module each week that includes one or more short lecture videos, quizzes, and a discussion or assignment prompt. Discussion and assignment prompts reflect the historical topic(s) assigned for that week. For example, during week three, students complete a primary source analysis on women's perspectives of the American Revolution. By dedicating assignments to that week's topics, students learn more about history as they complete the work. During the first two weeks of my online US survey course, I assign two worksheets instructing students on reading secondary sources. My feedback furthers this instruction by providing examples of locating the argument and summarizing information. I also elaborate on interesting details not covered in that week's course materials. Taking the feedback as instruction approach allows me to pepper instruction from the first day of the module until the week after the module ends, when I grade their work.

My secondary source analysis assignment begins with summarizing that week's readings. I then discuss the difference between primary and secondary sources. I also post a brief video where I analyze a secondary source about Native Americans in colonial America. I demonstrate how first to read the introduction and conclusion and then locate an author's argument. I also explain why reading each paragraph's first and last sentence can help the reader grasp the author's objective. Finally, I dig into the footnotes to evaluate the types of evidence authors used to support their arguments. By exhibiting how to effectively read sources, I provide students a guide applicable to all course readings.

After demonstrating how to read a secondary source, I assign a worksheet that gives students the opportunity to practice what they learned. I ask them to read a peer-reviewed article about colonial America. First, the instructions prompt them to study the introduction and conclusion and to summarize what they learn in the article. I then prompt students to identify the argument (I provide the argument's page number) and to practice paraphrasing and citing the argument.[8] The assignment also instructs students to examine three footnotes to determine if the evidence supports the argument and explain why or why not. The final question asks students to reflect on what they learned and how they will apply the skills they developed to future reading and writing assignments.

I repeat the process during week two but assign a blog post. That way, students consider the difference between peer-reviewed versus non-peer-reviewed writing. The worksheet asks students to evaluate the use of cited evidence. The blog post does not cite their use of evidence, which is something that students note in their responses. By introducing students to two types of historical writing, they are prepared to read and write critically throughout the course. Instructor feedback is an essential aspect of the online learning environment. Students rely on instructor feedback to understand how to improve their work and to learn more about historical topics.

One method of effective teaching is to imbue in students the feeling of social connection with their instructor and the course.[9] Positive feedback that encourages students fosters social connection between students and instructors. The instructor recognizes the student's work, applauds their achievement, and offers constructive tips for improvement, which helps develop a safe and effective online learning environment. Studies show that students feel "dissatisfied" or even "shut down" when receiving unclear instructor feedback.[10] Feedback is effective when it is delivered positively, written in lay terms, and provides examples.[11] Feedback is also well-delivered when it expands on historical topics covered in student responses. Teachers' feedback is one of their primary forms of communication with students, and students' trust in their instructors is deeply rooted in the feedback they receive.

The feedback I write for the secondary source analysis worksheets employs methods of providing detailed instruction that includes examples. It begins with an encouraging observation of something the student did well. Even those students who rushed through the assignment or did not understand the objectives did something well. For example, a student who shared their opinion about what they thought of the article rather than dissecting its contents could receive positive feedback such as, "Excellent job articulating your opinions about the contents of this week's article." This validates the student's ideas and creates a foundation to further instruct the student.

My next step in writing student feedback is to address sections of the response where students could improve their work to meet course objectives. First, I outline the objective of the worksheet, which is to analyze a secondary source rather than to reflect on what we think about the subject or the author's writing or share what we already know about the topic. The student can then differentiate between their approach and the assignment's primary objective. I then provide an example of how to answer the second question that asks to locate, summarize, and cite the argument. I give the page number and paragraph of the argument and the citation. This feedback provides students with a visual representation of how to complete the worksheet's argument section. Finally, I list tips for improvement, illustrating them with details from that week's readings. I also guide students to study the example worksheet I completed and posted to the assignment prompt.

Many students benefit from instruction on how to navigate online classrooms. Feedback guiding students to instructional materials posted at the beginning of each week and reminding them to review it before the due date helps them develop strategies to succeed in online courses.

After my encouraging observation and tips for improvement, I weave additional historical context into my feedback. For example, when students complete a project about death and the Civil War, I include some statistics in the feedback, building on content from my lecture. Sometimes, I reflect on detail or a quote students used in their work, adding information and suggested readings to encourage further study. Teaching about history in my feedback encourages students to find patterns and see how information, assessment, and feedback interconnect. I wrap up my feedback with a positive closing line, highlighting something interesting the student wrote or did well. This feedback allows students to reflect positively about their work.

Writing the amount of feedback described above sounds laborious. However, instructors do not need to start fresh with each student. My strategy is to write feedback in a Word document. I can then edit several versions of that feedback tailored to particular students. This takes time for the first few students, but then it becomes easy to tailor different versions for different students as I grade. Not every student needs the same feedback, but on average, multiple students will benefit from the same instructor guidance. Misspellings, for example, are a standard tip I include in my feedback: "I recommend using spell check before submitting your work." I personalize the feedback for students with misspellings or delete that line for those without misspelled words. For example: "'slave' is misspelled in your document. 'Salve' is a common misspelling for 'slave'! Sometimes my brain works faster than my fingers, and I misspell words too." By identifying the mistake and then personalizing it by demonstrating I also make mistakes, students feel safer and are more willing to incorporate feedback into future work.

How does an instructor ensure their students read and apply feedback? I encourage reading feedback by prompting frustrated students to ask me questions about my feedback. Recommending students revisit my feedback with additional clarification helps them get on the correct path. Future student email questions also tend to be more focused on how to complete assignments or asking me to review their work before they submit it. I don't answer questions about an assignment grade in an email until after I encourage them to study the feedback and ask me specific questions about it.

I also use the discussion board, which provides students opportunities to hone their writing by responding to prompts with well-analyzed and cited responses. Students interact with me on the discussion board as I respond to their posts with cited information, questions, and ideas. For example, in the Cold War module, I ask students to juxtapose the historic videos *Duck and Cover* (1951) and *Dating Dos and Don'ts* (1949). I ask students to draw on the textbook chapter about the Cold War and consider how each video fits into that historical context.

I also assign two peer responses, or engagement posts. Students must respond to at least two peer posts, engaging with what that student wrote and citing historical evidence. This method enhances the quality of the content on the discussion board, which becomes a space for well-thought-out answers complete with analysis and supporting evidence. I read student posts and respond to at least half of them with additional historical information.

Student evaluations reveal they enjoy reading instructor responses on the discussion board. They learn as much about the assigned topic from those as from weekly readings and videos. Discussion prompts are an effective way of helping students learn how to communicate effectively using evidence-based ideas and analysis. Instructor responses validate student ideas while providing them with more historical information. They make discussion boards valid online learning spaces rather than "busy work."

Once students learn to analyze primary and secondary sources, they are prepared to defend an argument and write short essays. I prepare my students to write their first short essay as their midterm project. That way, I can grade the assignment with a flexible rubric and add comments that prepare students to write more detailed papers for the final. I have found that if I want students to meet a certain level of proficiency, I need to break the process down into manageable steps over the course of several weeks. In other words, to scaffold the process.[12]

By designing interconnected assignments complemented by constructive and straightforward feedback, my students learn the skills they need to write an argument and evidence-driven essay, which are abilities they can use in other courses and in everyday life. Additionally, students feel validated and recognize the importance of student and faculty interaction. In short, using interconnected assignments followed by clear and positive instructor feedback serves as important teaching tools for helping students develop a strong understanding of the past and its application to the present. Assessment and feedback also help students continue developing the analytical and communication tools applicable to other academic courses and their professional and personal lives.

Notes

1. Alan Booth addresses the challenge of historian training to speak to one another in his book, *Teaching History at University: Enhancing Learning and Understanding*. New York: Routledge, 2003, 2–3. Students not majoring in history take courses to fulfill college and degree expectations and for interest each semester. Additionally, first-generation college students and individuals from marginalized or varied backgrounds can lack the tools to succeed in the academic classroom. Students learn more when their instructor presents information in various ways that meet their educational experience and individual learning needs.
2. Tierney, William G. and Suneal Kolluri, *Diversifying Digital Learning: Online Literacy and Educational Opportunity*. Baltimore, MD: John Hopkins University Press, 2018.

Brian Jacob, Dan Berger, Cassandra Hart, and Susanna Loeb discuss in their study of digital learning in K-12 how "recent technological innovations have expanded the capabilities of digital learning tools in ways that booster argue offer new potential to 'disrupt' the provision of education and reduce disparities in educational opportunities." However, most importantly, eLearning does not guarantee that all students will flourish. Strategic instruction and design are needed to monitor student learning and adjust when needed. See "Can Technology Help Promote Equality of Educational Opportunities?" *RSF: The Russell Sage Foundation Journal of the Social Sciences 2*, no. 5 (2016): 242–271.

3 Cerezo, Alison and Amaranta Ramirez, "Navigating New Terrain: Sexual and Gender Diverse College Students Who Are the First in Their Families to Attend College," in *Affirming LGBTQ+ Students in Higher Education*, ed. D.P. Rivera, R.L. Abreu, and K.A. Gonzalez, 162–163. Washington, DC: American Psychology Association, 2022, 161. See Lareau, Annette. *Unequal Childhoods: Class, Race, and Family Life*. Berkeley, CA: University of California Press, 2011.

4 Cerezo and Ramirez, "Navigating New Terrain," 162, 163, 164–165.

5 Eunjyn Yu outlines the advantages of online learning that include accessibility and the opportunity for self-paced learning, "Student-Inspired Optimal Design of Online Learning for Generation Z." *Journal of Educators Online 17*, no. 1 (2020). www.thejeo.com/archive/2020_17_1/yu.

6 bell hooks demonstrated the importance of the classroom as a place where students can authentically express themselves, *Teaching Critical Thinking: Practical Wisdom*. New York: Routledge, 2010, 2, 8, 21. Unclear assignment instructions and primarily negative and condescending instructor feedback can discourage and prevent some students from feeling confident enough to learn. Clear, positive, and informative information delivered through assignments and instructor information contributes to a positive classroom environment where students feel safe and excited to learn.

7 Zhang, Zhe (Victor). "Promoting Student Engagement with Feedback: Insights from Collaborative Pedagogy and Teacher Feedback." *Assessment & Evaluation in Higher Education 47*, no. 4 (2022): 540–541.

8 Not every student quickly identifies an argument. Many students, especially in survey courses, have not learned about paraphrasing, citations, or other vital skills expected in a collegiate learning environment. By identifying the page number and general location of the argument, the assignment challenges them to find the argument in a setting that validates that not everyone learns the same way. Validation is key to creating a safe online learning environment.

9 Lang, James M. *Small Teaching: Everyday Lessons from the Science of Learning*. San Francisco, CA: Jossey-Bass, Wiley, 2016, 176.

10 Zhang, "Promoting Student Engagement with Feedback," 543.

11 As a student, I received discouraging feedback from multiple professors. Examples include "this is stupid," "this is unclear," and scribbled phrases impossible to decipher. "This is stupid" is not appropriate terminology to explain why you disagree with a student's statement. Additionally, "this is unclear" is not helpful. Explaining why you are confused helps the student identify why the information is unclear to them. In short, avoid using feedback that demeans the student.

12 James Lang explains that if "we want students to become proficient at the specific mental tasks that we are planning to assess—such as writing formal essays or responding to essay exam questions, writing lab reports, taking multiple-choice or true-false or short-answer examples—we have to give them extended practice at those tasks" Lang, *Small Teaching*, 118.

Chapter 12

Games and Gamification in Online History Classes

Mary A. Valante

"Gaming" classroom learning is nothing new; teachers have been using role-play, debates, scavenger hunts, Jeopardy-type trivia quizzes and more for about as long as there have been teachers with students. Games are fun, and because they are fun, games can promote community building, keep students engaged, and provide a much-needed break from everyday routine. The "fun" is also a powerful learning tool, breaking down complex concepts into memorable pieces that students interact with and act on. Online learning presents both new opportunities and new challenges for instructors to game their own classes, especially when it comes to experiential learning. Whether in a traditional classroom setting or online, the key to successfully bringing games into the classroom remains the same. The game itself is never the point – gaming serves education, so however much fun it may be, to be successful, the mechanics of the game should require students to practice the skills and learn the content being taught.

Johan Huizinga's 1938 *Homo Ludens* remains the starting point for any serious inquiry into the history and anthropology of games and play. He demonstrated that "play" is always deliberate and purposeful. Importantly, though, he also argued that games and play are not training exercises; it is key that they are FUN. Bernard Suits' charming 1978 *The Grasshopper*, a philosophical dialogue between a Plato-esqe version of Aesop's grasshopper and his disciples Skepticus and Prudence, argues that a game is "a voluntary attempt to overcome unnecessary obstacles."

Building on these definitions of "play" and "game," in 2014 in *Gamify*, Brian Burke took on the concept of "gamification," distinguishing it from "game."[1] Burke argued that turning ordinary and even unpleasant tasks into a game-like system with *intrinsic* rewards (like badges and leveling up) could provide very powerful behavior motivation. Ian Bogost took a very different tack in his classic 2011 web essay "Gamification is Bullshit," (a longer version called "Why Gamification is Bullshit" was published in 2015)[2] demonstrating the ways corporations have interpreted "gamification" (such as racking up points for air travel) have little to do with games and much to do with tricking consumers out of their money.

DOI: 10.4324/9781003258414-15

In the classroom, gamification might resemble a rewards system, like the old-fashioned "gold stars" charts, or more modern point systems or treat boxes. The problem, though, is that a significant body of research over the past 20 or more years demonstrates reward systems do not work. Instead, as with corporate gamification, students work for the reward and not their education. In addition, classroom motivation by reward systems seems to work only temporarily. Its effects soon wane.[3] For example, Kahoots, a popular app often used by instructors to review material, is really a form of gamification. Students get those intrinsic rewards and they do have fun – but they "win" through speed instead of accuracy, meaning they quickly realize that jamming buttons on their phone is more likely to bring a winning result than patiently waiting to guess the correct answer.

So, Burke is correct about the power of gamifying, but Bogost is also right – gamifying may not bring about the desired educational result. Adding games to any class must have a clear pedagogical purpose that does not reward "winners" academically, but instead allows the fun, the play, to motivate students to dig deeper into class material, encouraging them to learn rather than just win.

Further challenges to adding games to classes come directly from the games themselves. Games may both encourage and discourage fostering an inclusive classroom, so instructors must choose widely. In discussions of board games, Faidutti, Trammell, Garcia, and Robinson described issues such as colonialism, racism, misogyny, Islamaphobia, and more that were encoded into games' artwork, physical components, mechanics, and even the "fun" of many board games, tabletop role-playing games, and even educational role-playing games.[4] To be clear, these do not mean faculty should avoid all potentially problematic games in the classroom. It does mean that students should not be forced to play at oppression. Some games might be better analyzed than played. Keeping in mind students' experiences of diversity and inclusion within a game are as important as any other classroom activity, since "it's just a game" cannot be an excuse for allowing students to play at oppression or othering one another.

There are special challenges to adding games to online classes, among them selecting or creating a game that works online, differentiating between synchronous and asynchronous gameplay, making sure students can manage the required technology, taking into consideration universal design principals, play testing, and making certain the instructor can keep up with and track gameplay. Adding games to a class also runs the risk of students who "lose" feeling there was no point to the exercise or becoming demotivated in their studies. Most importantly, as Darby and Lang point out, "edu-tainment" is never the goal.[5] A successful online game empowers students to take control of their learning experience. Winning, while fun, is not the objective. The game should never distract from reaching learning objectives. It should lead students to them. With some thoughtful preparation it is possible to add games to online classrooms successfully and meaningfully.

Teaching with games online presents challenges but is well worth the effort. Adding games to synchronous online classes helps maintain an immediacy in class interactions, though gaming can be quite successful in asynchronous classes as well. The simplest tech can do wonders, ensuring students' focus is on the game and learning. Exercises that "game" specific learning experiences (closely related to James M. Lang's "small teaching"),[6] role-playing games, and yes even board games, can all be used in synchronous and non-synchronous online courses.

Of these three types of games, adding board games to an online class may seem impossible, but it can be done easily if the instructor is flexible about the games they use. Board games can be analyzed as texts, just like films and novels and any other type of media. They provide a fresh way for students to analyze public perceptions of a subject.[7] In many disciplines, board games have been designed for education, or can be analyzed as teaching tools. In my own classes I have students play and/or analyze games like Carcassone, Crusaders: Thy Will be Done, and Splendor to interrogate how each presents history, what (or who) is left out of the game narrative or is rendered without agency, and to consider how themes such as economics, violence, gender, colonialism, orientalism, and more, are presented (or ignored).

The simplest way to add a board game or two to a class is use an online gaming site like Board Game Arena. At the time of this writing, some of the games can be played for free, while others are behind a "premium" paywall. The current paywall, however, is only $5/month or $30/year, and only one player needs a "premium" membership for others to play. While the complement of games is far from exhaustive, there are many choices that fall across a variety of disciplines.

In a synchronous class, board games can be played in class or as homework. In classes held over Zoom or in Teams, one group can demonstrate gameplay on the main screen, or smaller groups can play games in breakout rooms. Students can play online games over a shared screen in Teams or Zoom, or they can use the game hosting site's own chat/voice protocols while playing on their own screens.

In asynchronous classes, students can similarly meet up online and play together as group homework, which provides a precious chance to meet other students from the course. In all cases, students must engage with the game, and therefore the class. The board games offer an opportunity to build community with a small number of others in the class, which can be less daunting than trying to navigate the full class all at once. As with all forms of classroom gaming, creating meaningful learning outcomes is key. Whether a student wins or loses is immaterial to their grade; all students can equally analyze any game they play or study.

Beyond board gaming, many "small teaching" techniques facilitate gaming in online classrooms. As Darby and Lang describe it, small teaching can incorporate anything at all: a specific skill, a quiz, a discussion. Most importantly, the instructor needs to practice "backwards design," which means starting from the learning outcome and then creating the exercise/game to match.[8] To provide a few examples of how to do this by gaming, instead of a more traditional syllabus quiz, I have created simple online "escape rooms" that students can only complete by reading the syllabus. Because there are specific parts of the syllabus I especially want my student to notice at the start of the semester – my contact information, my DEI statement, the grading section, and the class schedule – I ensure that the solutions to the puzzles point the students directly to those sections. An online scavenger hunt would be equally effective and possibly even simpler to create. In a synchronous class, I often have students work in small groups in breakout rooms on the first day of class, because it gives them a chance to meet a few other students, engage with each other and the class, and most importantly, it gets them to review and read key elements of the syllabus. In an asynchronous class, even working individually and at their own pace, students still review and read key elements of the syllabus and will have a shared though separate experience.

Another example of an asynchronous "small teaching" game is my online upper level history course on the Viking Age. I needed to create an exercise that would ensure students had read and understood a selection of primary sources, and ideally engage with those readings meaningfully. Creating a discussion board where students post and then respond to each other on the course LMS is one effective way to do this. Another way to accomplish the goal is to use a social annotation tool, like Hypothesis or Perusall, which encourages a collaborative, interactive approach to close reading of assigned texts. Both approaches are effective, but even effective assignments can feel repetitive over time. So for one set of readings, I created a collaborative story exercise instead. Playing off a popular meme:

> Tired: online discussion boards
> Wired: class annotations of texts
> Inspired: a collaborative storytelling game

In this exercise, I gave students the image, name, and birth and death dates for a fictional character. They drew from a stack of index cards the sources they were responsible for, and the date/time when they needed to add to the story. Over the course of several days, the class worked together on a shared Google Doc to create the character and weave his life and story into the primary source readings. Because they were not allowed to contradict anything that came before, students had to read all primary sources as well as the emerging story before they added to it.

They loved doing it. Their "Tale of Áki" was creative, charming, and at times even heart-wrenching. More importantly, it was entirely historically plausible. Since the storytelling game took place online and outside of class time, it works easily for a synchronous class, but can be adapted for an asynchronous class if there are a series of deadlines within the overall class structure.

Debates, simulations, and role-playing games can also be used in online classes. Mark Carnes has written about the power of role-playing games in learning history, referring especially to the Reacting to the Past series of games.[9] In *Minds on Fire*, Carnes argues teaching intellectual history through role-play can be especially powerful, though he leans towards a certain both-sidesism when he discusses the ways role-playing can lead to empathy for all points of view.[10] More recently, the Reacting to the Past board of directors has taken a more protective stance towards students when it comes to playing roles where voicing racist ideology is written into the game.[11] But the effectiveness of a well-crafted role-play in the classroom is undeniable; similar to the power of immersive play in video games as described by Murray in *Hamlet on the Holodeck*,[12] role-play can be used to teach more than intellectual history. As students inhabit characters and people in historic periods, they can learn to identify with the very real struggles people in the past have faced, articulate ways humans in the past have worked together to overcome obstacles, and at best come to empathize with marginalized people from history.

The Zinn Education Project, while designed for high school teachers, provides valuable ideas for expanding the possibilities of role-play in college classrooms. In debates, students take a side and argue for it based on evidence, but they may or may not take on roles or characters when doing so. In simulations (think Model UN) or role-playing games, students inhabit a role or even a specific person. This carries risks, since historical figures could believe in a variety of oppressive and noxious ideas, whether racist, misogynistic, homophobic, heavily biased towards one religion or another, or worse. The Zinn Education Project includes an important article on "How to – and How Not to – Teach Role Plays." An older version of the article offered some sage advice university faculty can use when assigning difficult roles to students. In brief: no student should be forced to accept a role they are uncomfortable playing, no role should ever have a student act out any traumatic experience, and finally, students acting in the roles of oppressors are articulating a point of view but they are not expected to identify with that perspective. The updated version argues that effective role-play in a classroom setting must engage with and help students understand complex social phenomena, center on marginalized groups and individuals who worked for justice, and "increase students' capacity for justice."[13]

In my own classes, I have successfully designed and used a number of debates, simulations, and role-playing games. All of these can work online, both synchronously and asynchronously, though it is more difficult to maintain tension and immediacy in an asynchronous class. In one simulation I created based on the 1998 Irish Peace accords, students represented various factions from Northern Ireland, the Republic of Ireland, and the UK. They came to the virtual table understanding they were looking to create peace. On the final meeting, just as in real life, Senator Mitchell's draft proposal of a peace deal pleased no one. Fellow faculty members agreed to drop in and play the prime ministers of Ireland and the UK, as well as the US president. The surprise appearance of our "guest stars" (and a few carefully crafted IMs to Sinn Fein leadership from the US) secured the deal at the last minute. This class met synchronously and fully online. Students mostly presented their arguments live, though they were all welcome to prerecord a statement. Breakout rooms were vital for hashing out details in smaller sessions. In an asynchronous class, all students would record their statements (Flipgrid is a simple tool for this, and integrates easily into our LMS), and everyone would watch on their own time and then respond by set dates and times. Using Slack or Discord for the meeting spaces works very well in an asynchronous online class, making it easy for students to work out the details of their peace agreement.

In the end, best practices for gaming in online classes are the same best practices for any online class. Clear structure and predictability are vital to student success, so games should be built into the syllabus, not added on. Games and any technology used for the games should enhance the class experience, not replace it. To allow technology to fade into the background during the game, instructors must devote some time to teaching students how to use the technology involved. The best gaming experiences always take into account the principles of universal design for learning. And of course, classroom games, whether board games, "small things," or lengthy role-playing experiences, no matter how exciting, are never the end; the games are a means to guiding students willingly towards the class learning objectives.

Notes

1 Burke, Brian. *Gamify: How Gamification Motivates People to Do Extraordinary Things*. Brookline, MA: Bibliomotion, 2014.
2 Bogost, Ian. "Gamification is Bullshit," 2011, http://bogost.com/writing/blog/gamification_is_bullshit. Accessed November 22, 2022; Bogost, Ian. "Why Gamification is Bullshit," in *The Gameful World: Approaches, Issues, Applications*, ed. Stephan Walz and Sebastion Deterdig, 65–79. Cambridge, MA: The MIT Press, 2014.
3 Wilson, Lucinda M. and Deborah A. Corpus. "The Effects of Reward Systems on Academic Performance," *Middle School Journal 33*, no. *1* (2001): 56–60.
4 Trammell, Aaron. "Misogyny and the Female Body in Dungeons & Dragons," *Analog Game Studies 1*, no. *3* (2014). https://analoggamestudies.org/2014/10/constructing-the-female-body-in-role-playing-games; Garcia, Antero. "Privilege, Power, and Dungeons & Dragons: How Systems Shape Racial and Gender Identities in Tabletop Role-Playing Games," *Mind, Culture and Activity 24*, no. *3* (2017): 232–246; Robinson, Will. "Orientalism and Abstraction in Eurogames," *Analog Game Studies 1*, no. *5* (2014). https://analoggamestudies.org/2014/12/orientalism-and-abstraction-in-eurogames.
5 Darby, Flower and James Lang. *Small Teaching Online*. San Francisco, CA: Jossey-Bass, 2019, 62–3.
6 Lang, James M. *Small Teaching: Everyday Lessons from the Science of Learning*. San Francisco, CA: Jossey-Bass, Wiley, 2016.

7 Murray, Janet H. *Hamlet on the Holodeck: The Future of Narrative in Cyberspace*. Cambridge, MA: MIT Press, 1997, is the foundational text in reading games as media.
8 Darby and Lang, *Small Teaching Online*, 5–26.
9 Please see the resources section in this book's appendix for links to Reacting to the Past and other gaming sites and resources.
10 Carnes, Mark. *Minds on Fire: How Role-Immersion Games Transform College*. Cambridge, MA: Harvard University Press, 2014, esp 207–227.
11 https://networks.h-net.org/node/950/discussions/10250560/reacting-past-removes-frederick-douglass-role-play-print-version.
12 Murray, *Hamlet on the Holodeck*, esp. 97–125.
13 www.zinnedproject.org/news/how-to-teach-role-plays.

Part 3

Online Discussion and Interactive Learning

Stephen K. Stein

Instructors approach online teaching in a variety of ways. No matter one's approach, though, active discussions are central to an effective online history course. Discussions help create a collegial, supportive environment, in which students showcase their knowledge, support one another as they progress through a course, and learn from both faculty and their fellow students. Discussion participation reinforces students' understanding of historical events and sharpens their critical thinking skills. Students who participate more in discussion often learn more in their courses. They also tend to show the most improvement in their writing.

As Tony Acevedo notes in his chapter "Creating Meaningful Online Discussions," the point of online discussion is not to send students on fact-finding missions. Rather, instructors must structure discussions to promote historical inquiry and stimulate a critical dialogue among students and between students and their instructors. One should open a discussion with a well-crafted question that encourages students to present their own perspective and showcase their reading and other research. Acevedo offers numerous ideas for these, as well as instructors' follow-up questions that keep discussions moving forward by encouraging students to dig deeper into historical sources, ask more profound questions, and critique their initial assumptions.

J.M. Wolfe's chapter "Managing Online Discussions in Larger Sections" builds on many of Acevedo's ideas to discuss the challenges of online classes with more than the traditional 25–35 students. As Wolfe notes, it is simply impossible for an instructor to have an individual dialogue with each of the 200+ students in a class. Nonetheless, many common discussion techniques can be scaled up without creating undue burdens on overworked instructors. Most learning management systems also provide tools to help monitor students, such as tracking how much time they spend in a course, what resources they access and pages they read, and even which discussion posts they read. Rubrics ease grading, as does providing collective feedback for each discussion, including a summation of important points and key take-aways on a topic.

Discussions can play an important role in scaffolding class assignments, a technique in which instructors design assignments to build on each other, culminating in a final project. In several of my own graduate seminars, students turned

DOI: 10.4324/9781003258414-16

in writing assignments of increasing length, culminating in a 2000-word essay. Starting with small writing assignments taught students to isolate and focus on critical points, which ensured a tighter focus in their longer essays.

Primary sources are a great way to kick off discussions, which Micki Kaleta covers in "Letting the Sources Guide the Way: The Dynamic Utilization of Primary Sources in the Online History Classroom." Analyzing primary sources improves historical literacy and builds critical thinking skills as students grapple with the context, significance, and legacy of documents, art, and other materials. Students learn to question and critique source material, a skill vitally important to historians, but also relevant in assessing contemporary media, including social media. Kaleta's chapter discusses integrating primary sources into online courses in meaningful ways and using them to support class discussion. She explains the types of sources one should use, the questions to ask about them, and where they can be easily found.

Discussions themselves can be scaffolded so each lays a foundation for the next, allowing students to progress through increasingly complex topics. Discussions also provide a forum to support the scaffolding of traditional assignments, such as research papers. As Leigh Ann Wilson shows in her chapter "It's All Relative: The Importance of Scaffolding and Course Design in the Online History Classroom," students share their work with one another and receive feedback from fellow students, in addition to the instructor, as they work through the essential steps to completing a research paper, from its original idea, thesis, and annotated bibliography to the final paper.

Timelines offer another way to help students grapple with historical complexity and the interconnectedness of diverse events. In "Interactive Timelines as the Center of Class Discussion" Brandon Morgan discusses how he employs interactive timelines to familiarize students with important historical characters and events, keep them engaged, and facilitate class discussion. Using Tiki-Toki, Timeline JS, and similar tools, students create and share timelines on important historical figures and events. In doing so, students begin to think like historians. They examine connections between diverse historical actors and events, assess and analyze their linkages, and determine cause and effect. The annotated timelines they create then become the basis for class discussion.

Christine Eisel and Brigitte Billeaudeaux build on Kaleta's discussion, showing how they used archival sources in online courses. As they note, archival sources are difficult to incorporate into classes, whether online or traditional. Yet, archival work is central to the historical profession. In their chapter "Using Omeka to Bring Women's History to Online Learners," Eisel, a historian, and Billeaudeaux, a librarian and archivist, showcase their collaboration, which provided new archival material to students in a women's history class. Students benefited from rich archival materials, used them in research papers, and showcased their work online, using Omeka, a new digital platform, sharing it with both instructors and fellow students.

Chapter 13

Creating Meaningful Online Discussions

Tony Acevedo

Introduction

Among the greatest challenges in developing effective online history courses is creating meaningful online discussions, both between professor and student and between students themselves. Discussion forums play a critical role in making the online learning space a "classroom." If not well crafted and facilitated, online discussions may make e-learning feel different from, and potentially substandard to, face-to-face courses. This chapter presents a variety of strategies for history educators to promote meaningful online discussions to foster historical thinking and student engagement.

The Purpose and Value of the Online Discussion-Question Forum

Discussion-question forums (abbreviated as DQ forums) hold an important place in online history courses because they aim to replicate the dialogue and community of face-to-face classes. Online courses also employ varieties of essays, quizzes, exams, reaction papers, and projects, but the heart of student interaction takes place in DQ forums. In their most common form, the professor asks one or more historical questions related to course themes and readings. Students must then contribute multiple response-posts in the forum throughout each week (usually two to four posts per DQ forum). Instructors assign one or two DQ forums per week through the semester with deadlines for students' initial and follow-up posts to limit last-minute posting. As John Lyons notes, online discussion "builds class cohesion and helps to break out of the isolation associated with online learning."[1]

Some educators argue that online DQ forums provide *better* opportunities to engage students than traditional courses. Douglas Fisher and Nancy Frey note that in some traditional classroom discussions, "when one student is provided the opportunity to answer, the ability to check for understanding with the larger group is lost."[2] Any professor can recall moments when – to avoid letting a few students monopolize the discussion – they call on "someone new"

DOI: 10.4324/9781003258414-17

or "someone who has not yet spoken." In online DQ forums all students must respond to professors' discussion prompts.

Other advantages of online DQ forums include the flexibility of virtual attendance, the ease of connecting web-based resources to the curriculum, the participation of students too shy to interact in face-to-face classes, and the lack of time constraints to compose responses.[3]

Challenges in the Online DQ Forum

Still, many challenges present themselves to the online teacher. One of them, particularly in asynchronous online classes (the most common modality), is overcoming feelings of anonymity seemingly inherent in distance learning. In student evaluations for my face-to-face courses, students often mention my *passion* for history and my *enthusiasm* for teaching. How do passion and enthusiasm manifest themselves online? How does one avoid making online history courses ones in which otherwise dynamic educators only ask students to accomplish numerous "tasks" before deadlines? When discussions are purposefully designed, they make online courses enriching experiences in which students are active learners and instructors do more than grade assignments.

Some challenges arise specifically from student DQ posts: summarizing rather than analyzing, shallow responses lacking detail and context, and "I agree" or "good point" posts that dampen intellectual engagement. In the *summary* posts, students respond by paraphrasing the readings and show little original thought. In posts *lacking detail and context*, students present their own ideas, but offer vague generalizations with little historical discussion and no evidence they completed assigned readings.

In *I agree* posts, which Lisa Lane calls "me too" responses, students agree with their peers or summarize what others have said (e.g., "I like how you said that _____ and agree with you that _____").[4] These half-hearted posts quickly dull the learning environment. As Suzanne K. McCormack notes, "the lack of disagreement in class discussions, especially early in the semester when students are not yet familiar with their cohort, stifles their critical thinking and the process of inquiry that is so important to academic interactions."[5]

Defining "Meaningful Discussions"

Meaningful online history discussions must promote historical thinking, be rooted in inquiry, and stimulate a critical dialogue. DQ prompts should not focus on sending students on fact-finding missions. They should allow "answers" to become arguments, discoverable rather than findable. Sam Wineburg called historical thinking an *unnatural* act.[6] It is what happens when students employ the same habits of mind as professional historians. These include marshaling primary and secondary sources, placing evidence within historical contexts, analyzing from multiple perspectives, producing sophisticated arguments underpinned by claim-evidence connections, and asking questions that lead to still more questions. Thomas Andrews and Flannery Burke provide a useful framework in their "Five C's of Historical Thinking": change over time, causality, context, complexity, and contingency.[7]

Online history courses would do well to begin with a discussion on the practice of history, especially in survey courses. For students to "think like historians," they must learn what this means. My online Western Civilizations 1 course begins with a DQ forum where students respond to two brief videos on historical thinking. The first, from the Minnesota Historical Society, explains the difference between primary and secondary sources (and includes a quiz on the topic).[8] The second, from the National History Education Clearinghouse (teachinghistory.org), explains historical thinking around five key concepts: multiple accounts and perspectives; analyzing primary sources; sourcing; understanding historical context; and the claim-evidence connection. The latter video is designed for teachers, but if students know from the beginning how their instructors want them to think about the assignments, they will be more likely to meet those expectations. After watching the videos, students respond to several discussion questions with a thorough and substantive initial post and two follow-up replies to their peers or professor:

1 How do historians know about the past?
2 What could make knowing about the past difficult?
3 If historians many years in the future wanted to write about your life, what primary sources would they utilize? Give multiple examples.
4 Are you familiar with any famous historical primary sources?

Students usually respond enthusiastically to the questions, and history becomes more than just dates and names. The discussion helps instructors identify students having trouble understanding the processes of historical thinking and provides a platform for instructors to discuss the types of sources students encounter in the course. The discussions are designed to move students beyond looking up answers. Consider how limited the discussion would be if the following questions were posed: What is a primary source? What is a secondary source? What is historical thinking?

Others have noted the utility of beginning with a discussion on historical thinking. To turn online DQ forums into "history labs," Lane begins the first weeks with posts teaching how to distinguish between primary and secondary sources.[9] When Kelly Schrum and Nate Sleeter created two online history courses for K-12 teachers in Virginia, they also began with introductions to historical thinking. They place "historical inquiry at the center… viewing history as a problem to be solved rather than as a narrative to be absorbed or consumed."[10] Their lessons include videos of historians analyzing sources, providing students real-life examples of historians' craft.[11]

The quality of instructor interaction – no less than the quality of student posts – is also important in creating meaningful dialogue in online discussions. A fellow educator once explained to me that while her professor in an online graduate course often responded with in-depth reply posts, these replies had little, if anything, to do with the particulars of her posts. The instructor's replies touched on the general topic of the DQ prompt but could have been responses to any student's post. The trend continued with each passing week, causing her to wonder "is he even reading my posts, or just pasting in replies that have nothing to do with what I said?" The discussions became disengaging, and she felt less incentive to do her best work. Just as in face-to-face settings, there is nothing inherently wrong with offering a similar reply to two students in different classes with similar questions. But this professor's disconnected replies worked against creating meaningful online discussion.

How often should instructors post in DQ forums? There is no set rule. It depends on the prompt and the extent to which the instructor needs to intervene to redirect conversations or clarify misinterpretations. John Lyons argues for a hands-off approach, so students reply to one another and not just the professor.[12] He recommends one weekly welcome post in which instructors set the historical context and one general feedback post at week's end. Carolyn Lawes takes a similar approach. She monitors the discussions and occasionally offers a comment or clarifies a misconception, "but by and large the students take the ball and run with it, developing new insights as they offer their own thoughts and respond to how others have interpreted the material."[13]

Will the instructor's missing presence in DQ forums give students the impression posts are not monitored or carefully read? Might this discourage students from making their best effort? I have found that responding to all or most student' posts stifles student-to-student interactions (in addition to being extremely time-consuming). Having *some* instructor presence in discussions, though, maintains accountability, reminding students the teacher is in the room. For this reason, I prefer to take an active and participatory role in the DQ forums, encouraging students and offering feedback while avoiding a domineering role. I treat the DQ forums no differently than in-class discussions: I facilitate discussion and help students put forth their best efforts and encourage peer-to-peer dialogue.

Meaningful Discussions Require Meaningful Prompts

Designing DQ prompts can be daunting, particularly in survey courses, where one or two DQ forums might correspond to a book chapter that covers dozens or even hundreds of years of history. Well-crafted prompts promote historical thinking while stimulating student dialogue. Instructors should begin by considering whether their prompts are asking students solely for facts. Students asked to explain Manifest Destiny will mostly paraphrase the definition from their readings (or a Google search) and posts will differ little from one another.[14]

Instead, one should give students open-ended prompts asking not only *who, what, when,* and *where*, but also *how* and *why*. Why was Manifest Destiny a popular *ideology among many mid-nineteenth century Americans? How did this rhetoric impact particular groups of people?* These questions integrate the "Five C's" into discussion. Students must consider the *context* of the mid-nineteenth century, *changes over time* influenced by Manifest Destiny, and how the advantages for some (newly acquired lands) were *contingent* upon disadvantages for others (displacement). It encourages diverse student answers that stimulate more discussion. And because the prompt says *many*, some students may point out examples of Americans for whom Manifest Destiny was *not* a popular ideology.

What if the instructor wants to ensure each student understands a key term, or a technical meaning from a primary source? Here it is useful to create prompts asking students to *define and explain*. In a two-part sequence, ask students to demonstrate they understand the technical meaning or basic information (*who, what, where, when*) and then explain its significance (*how, why*). After reading the first chapter of Eric Foner's *Give Me Liberty*, students discuss the following questions: *There were differing versions of "freedom" or "liberty" among the various groups you read about in Chapter 1. What are examples of these differing versions, and how did they shape early encounters between Europeans, Native Americans, and Africans?* The first part clarifies a point, or "gives an answer": there were competing notions of liberty in early America (an important theme of Foner's book). Students are asked to define these distinctions, which reveals which students have read and understood the chapter. If I notice any misinterpretations, I interject. If the DQ prompt ended here, there would be little distinguishing most student answers. But in the latter portion, in which students discuss the more abstract *shaping of encounters*, responses vary considerably.

Another strategy is to ask multiple questions in a prompt and allow students to decide which to answer. This offers students flexibility in their responses and produces a greater variety of responses. McCormack highlights the value of asking multiple questions:

> When I first began teaching online, I made the mistake of posting a single question to the board and expecting everyone to answer it in detail and respond to one another. This exercise proved not only redundant but also quite boring, and I realized very quickly that the students need options that enable them to explore more than one topic in the discussion over the course of a week's assignments.[15]

In my Western Civilizations II class, after reading a textbook chapter on absolutism and excerpts of Thomas Hobbes' *Leviathan*, students may select *any three* of the following questions:

- Hobbes states that humans are naturally equal in their faculties of mind and body. He would also probably say that humans are equally _____. Explain your answer.
- What is at the heart of most human conflict, according to Hobbes?

- He mentions people needing a power to "overawe them all." What do you think he means by this?
- Is he a pessimist or realist about human nature? Explain your answer.
- What does he argue will happen without a *Leviathan*? What would be the overall effects?
- What do you think Hobbes would say people should do if they feel a monarchy becomes oppressive?
- Is Hobbes promoting dictatorship? Or not?

Some questions focus on comprehension, others on interpretation. Student selections usually come from across the board and the follow-up replies tend to be more intriguing because students are interested in discussing the questions they did not answer in their posts.

Professors can also create DQ prompts that require students to respond with their own questions. For example, instructors may ask students to include in their initial posts two responses: 1) an answer to the prompt's question[s], and 2) a related question of the student's choosing, to which other students must respond. For example:

> How did the Market Revolution impact the lives of women in the United States? And what is one question you have about women's experiences during the early to mid-nineteenth century? (Please respond to another student's question by the end of the week).

Students may become so interested in a classmate's question they do outside reading to answer it or offer their best answer based on what they learned in assigned readings. In such scenarios the professor can intervene to help students consider how best to answer one another.

Carla Vecchiola also encourages questions as responses. She asks students to read a primary source from a database and respond with their own related discussion question (along with a link to the source).[16] For their follow-up posts, students must respond to a peer's question, requiring them to analyze the primary source their classmate chose. Having students pose questions promotes reciprocity in online classes by inviting students to participate in the production of knowledge.

DQ prompts can reinforce the point that student posts should be rooted in the knowledge they acquired from the assigned readings. Signal phrases can be utilized: "Given what you read in Chapter 4…" "After reading the primary sources on Spartan women…" or "Based on your interpretation of Equiano's description of the Middle Passage…" Instructors can also cross-reference multiple readings so that students synthesize their understanding of important themes across assigned texts. In my Honors Western Civilizations II course, in addition to their textbook chapter on nineteenth-century national unification movements, students read excerpts from Benedict Anderson's *Imagined Communities*.[17] A DQ prompt reads:

What were two or three main takeaways that you had when reading excerpts from Benedict Anderson's *Imagined Communities*? What do you think the idea of a "nation" meant to some of the prominent figures discussed in this week's chapter (e.g., Mazzini, Cavour, Garibaldi, Bismarck, or others – you can pick whomever you'd like)? What do you think "the nation" means to Americans today?

Some questions ask students to respond to a specific point in their readings. Others ask them to broadly synthesize their interpretations. At its core, the prompt asks students to think about the lesson's central theme (nationalism) from multiple perspectives: what they learned from their textbook, the related ideas of another linked reading, and their own society.

One effective design for discussion prompts poses no questions at all, asking students instead to respond to historical claims. One of the most useful practices that I have used is David Voekler's "for and against" model.[18] Voekler asks students to write two paragraphs in response to a historical claim put forth by the professor: one "for" paragraph and one "against" paragraph. The claims cannot be historical facts (e.g., "the French Revolution began in 1789"). They must be what Voekler calls "half-truths: claims that contain scraps of truth that obscure more than they clarify."[19] These are claims for which one could make reasonable arguments both *for* and *against* (e.g., "The French Revolution lived up to the slogan Liberty, Equality, and Fraternity"). Students must present their best arguments for the claim in one paragraph and a counterargument against it in another paragraph. The prompt explains that the best arguments will be those supported by historical examples. Well-crafted for-and-against claims help students think about their readings in context. For instance, in their arguments both for and against the claim that "President Lincoln deserves the title The Great Emancipator" students often incorporate key terms from their readings, such as *colonization* or the *Emancipation Proclamation*, but as part of an explanation in which they demonstrate their understanding.

It is important to anticipate and mitigate challenges when designing DQ prompts. In the "for and against" prompt, for example, the point of students putting forth original arguments will be undermined if students can simply log on and review what others have already stated. Learning management systems usually offer options to hide DQ forum responses until students have submitted their first post. The instructor should also ensure prompts are "Google-proof," preventing easy copying and pasting from popular websites or message boards. For instance, if a prompt asks students to explain differences between ancient Athens and Sparta, they could go to sites like DifferenceBetween.com to find ready-made answers detailing their distinctions. Wording DQ prompts to discourage plagiarism helps ensure student posts are interesting and original.

Incorporating Primary Source Analysis into Online Discussion

Online discussion forums can be excellent platforms for students to work with first-hand historical evidence. Whereas mid-term or final papers are high-stakes assignments in which students only have one or two opportunities to demonstrate their historical thinking about primary sources, weekly DQ forums make thinking like a historian habitual. Analyzing primary sources in active, ongoing discussions allows professors to highlight important course themes and guide students through the types of contextualization and sourcing discussed in the historical thinking module. As Grant Miller and Shannon Toth explain, "teachers cannot simply give their students a primary source and hope that they figure out its meaning, context, or significance." Instead, sources and history concepts need to connect "to a context, a topic, or a question."[20]

The wide availability of excellent free online primary source databases makes their incorporation into discussion forums easy, allowing instructors to avoid pricey course readers. DQ forum prompts can link students directly to primary sources or primary source databases, allowing students to find sources of interest and report back in the DQ forum. To discuss the 1911 Triangle Shirtwaist Factory fire, for example, Vecchiola sends students to Cornell University Library's primary source database on that tragedy.[21] Mark Pearcy asks students to visit the University of Virginia's "Geography of Slavery in Virginia" database to analyze eighteenth-century newspaper advertisements.[22] Lawes sends students to "Virtual Jamestown," a database where they can find original maps, freedom lawsuits, and images of artifacts ranging from drinking jugs to chamber pots.[23] Similarly, in a discussion on World War I posters, I ask students to upload and explain a poster from a Library of Congress database.

Other free primary source databases include Fordham's Internet History Sourcebooks Project, George Mason University's Women in World History Primary Source Collection, the American YAWP Reader, and Yale's Avalon Project. Many textbooks offer adoption options "with documents" in which texts include one or more primary sources per chapter. Whether using a single primary source, multiple sources, or sending students to research in databases, the opportunities for students to have enriching encounters with historical evidence in the DQ forums are many.

Using primary sources in the DQ forums helps establish course themes and prepares students for other class assignments. In my US History I course students read the Declaration of Independence and excerpts from Thomas Paine's *Common Sense*. Later in the course, a DQ prompt asks students to analyze an excerpt from David Walker's *Appeal to the Colored Citizens of the World* (1829). One student connected this with the earlier *Common Sense* discussion, writing:

> His Appeal reminded me very much of Thomas Paine's Common Sense… both are emotionally charged and use religion to appeal to the

religious majority of the American people. Walker's view of the people seems to be that they have definitely been hypocritical in their treatment of slaves and makes direct comparisons between the American sufferings under Great Britain. It seems to me that he is saying, and I'm paraphrasing here, "If you fought for your freedom under the minor infractions that Great Britain caused you, then African Americans have every right to fight you on your injustices to us."

This student referenced an important course theme that appeared across multiple course readings (the meaning of liberty), even though only the *Appeal* was assigned in the prompt. Students cross-referencing earlier sources in this way is not uncommon when incorporating primary sources in DQ forums. This discussion primes students for the final course paper on Frederick Douglass's "What to the Slave is the Fourth of July?" In that speech, Douglass also uses both the revolutionary ideals of the founders and Christianity to present slavery as immoral and argue against it.[24] Douglass' speech is lengthy, and students might have had difficulty digesting it in the first weeks of the course. By the end of the semester, though, students are accustomed to analyzing primary sources, guided by instructor feedback. In this way DQ forums play integral roles in the scaffolding of assignments throughout the term.

Incorporating Digital Media in the DQ Forums

Students today live in a world of ever-increasing digital engagement. According to an Edison Research study, the percentage of Americans (12 and older) who own a smartphone rose from 10% in 2009 to 88% 2021.[25] While the amount of information students hold in their pockets would leave the likes of Diderot astounded, the ubiquity of history-related blogs, video channels, podcasts, and other digital media presents difficulties when teaching online history courses, particularly when students rely on questionable sources to complete assignments. Nevertheless, there are excellent academic digital resources that, when purposefully paired with assigned secondary and primary source readings, offer students a comprehensive set of tools to learn historical thinking.

Podcasts can help students think *in conversation* about the course material in ways traditional readings may not easily allow. By 2021, an estimated 162 million Americans had listened to podcasts, with 41% of Americans (12+) listening to podcasts on a monthly basis (a dramatic rise from 9% in 2008).[26] History podcasts are especially popular. Several are hosted by professional historians. *Backstory* (Virginia Humanities), *15-Minute History* (University of Texas at Austin), and podcasts from the Gilder-Lehrman Institute feature academic historians discussing some of the most important topics examined in college history courses. Examples include *15-Minute History*'s "Urban Slavery in the Antebellum United States" with Professors Daina Ramey Berry and

Leslie Harris and *Backstory*'s "Red in the Stars and Stripes? A History of Socialism in America" with Nick Salvatore.

One approach is to pair podcasts with assigned readings in DQ prompts to give students multiple ways to examine course themes. I have incorporated podcasts to discuss causality. The tidy presentation of events in textbooks can make students lose sight of complexity and contingency. "Far too often, history classes and textbooks present students with a singular cause as to how historical events unfolded," writes Scott M. Waring. "One of the most dangerous practices by history teachers is allowing students to believe that there are simple, monocausal explanations for why and how history happens."[27] For my US History course, I ask students to first read the assigned chapter from Foner's *Give Me Liberty!*, then listen to a two-part *15-Minute History* episode on the causes of the Civil War with George B. Forgie (University of Texas). In that episode, which includes a text transcript, Forgie discusses five major scholarly interpretations for secession and the outbreak of war: slavery, economic differences, constitutional differences, the "two divergent societies" interpretation, and the "blundering generation" interpretation. The podcast does not replace assigned readings, but gives students a sense of historiography, reminding them history is interpretive and based upon evidence. Students have responded well to the prompt. One stated:

> After listening to the podcast, I think slavery and economics worked hand in hand to cause the war between the North and the South. Though Forgie makes a compelling argument that the majority of people who benefited from slavery were the wealthy plantation owners in the South, this group of people had enough influence within Congress and the South to rally people into maintaining the institution.

By week's end, most students will have presented sophisticated arguments explaining that slavery underpinned all the interpretations discussed in the podcast. Podcasts allow students to hear enthusiastic and well-informed conversations in a familiar digital media platform, which helps them become comfortable discussing their own ideas.

Video and film present another way to integrate digital media into discussion forums. The best results come when videos are methodically incorporated with clear connection between assigned readings and what they are learning from the professor. In my Western Civilizations II course students are linked in a DQ prompt to the full-length film *They Shall Not Grow Old* (2018), licensed by our college library. In the film, director Peter Jackson used modern technology to enhance original footage of the war (points to which students were caveated): colorization, added sound effects, and an overlay of interviews of Great War veterans aligned with the visual content. The prompt asks students to draw connections across *all* the sources for the unit. Here again students must synthesize:

You learned a lot about the causes and effects of World War I in this week's assigned textbook chapter, and you learned a lot about the experiences of soldiers in the war in your primary source readings. In what ways did aspects of these readings manifest themselves in *They Shall Not Grow Old?* Did you get any sense that the soldiers' expectations and attitudes changed as the war (film) dragged on?

Student responses to this prompt reveal interesting connections, and because there are many ways to answer the prompt, they are fun to read. Students identify particular themes in all the sources, be it the conditions of the trenches, the role of modern technology, nationalism, and the plight of young soldiers. Students also explain what most surprised them and how sources diverged from one another. The DQ forum does not just ask students to locate and repeat information (e.g., "discuss the causes of World War I"). It asks them to think historically.

Conclusion

As online learning grows in popularity, history educators are likely to find themselves teaching some of their courses in a remote setting. Whether in synchronous, asynchronous, or hybrid modalities – or perhaps even as a supplement to traditional on-ground learning – DQ forums will play important roles in online history curricula. Online discussions offer several advantages: all students must participate, they allow students to fully gather their thoughts when responding to their peers, they can be seamlessly linked to online resources, and they allow students to consider important ideas beyond the confines of traditional class time constraints. Yet, poorly crafted prompts risk making DQ forums tedious exercises, in which professors pretend to teach and students pretend to learn. History educators have developed many strategies to ensure that online discussions reach their full potential. When DQ forums promote historical thinking, inquiry, and foster a critical dialogue, they are wonderful spaces where students and instructors partner in the transformative power of learning.

Notes

1 Lyons, John. "Teaching US History Online: Problems and Prospects." *The History Teacher 37*, no. 4 (2004): 447–456, 450.
2 Fisher, Douglas, and Nancy Frey. *Checking for Understanding: Formative Assessment Techniques for Your Classroom*, 2nd ed. Alexandria, VA: ASCD, 2014, 20–21.
3 Lawes, Carolyn J. "Talking Less but Saying More: Teaching US History Online." *Journal of American History 101*, no. 4 (2015): 1204–1214, 1204.
4 Lane, Lisa. "Constructing the Past Online: Discussion Board as History Lab." *The History Teacher 47*, no. 2 (2014): 197–207, 197.
5 McCormack, Suzanne K. "Teaching History Online to Today's Community College Students." *Journal of American History 101*, no. 4 (2015): 1215–1221, 1219.

6 See Wineburg, Samuel S. *Historical Thinking and Other Unnatural Acts: Charting the Future of Teaching the Past*. Philadelphia, PA: Temple University Press, 2001.
7 Andrews, Thomas and Flannery Burke. "What Does It Mean to Think Historically?" *Perspectives on History* (2007). www.historians.org/publications-and-directories/perspectives-on-history/january-2007/what-does-it-mean-to-think-historically. Accessed July 30, 2022.
8 Minnesota Historical Society. "Primary vs Secondary Sources," YouTube video, 4:18, September 14, 2015. www.youtube.com/watch?v=TgU1BcDStK0. Accessed June 20, 2022.
9 Lane, "Constructing the Past Online," 200.
10 Schrum, Kelly, and Nate Sleeter. "Teaching History Online: Challenges and Opportunities." *Organization of American Historians Magazine of History 27*, no. 3 (2013): 35–38, 35.
11 Schrum and Sleeter, "Teaching History Online," 36.
12 Lyons, John. *Teaching History Online*. New York: Routledge, 2009, 38.
13 Lawes, "Talking Less," 1208.
14 Fisher and Frey, *Checking for Understanding*, 20.
15 McCormack, "Teaching History Online," 1219.
16 Vecchiola, Carla. "Digging in the Digital Archives." *The History Teacher 53*, no. 1 (2019): 107–134, 112.
17 Anderson, Benedict. *Imagined Communities*. Revised Edition. New York: Verso, 1991.
18 Voekler, David J. "Assessing Student Understanding in Introductory Courses: A Sample Strategy." *History Teacher 41*, no. 4 (2008): 505–518.
19 Ibid., 509.
20 Miller, Grant R., and Shannon Lindsay Toth. "To Dismantle an Idle Past: Using Historiography to Construct a Digital Learning Environment." *The Social Studies 103*, no. 2 (2012): 73–80, 73.
21 Vecchiola, "Digging in the Digital Archives," 111.
22 Pearcy, Mark. "Student, Teacher, Professor: Three Perspectives on Online Education." *The History Teacher 47*, no. 2 (2014): 169–185, 181.
23 Lawes, "Talking Less," 1214.
24 Douglass, Frederick. "What to the Slave Is the Fourth of July?" Speech, Rochester, NY, July 5, 1852. https://teachingamericanhistory.org/document/what-to-the-slave-is-the-fourth-of-july/. Accessed November 22, 2022.
25 Edison Research. *The Infinite Dial 2021*. March 11, 2021. www.edisonresearch.com/wp-content/uploads/2021/03/The-Infinite-Dial-2021.pdf. Accessed November 22, 2022.
26 Edison Research, *The Infinite Dial 2021*.
27 Waring, Scott M. "Escaping Myopia: Teaching Students about Historical Causality." *The History Teacher 43*, no. 2 (2010): 283–288, 287.

Chapter 14

Managing Online Discussions in Larger Sections

J.M. Wolfe

Introduction

One of the challenges of online learning is maintaining the frequency and quality of interaction present in in-person courses when operating in a virtual environment. Many educators, myself included, utilize discussion forums to facilitate student engagement for their courses, especially those with larger enrollments. This chapter explores strategies and best practices for managing discussions in larger classes to promote substantive exchange and intellectual discourse without creating an undue burden on the instructor in interacting, assessing, and developing these forums. My personal experience employing these techniques comes from courses with enrollments ranging between 20 and 300 students. I have over 15 years' experience teaching in online formats and now employ some of the practices from that modality in my on-campus offerings too with great success. This chapter shares advice borrowed from other experienced teachers and how my lived experiences have shaped my current approach pedagogically.[1] Current scholarship from Education, the Arts and Humanities, and other disciplines is included to offer multiple examples of tactics to explore, providing options to compliment ones' individual teaching style and delivery modality.

A goal in my courses is to help students take their virtually unlimited access to information and show they can generate knowledge and effectively communicate their understanding to others. Regardless of a student's major, future profession, or personal life, intentional course design can foster communication skills as well as "problem-solving and critical-thinking skills," thus transferable skills that create future generations of life-long learners.[2] As such, I do my best to intertwine skills development with content mastery even in my survey-level courses. To achieve communication skills development, I employ online discussion forums in both my in-person and online offerings due to the many advantages provided by the modality.[3]

DOI: 10.4324/9781003258414-18

Benefits of Online Components

Technology helps us "add value and depth to the learning experience by creating a bridge between classroom and independent (out of school) study."[4] Forums are excellent tools to achieve this process. When employed asynchronously they create a level of comfort and flexibility that gives learners greater control over their own success.[5] As discussed later, I allow the student some control over their level of interaction and investment but leave room so they can still pass graded assignments without talking to others, though they are always encouraged to do so. Research demonstrates that online communication in forums fosters social interaction and metacognitive development. It provides an avenue to encourage students to "think about thinking" when they explain to peers their understanding of course content or a discussion prompt.[6] Forums also offer multiple layers of interaction: student and instructor; student to student; and students with content.[7] Source-driven discussion forums encompass all these interactions in the same assignment. When students engage with the exercise, they benefit from the dense and diverse interactions happening.

Another reason to employ online, asynchronous discussion forums in conjunction with your course, regardless of delivery modality, is that it promotes diversity and inclusivity while ensuring accessibility. This process generates confidence and increases chances for students to learn from each other.[8] Additionally, students who employ English as a second language may feel more comfortable with the asynchronous format, which offers more time to frame responses and interact with their cohort than "on-the-spot" classroom situations. Online forums offer a wonderful opportunity for all students to express their voice and agency in ways difficult to achieve in large, in-person classrooms.

Intentionality and Design

Merely having content online does not improve student performance.[9] It is imperative that online assignments and course development be approached intentionally. For my forums, I generally have an ungraded assignment during the first week of the course nested as an "About me" section. Here, students give brief biographies of themselves, including major, reason for taking the class, hobbies, favorite areas of history, etc. to foster familiarity with how to post to class forums. I, too, participate in this social setting to foster a sense of rapport and comfort with the forum's interface. I include all students enrolled in the class in this forum, but for subsequent forums I divide the course population into smaller groups of 10–15 students to foster successful interaction without overwhelming students.

Ultimately, educators must know their audience. Figure out where your students are and chart a path to where you want them to end up. This edifying mantra should be tempered slightly. One also must be realistic in this process. In my experience some students refuse to interact in the forums or are otherwise uncomfortable with taking responsibility for their learning. This may be true for incoming freshmen, non-majors taking their first college history course, or returning students who have been away from college for some time.[10] Their decision, of course, is a calculated risk. I clearly state the grade impact in the syllabus and in early-semester course walkthroughs and explanations. Overall, intentional design makes the forums as inviting as possible while overlapping with other course content and minimizing the number of students who opt out of online discussion.

Aligning Learning Outcomes

When creating online discussion forums, one must take into consideration the purpose and desired function of assignments in relation to course objectives, aligning assignments with learning objectives. I use the forums to assign short primary or secondary source readings so students can interpret these documents within their historical context and elaborate on the impact or legacy of particular sources (usually aligned to one of the class's overarching themes – religion, human migration, social inequity, globalization, spread of ideas and technology, etc.). Doing so reinforces content delivery and skills development. Since many students compartmentalize assignments in survey courses, I try to be as explicit as possible in explaining how the different assessments and exercises in the course are designed to complement each other to reinforce learning and skills development.

Structural Preparation, Creating Groups

I suggest instructors initiate forum posts through a guided prompt, then allow the students to respond, followed by peer interaction. Once forums are closed, the instructor grades them and broadcasts collective feedback and observations to students. In this framework, students realize that they are producing posts, thus creating knowledge, that their peers will view. I hope students will become conditioned to producing work for a wider audience, not just the grade giver. My goal is to foster an interactive environment and an exchange of ideas ranging from affirmation to actual debate. Starting the forum with a guided prompt then stepping back until after the students have interacted also prevents the instructor from accidentally dominating the conversation. Research indicates "students may contribute more to forums and pursue discussion threads at greater length if instructors intervene in a minimal way."[11] My experiences support these findings.

Another important aspect of fostering a productive online discussion forum is accounting for the frequency of assignments, size of cohort, overall reading burden, and expected time investment for students. Earlier in my online teaching experience, I employed a discussion forum for each module/week of class. Though some of the reading assignments were only two to three pages long, I discovered the cumulative time investment between reading, writing, and interacting on these assignments created more work for students than necessary to achieve learning outcomes – especially considering these were survey-level courses. Two colleagues from English compared their respective composition courses' rough word-count expectations with my requirements, and I realized I may have been overwhelming the students – not to mention making more work for myself. Over the past decade, I have reduced these assignments from 15 to 9 (with the caveat that the three lowest grades are dropped from the gradebook). Here, too, I give students agency over their time in relation to course assignments.

Creating cohort groups of 10–15 students offers an increased chance of comfort and collegiality between students who may not otherwise know or meet each other in-person. The consistency of weekly group composition tends to ease students into discussing topics over the course of the semester, especially if the subject matter delves into sensitive topics. Larger groups can foster too much anonymity, leading some students to feel invisible, or appear intimidating, diminishing student participation. In contrast, too small a group increases the chance of insufficient interaction. Students need to know they have a voice and that they are expected to communicate their knowledge and informed opinions. Students increase their self-confidence by expressing themselves on a regular basis, in a controlled environment. For large-enrollment classes, the sophisticated discourse between students availed by asynchronous forums is nearly impossible in a traditional classroom without multiple breakout groups and Teaching Assistants to help manage the discussions. Outside research aligns with my experiences, concluding that online discussion forums help ensure a broader range of activity than in-class discussion sessions and may be superior for larger surveys.[12]

Making Prompts

Once discussion groups are created it is time to set the stage for interaction. Set question prompts with some level of flexibility allowing for differed responses. When creating prompts tied to assigned readings or other course material, offer some level of choice in the questions to give students agency in how they post based on what resonates with them or what they are comfortable discussing in a shared forum. This is not to say one should have full choice within the prompt, especially if an assigned source has paramount significance to the rest of the course content or themes of the class. I often have a mandatory question in the prompt, then options among subsequent questions. When discussing the French Revolution, I have students read the "Declaration on the Rights of Man and Citizen" but also include Olympe de Gouges's "Declaration on the Rights of Woman and the Female Citizen." I have a mandatory component asking for evidence from the first source about why the demands of the Third Estate were revolutionary in the context of the Ancien Régime.

Next, I ask them to engage with de Gouges's treatise, responding to one of two options. The goal is to evaluate students' understanding of the source(s) within the course context, but also allow them to express their own perspective. Forums allow students a better avenue to learn from one another in addition to merely providing a means of assessment.[13] Reading their peer's responses also highlights divergent perspectives, encouraging the class to revisit the material and analyze these. Usually, though, most student posts complement one another, demonstrating to students their ability to engage with the content and forge their own path to success in the course, which builds self-confidence.

I also recommend diversifying source materials used in discussion forums.[14] Examples can obviously be primary- or secondary-printed sources, but excerpts from literature, visual depictions of art or architecture, or even material culture like clothing or tableware can generate discussions when placed in proper context. The success and popularity of Neil MacGregor's *History of the World in 100 Objects* and the many curricula and lesson plans it spawned demonstrates the value of non-textual source materials.[15] When using a variety of sources, students better recognize the existence and value of the human story across formats and media – hopefully helping spark curiosity in their daily lives. Using materials other than printed documents, though, generally requires a lengthier introduction to explain the assignment to students.

Grading Using a Rubric

Rubrics make managing larger discussion forums easier. This ties back into the intentional design process, but also serves to detail one's expectations for students before their first assignment. Being upfront about expectations and assessment is critical for students to understand how they can succeed.[16] Clarity in how students will be graded is important for all classes, but especially so for large sections. One receives fewer emails about grades and grading if when giving feedback one can refer students to rubrics, examples of prior students' work, and pre-recorded walkthroughs or instructional materials.

As a confession, I avoided standardized rubrics for many years. Usually because the examples I consulted had very strict point breakdowns and I believed the topics covered in my assignments benefitted from the latitude offered by extended comments rather than "ticking boxes." I also allowed my earlier experiences as a student on the receiving end of rubrics to form a basis against them. The ones that left a negative impact were from professors who printed off a rubric for the assignment and checked off boxes or highlighted score components without any comments on the work, considering any deductions as self-evident without reflecting on the quality of the work or providing constructive feedback or validation. However, as my forum assignments evolved, I realized that a generalized rubric instead of a rigid one would serve to express expectations and describe the qualitative differences in students' posts.

As my teaching load increased, and course enrollments crept over 100 students per section, I finally succumbed to rubric implementation. When I laid out my first drafts, I realized that a good rubric merely articulates the grading expectations one already employs. Creating a generic rubric for discussion forums that explains the overarching expectations for how submissions will be assessed provides students insight on what they need to do to be successful. It also provides the instructor with a baseline to refer to if students have initial concerns about their scores. Remember that in a rubric, some indication should be made as to how points will be earned.[17] Doing so provides students with a resource that can be used in conjunction with examples to show the expected level of effort needed to earn their expected grade. Being explicit in expectations also helps students understand the differences between under-investing and overinvesting in these assignments. Too often, I have students write one-sentence responses that demonstrate neither understanding nor effort. Yet, I also have students who write small essays, overinvesting in the assignment. They should not be seen as merely overachievers. There are two negative ramifications from over-doing an assignment. First, the student is stealing time from their other responsibilities. I encourage them to effectively manage a school-work–personal life balance. Secondly, these excessive posts sometimes intimidate shy or struggling students, defeating the goal of fostering interaction and growth. So, rubrics are a first line of defense. They help ensure student success and save time for the instructor.

Table 14.1 shows the discussion forum rubric I use for my survey courses. It is broad enough to encompass different subject areas and speaks to the components I'm looking for in quality posts. This rubric will need adjustment depending on how one balances content acquisition and skills development.

Collective Feedback

Once you frame a rubric you are ready for the greatest time-saving component of online forums – collective feedback. Assessing forums in large-enrollment courses does not have to consume an inordinate amount of time. I read and grade every student's work, but do not give explicit individual feedback for each post. While grading, I take notes on the side, indicating trends, kudos, correctives, etc. I then write up two to three paragraphs addressing the assignment responses collectively. Adopting this format has cut untold hours from my grading routine, yet still lets students know I am engaged with their written work. This process has also cut back on simple questions and emails from students inquiring about grades. One can re-direct the student to the rubrics, examples, and collective feedback, offering individual coaching on

Table 14.1 Discussion grading rubric

Points	7–6	5–1	0
Quality of Post	Clear grasp of material; addressed all required questions posed; placed sources in historical context; sources and relevant historical figures identified in post	Moderate to minimum effort given to each aspect of discussion prompt(s); ideas or explanations of sources need clarification; failure to identify source or historical figures in question	No posting or posts after the due date
Relevance of Post	Posts topics related to the discussion prompt; fostered further discussion of the topic	Posts topics which do not directly relate to the discussion content; makes short or irrelevant remarks	No posting or posts after the due date

Points	3	2–1	0
Contribution to the Learning Community	Appropriate comments: thoughtful, reflective, and respectful of others even when presenting differing opinions; presents unique perspective of the topic; and/or, offers productive question(s) based on another's post	At least one response to another student's post; responds with minimal effort (e.g. "I agree with…"), but includes some evidence showing engagement with another's post	No feedback provided to fellow student(s) or posted after the due date

responses on a case-by-case basis. Responding to the assignment as a whole allows one to clarify content understanding and answer questions students did not explicitly bring up in discussion rather than allowing them to linger in the land of assumptions.

Another advantage of this process is that one can build a repository of feedback across semesters. This allows you to read through all responses, take notes, then edit your earlier feedback accordingly. Doing so allows the delivery of an informative and critical feedback message to students without having to compose it from scratch. Some educators advocate the use of this collective feedback approach or close variations thereof, but also include the practice of random sampling when grading in larger courses. Taking this route cuts down time invested in assessing student work, but requires planning in terms of frequency, setting rules on participation, and emphasizing to students the necessity to take ownership of their grade.

New Approaches

As many of us become comfortable with the use of technology in and out of the classroom, there are more avenues to humanize the online format for larger enrollment courses. I employ short videos in my classes to serve as course introductions and provide study tips and pep talks for exams. I have also explored utilizing video/audio recordings for each discussion forum to provide a short introduction with extended context outside of the written portions already included. As time and energy allow, I may use videos to deliver my collective feedback. I already tailor those responses, but adding a visual component further humanizes interaction despite the asynchronous delivery.

Drawbacks

I would be remiss in not exploring some of the disadvantages of online forums. If one uses the same sources each year on a consistent basis, that information will likely be shared with siblings or cohorts. I have come to this conclusion from talking earnestly with students and examining the activity reports and analytics available from my learning management system (LMS). There are times when I am disturbed by the number of students who never access source documents, yet somehow produce strong posts in answer to prompts, leading me to believe they are turning to their peers or internet searches. Adjacent to this problem are students who merely mimic earlier interaction posts. My LMS is designed to employ a one-hour time lock after the student's initial post before they can see or interact with others. Once the forum opens, however, no apparatus prevents a student from reading another's post and paraphrasing it to submit as their own. I have instituted a couple of mechanisms to combat this behavior, but they are not fail-safe. The most effective method to prevent this behavior is to have diminishing scores for interaction posts that merely reiterate earlier posts.

Conclusion

Overall, discussion forums in a large-enrollment course can be fruitful and engaging without creating an undue burden on the instructor (or grading assistants). To do so requires planning and implementation of pedagogical strategies based on best practices while curating and modifying assignments to fit one's teaching style and learning objectives.

Notes

1 I would like to thank the years of interaction, edification, and growth fostered by the Communication Across the Curriculum (CxC) program at Louisiana State University. Annemarie Galeucia, Rebecca Burdette, Jennifer Baumgartner, and Boz Bowels have worked to expose faculty members to various pedagogical techniques and innovations to keep our respective classrooms infused with best practices and introduce us to forms of assignments and assessment we may not otherwise encounter within our departments.
2 Condie, Rae, and Kay Livingston. "Blending Online Learning with Traditional Approaches: Changing Practices." *British Journal of Educational Technology 38*, no. 2 (2007): 337–348, 339. See also, McCormack, Suzanne K. "Teaching History Online to Today's Community College Students." *Journal of American History 101*, no. *4* (2015): 1215–1221, 1218 *ff*.
3 I forego some of the acronyms and buzzwords to help make this chapter more accessible to those from a host of silos, so to speak. But for those of you interested, feel free to review pedagogical discussions from our colleagues in Education who weigh the pros and cons of Information and Communication Technology (ICT) and Computer Mediated Communication (CMC). The duo most cited in materials I've seen are Mazzolini and Maddison. See: Mazzolini, Margaret, and Sarah Maddison. "Sage, Guide or Ghost? The Effect of Instructor Intervention on Student Participation in Online Discussion Forums." *Computers & Education 40*, no. *3* (2003): 237–253.
4 Condie and Livingston, "Blending Online Learning," 341.
5 See also Mtshali, Muntuwenkosi Abraham, Suriamurthee Moonsamy Maistry, and Desmond Wesley Govender. "Online Discussion Forum: A Tool to Support Learning in Business Management Education." *South African Journal of Education 40*, no. *2* (2020): 1–9, 1.
6 Marra, Rose M., Joi L. Moore, and Aimee K. Klimczak. "Content Analysis of Online Discussion Forums: A Comparative Analysis of Protocols." *Educational Technology Research & Development 52*, no. *2* (2004): 23–40, 25 *ff*.
7 Nandi, Dip, Margaret Hamilton, and James Harland. "Evaluating the Quality of Interaction in Asynchronous Discussion Forums in Fully Online Courses." *Distance Education 33*, no. *1* (2012): 5–30, 6.
8 Mtshali et al., "Online Discussion Forum," 2–7; and Ter-Stepanian, Anahit. "Online or Face to Face?: Instructional Strategies for Improving Learning Outcomes in e-Learning." *International Journal of Technology, Knowledge & Society 8*, no. *2* (2012): 41–50, 42.
9 Lawes, Carolyn J. "Talking Less but Saying More: Teaching US History Online." *Journal of American History 101*, no. *4* (2015): 1204–1214, 1205.
10 Condie and Livingston, "Blending Online Learning," 345.
11 Mazzolini and Maddison, "Sage, Guide or Ghost?" 237, 245.
12 Lawes, "Talking Less but Saying More," 1208–1209.

13 Ibid., 1212.
14 McCormack, "Teaching History Online," 1218–1219.
15 MacGregor, Neil. *History of the World in 100 Objects*. New York: Penguin, 2010. The book was a companion to a 20-week radio broadcast on BBC Radio 4 in 2010. There is educational value in the work regardless of where one stands on the issue of decolonizing museums by re-patriating artifacts to the current nations from where these items originated.
16 Nandi et al., "Evaluating the Quality of Interaction," 23.
17 I am a firm believer that students earn grades in contrast to having points deducted for assignments.

Chapter 15

Letting the Sources Guide the Way
The Dynamic Utilization of Primary Sources in the Online History Classroom

Micki Kaleta

The usage of primary source material is the basis of all historical research and writing. It is the process of interacting with and analyzing these sources which builds historical curiosity and stands as key to the development of critical thinking skills. Many online history courses drive assignments and/or discussions by asking questions based on textbook or article readings. Though content mastery is meaningful and necessary, utilizing the content to engage with primary source material builds complex thinking, and moves the learner from simple remembrance of facts to building skills of evaluation and analysis.[1] In grappling with primary sources learners look at history from a lens not their own. This process not only challenges one's own thinking and ideas, but teaches learners to question source material, a skill that is vital in today's social and political climate.

Including historical primary source material in online history courses increases the development of key critical thinking skills.[2] John Stanrock, Professor of Behavioral and Brain Sciences, explains critical thinking "[i]ncludes asking not only what happened, but how and why; examining supposed 'facts' to determine whether there is evidence to support them; evaluating what other people say rather than immediately accepting it as the truth; and asking questions and speculating beyond what is known to create new ideas and acquire new information." Building this critical thinking stands as the principal learning objective when utilizing primary source material as the centerpiece of one's online history course. In focusing on analyzing sources, a skill where learners actively question material and engage dynamically in the course, one is teaching learners a useful skill as opposed to simply covering the material.[3] It is a paradigm switch from passive to active learning.

Before utilizing primary source material in the online classroom, one must establish clear and nuanced student learning objectives for the individual unit. What are the goals for the course? What skills and objectives should the learner master upon the completion of the unit? These goals must be specific, for example the learning objective of having a student display critical thinking competency is too broad for an individual unit.

Craft nuanced objectives for each unit. For example, in an American History unit on Franklin D. Roosevelt's 1930s New Deal programs, one could

DOI: 10.4324/9781003258414-19

focus on a few New Deal initiatives such as the Tennessee Valley Authority (TVA), The Civilian Conservation Corps, and/or the Works Progress Administration. In specifically crafting objectives based on those programs, one might include objectives such as: The learner will be able to evaluate differing perspectives of the impact of the TVA, discuss the goals of the Works Progress Administration and how those programs combatted unemployment, and/or determine how the Civilian Conservation Corps affected the lives of those it employed. Specific objectives must be established so one can work backwards to craft prompts and find appropriate primary source material to meet those objectives.

Historical primary source material works with and supports the chosen textbook or contextual materials. Assigning a required reading to establish context is useful as a basis for including primary source material in the online history course. There is currently an array of open educational resource textbooks one can utilize, providing free textbooks and resources for learners. The contextual reading assigned also must support the learning objectives that were established for the unit. It is in this contextual reading that learners build connections between the time period, the primary source material, and within their own lives.

One way to ensure contextual reading is completed is to include short quizzes, which ensure students master the foundational historical reading. Utilizing self-grading quizzes within the learning management system (LMS) is an easy way to ensure that contextual knowledge is included in the course without additional burdensome grading. Many textbook publishers include instructor resources, such as test and quiz question banks, which again make these self-grading quizzes a less onerous added component to the course.

After establishing specific and nuanced learning objectives for the unit, one can establish one or more prompts which support those objectives. These prompts offer the student guidance and structure while engaging with the primary source material. The prompts should also invoke the learner's critical thinking skills and be open ended enough to engage various opinions. Returning to the example of the TVA, one might craft the prompt "on May 18th, 1933, President Franklin Delano Roosevelt passed the TVA Act which transformed Tennessee Valley. Was this a positive force for change for everyone in the region? Give specific examples in your response." This prompt addresses the TVA's effect on various demographics, and whether people agreed or disagreed with its goals.

After establishing open-ended and thought-provoking prompts one can begin the process of mining differing sources for relevant primary source material which serves to support the specific student learning objectives, in addition to engaging the prompt. It is key to include numerous types of primary source material in building your source set which aid in accommodating numerous learning styles evident in student learners. These would include written sources (speeches, diaries, manuscripts, letters, newspaper articles, pamphlets, etc.), visual sources (maps, art, sculpture, artifacts, etc.), audio recordings, video

Letting the Sources Guide the Way   135

recordings and films, oral historical accounts, etc. Including numerous sources from which learners can choose gives learners options to find sources which speak to them and with which they feel comfortable engaging.

The mining for primary source material can be an overwhelming endeavor and can sometimes feel like finding the proverbial needle in a haystack. Search engines can easily bring up endless droves of primary material that one might include in a class, but where should one start? Begin with a plan of establishing a robust primary source set which speaks *specifically* to the prompt. A set that responds to the aforementioned TVA prompt might include the following primary sources:

1. Tennessee Valley Authority Act (1933). Government document explaining the plan for establishing the TVA and its goals. www.docsteach.org/documents/document/tennessee-valley-authority-act.
2. TVA pictorial map (US GPO, 1939) detailing the proposed location of the TVA dams. www.loc.gov/item/2008628288/.
3. Film. *The TVA at Work, 1935*. Department of the Interior. Division of Motion Pictures. (1935) https://youtu.be/idCwqXju7w0. Thirteen-minute film detailing the control of water flow utilizing various techniques in the Tennessee Valley.
4. Photograph. Better Sight for Better Living (Display #6, TVA RG 142, 1948). A photograph highlighting the benefits of the TVA program. www.docsteach.org/documents/document/better-sight-better-living.
5. Photograph. Photograph of School Lighting in a 5th Grade Class in Florence, Alabama (TVA RG 142, 1946), which highlights the benefits of the TVA for schoolchildren. www.docsteach.org/documents/document/photograph-of-school-lighting-in-a-5th-grade-class-in-florence-alabama.
6. TVA Song by Jean Thomas (1939). Song from the Works Progress Federal Theatre Project production "Power." https://memory.loc.gov/cgi-bin/ampage?collId=ftp&fileName=fprmus/1309/13090003/ftp13090003page.db&recNum=0.
7. Memorandum Relating to the Relocation of the Randolph Family (1935), TVA Record Group 142. Details efforts to relocate a family when the TVA exercised right of eminent domain. https://catalog.archives.gov/id/656693 and https://catalog.archives.gov/id/656692.
8. Photo of Removal and Reinternment of Graves, Brown Cemetery 6/1/1942, following the TVA's exercise of eminent domain. www.docsteach.org/documents/document/south-holston-reservoir-removal-and-reinterment-of-graves-brown-cemetery-disinterment-cemetery-no-20.
9. Clayton, Cranston, "The TVA and the Race Problem," *Opportunity, Journal of Negro Life 12*, no. 4 (1934): 111. Details the lack of African Americans employed by the TVA and limited access to TVA training. http://newdeal.feri.org/opp/opp34111.htm. New Deal Network: http://newdeal.feri.org.

The above source set includes a government document, a map, photographs, a film clip, a transcript of an oral interview, lyrics from a song, and a journal article. This variety of sources speaks to differing learning styles and includes sources which will invoke numerous perspectives both for and against establishing the TVA. Including sources that spark various perspectives or potential academic debates will invoke creative and critical thought in learners. Having a specific prompt as a starting place will narrow down the search for primary sources; instead of a broad and likely overwhelming search for primary documents on Franklin D. Roosevelt's polices, one can search specifically for documents on the TVA. The results that return are a manageable amount that can be mined quickly and efficiently.

Once primary source material is mined for use, it is up to the instructor to determine how best to embed the sources into the course itself. For example, one must make the decision to upload the material directly to the course, or to offer the material as an outside link(s). The benefits to uploading the materials directly to the course include the avoidance of dead links and encourage the learner to quickly view the material, avoiding the additional step of leaving the LMS. Leaving the LMS for outside material could sidetrack the learner, possibly detracting from returning to the course itself. One of the disadvantages of uploading material directly into the LMS is possible copyright infringement. Material uploaded to a course must either be public domain, must utilize the doctrine of Fair Use, or have the author's permission for use. (See Chapter 6 for more discussion of this topic.) Another disadvantage in uploading the material into the LMS is the space available on one's institutional server. Uploading large files and recordings can take up considerable digital space and may be prohibited by one's institution. Using links to outside sources decreases the size of the course on one's institutional server and it decreases the risk of intellectual property and copyright infringements. Using direct links to outside sources can, however, create issues of source availability, namely links can and do break. Broken or dead links quickly inhibit a student's learning if those are not fixed in a timely manner, preferably before a student reaches out to the instructor. Monitoring these links consistently in a course can be a time-consuming and tedious process. The decision on how best to embed or link sources to one's course depends on time availability and one's institutional preferences.

Primary source material can be utilized in numerous places within an online course. One might consider using sources in assigned writing assignments, journal prompts, or discussion boards. When using writing prompts or journal entries the prompt is offered as well as the primary source set and the learner is asked to respond using a certain number of primary sources, for example three to five sources. The use of a discussion board for engaging students with primary material is robust and involves more interaction among learners and instructors. Online discussions offer rich engagement by facilitating diverse viewpoints in which learners and instructors can challenge one another.

Engaging with primary source material is a skill that is learned and built over time and requires practice. It is not a skill learners naturally are accustomed to and many have not engaged with primary sources previously. Modeling the process of analyzing sources for learners before requiring them to write a response or post in a discussion board is useful and serves learners well. Offer learners an example of what responding to a prompt and utilizing the primary material entails. One might offer examples or quotes from the documents to support the argument established in responding to the prompt. Historian Sam Wineburg offers a metaphor of a courtroom to use when building an argument utilizing primary source material.[4] Ask the learners to assume the role of an attorney. They must see their classmates as a jury, a jury they must convince that their argument is correct. The primary source material is the evidence.

There is also a vast array of worksheets that one might offer at the beginning of a course to guide learners on how to analyze primary source material. These worksheets can be utilized as supplementary resources or as additional assignments for the unit. The National Archives offers a large assortment of primary document worksheets for written documents, photographs, maps, cartoons, sound recordings, artwork, artifacts, and videos at the following link: www.archives.gov/education/lessons/worksheets. This is a good starting place for learners who have had little to no experience in analyzing primary source material.

Early and consistent interaction with learners after they have answered the prompt and engaged with the primary source material is imperative. Learners must have a sense of instructor presence. "The feeling that someone is interested is so very important in all types of learning situations, but may be more so online where everyone is physically isolated. Instructors noted that student anxiety was highest in the beginning stages of each course and, in addition, students had differing needs for support."[5] Some learners will need more leading than others. Offer encouragement and constructive feedback privately to learners. When engaging with a new skill, such as working with primary source material, public feedback can be intimidating for learners and may shut down future engagement. Publically within the discussion, offer leading questions to further the discussion both for the posting learner and others within the course.

It is paramount to monitor learner activity during online discussions. Utilizing primary source material can and should invoke numerous responses with a vast array of perspectives. It is in this vein of thinking that issues may arise. Some learners may promote problematic viewpoints that could alienate their classmates. These types of responses must be handled quickly in order to keep the discussion fruitful. Learners who feel invalidated by their peers will shut down, halting the potential for learning. It is a good idea to post reminders for respectful dialogue at the opening of discussion boards.

When the discussion board closes, an instructor's job is not done. Upon the closing of the discussion board offer a synopsis of the prompt, how the sources and prompt speak to and support the student learning objective, and any new exciting viewpoints and perspectives that might have been uncovered on the discussion board. This is the exciting part of teaching using primary source materials; learners consistently discover new and impactful ideas in every course. This is an excellent place to draw connections from the sources and historical topic covered to students' own lives. This makes the primary material relevant and useful for learners, truly making history come alive.

The initial constructing of a course utilizing primary sources is not an end in itself. A dynamic course constantly evolves. Instructors should continue to review the course and how learners interacted with it for improvement. Not all lessons go as planned and some sources may not resonate with learners as intended. It is then important to adjust, delete, and add sources as the course progresses. Being malleable and open to where the learners are leading is integral to creating and maintaining a dynamic course.

Not all sources are readily available, and it can be overwhelming to create a primary source set for an online course lesson. The sites listed in Appendix 2: Website and Additional Resources, such as the Library of Congress and the Gilder Lehrman Institute, have an array of material including photos, music, and documents of various lengths for use in an online history course.

Utilizing primary material in the online history classroom is not new pedagogy but utilizing it in dynamic and effective ways can transform an online classroom. Offering a variety of source mediums which spark numerous perspectives can make history seem relevant and tangible to learners. It is a constant battle for educators to get and keep a learner engaged, and using primary source material effectively can be the engine to make this a reality in the history classroom.

Notes

1 See Bloom's Taxonomy in Bloom, Benjamin S. *Taxonomy of Educational Objectives: The Classification of Educational Goals.* London: Longman Group, 1956.
2 Santrock, John W. *A Topical Approach to Life-Span Development.* New York: McGraw Hill Education, 2014. See also Caudle, L., and T.H. Paulsen. "Evidence of Critical Thinking in a Capstone Course." *NACTA Journal 61*, no. 3 (2017): 208–218.
3 Sipress, Joel M., and David J. Voelker. "The End of the History Survey Course: The Rise and Fall of the Coverage Model." *Journal of American History 97*, no. 4 (2011): 1050–1066.
4 Wineburg, Samuel S. *Historical Thinking and Other Unnatural Acts: Charting the Future of Teaching the Past.* Philadelphia, PA: Temple University Press, 2001, 77.
5 Duncan, Heather E., and Suzanne Young, "Online Pedagogy and Practice: Challenges and Strategies," *The Researcher 22*, no. 1 (2009): 17–32, 23.

Chapter 16

It's All Relative

The Importance of Scaffolding and Course Design in the Online History Classroom

Leigh Ann Wilson

Teaching history requires a unique skill set separate from our subject matter expertise. In graduate school, many of us were taught how to be scholars and researchers first and teachers second. Some institutions do not require their graduate teaching assistants to complete any coursework in teaching methodologies. This lack of formal preparation may cause faculty to stumble when creating classes requiring virtual components or that are fully online. While the number of electronic resources and websites available on the internet can be overwhelming, navigating these resources and presenting them in meaningful ways to students are essential skills.

This chapter discusses "scaffolding," a course design technique that engages students, encourages them to take greater ownership of their learning experiences, and guides their progress from one assignment to the next.

The concept of scaffolding is twofold. First, the scaffolded classroom is built around assignments that are interconnected. Each subsequent assignment becomes more rigorous and requires a more sophisticated skill set than previous assignments. Additionally, scaffolded assignments are written so that students take on a greater degree of autonomy and pedagogical responsibility, with less instructor oversight.

The days of endless lectures where silent history students took copious notes in face-to-face classes are behind us. Scaffolded history classrooms are dynamic and interactive, encouraging students to reflect on the material and collaborate on projects. Depending on the course, student skill level, and length of term, faculty can create scaffolded assignments to teach the desired historical content while creating a safe space for student self-discovery and reflection.

Origins of Scaffolding

Scaffolding was first applied in education to facilitate learning for children during the 1950s.[1] However, there is substantial debate around when the concept of scaffolding was created. While many credit Lev Vygotsky[2] with the naming and creating this concept in the early 20th century, other scholars such as Anna Shvarts and Arthur Bakker argue scaffolding was first explored a century earlier by Karl Marx and Georg Hegel.[3]

Regardless, this concept first found success with student athletes in higher education. As Jillian McNiff and Thomas Aicher explain, student athletes face challenges due to travel and training schedules. Scaffolding assignments helped them meet course objectives and support those student athletes who needed remedial work, helping learners independently compensate for any past educational discrepancies. Scaffolded assignments within online courses, which offer greater scheduling flexibility, proved particularly beneficial.[4] Students with learning disabilities or in remedial or special education classes also found success in scaffolded classrooms.

A wide range of scholarship addresses scaffolding and the various approaches to applying it to diverse academic disciplines.[5] This chapter addresses its use in the college history classroom on which very little has been written.

How Does Scaffolding Work?

The theory behind scaffolding is that if assignments throughout a course are entwined and build upon each other, students will develop critical thinking skills, writing skills, and research expertise. As students gain confidence and knowledge about their topics and improve their writing skills, they take increasing responsibility for their learning. They are empowered to pursue their studies both independently and collectively as part of a class. Correspondingly, scaffolding reduces some of the burden on faculty, allowing them to focus more attention on developing students' critical thinking skills.[6]

Before we look at a specific example of how scaffolding can work in the online classroom, it is significant to note that the atmosphere of the scaffolded class will differ from typical lecture-style history classes. Treating the scaffolded course as a "workshop" or a "studio" style course, akin to a visual artist's studio, is beneficial for several reasons.

First, the workshop or studio mentality encourages the student to think of the faculty member and other students as allies in the course. Imagine the scaffolded classroom as an artist's studio in a giant warehouse, with drop cloths on the floor and art supplies strewn about. Rather than competing for the highest grade or the flashiest topic idea, faculty encourage students to think about self-expression and topics are of individual interest in their educational journeys. No two projects will be alike because no two students are alike, nor are their educational goals and professional pathways. Since all projects will be different, students will be motivated to provide constructive feedback and suggestions for improvement to each other. This perspective has the added benefits of encouraging students to attend class regularly and participate frequently in class discussions and activities.

Faculty will encourage students to view each assignment as a rough draft or a preparatory assignment for the next step in the process. The studio concept instills the "long view" perspective of the course. Students will begin with a nascent idea and develop it over time into a university-quality project. The finished product will be a valuable example to prospective employers or to graduate school admissions committees. Project management and completion of a task that can span several months can be a new growth experience for students. This approach encourages students to develop self-confidence, autonomy, and independence,[7] which are skills that may be nascent in traditional students.

Below is an example of how scaffolding is currently applied in my 300-level online History of the Vietnam Conflict class taught at University of Massachusetts Global (formerly Brandman University). It is an elective, eight-week course conducted using the Blackboard learning management system.

From the beginning of the course, weekly discussion board prompts encourage students to thoughtfully approach course content and reflect on their learning goals for the course and their research project. Week One's discussion prompt asks:

> Describe the most notable person/place/event that you associate with the topic of the Vietnam conflict. This does not have to be a factually specific or detailed post; in fact, it may be more reflective than factual, which is perfectly fine. It is merely a yardstick to measure your favorite topics of the Vietnam conflict prior to our intensive study of it. Doing this will help you gauge your current knowledge base and to assist you in seeking out a topic for the research paper. However, it should still be about 2–3 paragraphs in length.
>
> Your post should address the following:
>
> - What person/place/event are you interested in concerning Vietnam? Why?
> - Do you think this person/place/event was integral in the outcome of the Vietnam conflict? Why?
> - How do you think events would have been different if this person/place/event had not been a factor?
>
> This week's post will also help you prepare for your research paper for the course, so think selfishly about what *you* are interested in learning more about.

In follow up posts, faculty ask students what aspects of the Vietnam conflict they are most familiar with, or to name three adjectives that correlate with their preconceived ideas about it. This exercise helps determine students' baseline knowledge. Students must be reflective, thoughtful, and courageous as a quality reply cannot be made hastily. Asking such questions requires students to trust the professor and classmates to avoid judgmental responses, if they know little about the topic.

During the last week of the course, Week Eight, students revisit their comments from the Week One discussion board and assess how their opinions from Week One have changed. This activity offers students a tangible way to evaluate their learning, which may happen in such small increments over the term that they may be unaware of the change. We conclude Week Eight's discussion by asking students what they will do with their new knowledge. This allows faculty to suggest directions for further reading and research or community activism, such as working with a Veteran's Administration hospital or charity for disabled veterans, which may lead to oral history projects. This encourages students to build on their new knowledge and put it to work.

For grading, students may earn a total of 600 points in the Vietnam Conflict course, of which 360 relate directly to the research paper. So, it is critical for students to understand that the project, a 10- to 12-page paper based on scholarly sources and original research, will require a significant time investment.

Early in the term, students submit a 500-word proposal on their topic in which they present their working thesis, cite at least four sources, and explain why the topic is important to them. This helps them organize their ideas. Although a brief assignment, it can be time consuming for faculty. Students often need direction choosing a topic, finding sources, and developing their ideas. Multiple proposal rewrites are common, as students develop their ideas and progress on their research.

Developing a proposal helps students take responsibility for their learning and choose a research topic that is both meaningful to them and relevant to the course. In this eight-week class, the scaffolded assignment due dates are:

1. Week 2: Research Paper Proposal.
2. Week 5: First Draft of Research Paper.
3. Week 7: Final Draft of Research Paper.
4. Week 8: Presentation to class (via the discussion board).

For students, the notion of writing a proposal is formidable. We provide students with detailed directions on selecting a topic and formatting the assignment. While the goal of the proposal is to be objective, this is undeniably an exercise in self-reflection, scholarly research, and academic writing. Previous students in this class, some of whom were Vietnam veterans, chose to write about specific battles or military units. One student shared with the class a digital copy of his 1973 draft card, requiring him to report for Basic Training. This, along with the student's personal reflections in online class discussions, demonstrated to other students the emotion and reality of being called into active duty. The drafted student's testimony profoundly affected younger students.

Several members of the class were children of Vietnam veterans service members and wrote about the mental and physical health challenges faced by returning veterans, including drug and alcohol addiction, reintegrating into civilian society, domestic relationships, and employment issues. Such papers generally include objective overviews of difficult issues, such as post-traumatic stress disorder (PTSD), and students often interview people with special insight into these. In one case, the active-duty son of a veteran who suffered from addiction issues sought work with returning service members who suffered from traumatic brain injury, suicidal ideation, and mental health challenges. The scaffolded classroom helped him become more familiar with the scholarly research on the topic, which supported his professional goals. It also helped him create a family history that was meaningful to his father and other family members.

The Research Paper Topic Proposal requires student to have regular and detailed interaction with faculty. Even the most knowledgeable and eager students need assistance assessing their topic's viability, refining the direction or their research, and locating appropriate sources. Providing detailed instructions about the assignment or a detailed checklist citing all the required elements is especially useful to students – even more so in courses like the Vietnam course, which are popular among non-majors. Having this assignment due in the early weeks of the course reduces student anxiety about the scope of the project, making it less formidable and more achievable. The same is true of lower division courses whose students are often new to the university experience and unfamiliar with research methodology. Scaffolded assignments due early in the term set the tone for the remainder of the course and make clear that earning a good grade requires regular time devoted to research and writing rather than a last-minute rush in finals week.

Requiring students to complete each assignment before moving on to the next step helps students see how all a project's assignments connect. Also, by requiring students to incorporate the instructor's feedback from each assignment into subsequent assignments, students gain experience with the concept of continuous improvement. Students must demonstrate that they have invested the time to seek out legitimate and relevant sources, explaining how the sources will be of use in the project. This also gives faculty the opportunity to discuss and cull out dubious or low-quality sources. When the research paper topic proposal is complete, students will be prepared to write the first draft of the paper. Due about two-thirds of the way through the course, this assignment provides students their first opportunity to fully explain their research agenda and its results. They are encouraged to treat this first draft as a "dress rehearsal" for the final paper. Having it due early in the course allows students time for additional research and revision. They are encouraged to leave notes, questions, or any other extraneous comments for themselves, peer reviewers, and the professor requesting feedback.

This feedback prepares students to compose their paper's final draft. As they finish and edit their papers, they also prepare to present their work, either orally in a traditional classroom, or via the discussion board in an online course. Students can use presentation tools such as Prezi or PowerPoint and make appropriate handouts. This final paper and presentation mark the culmination of the student's scaffolded assignments and research and allow students to present themselves as experts, educating one another on their research projects. They again get practical experience demonstrating their knowledge and answering questions from peers and professors.

Beyond the Research Paper

If the length of the term allows, adding assignments such as annotated bibliographies and peer reviews are excellent additions to the research paper process. Further, there are other ways that scaffolding can include tangential assignments that are not funneled directly into the final paper. Specifically in the Vietnam class, faculty have included disciplines such as journalism and communications, nursing, psychology, sociology, and social work. In the Vietnam Conflict class, the topic of United States soldiers' addiction and psychological issues could present students with the opportunities to build upon professional interests and career paths. One recent student, a psychology graduate student and National Guard member, sought to learn the timeline by which "PTSD" replaced "shell shock" as the preferred term.

Faculty can also ask students to find relevant, current media coverage that relates to the students' topics. The US military withdrawal from Afghanistan offers numerous comparisons to Vietnam. Asking students to seek out quality analyses is an important critical thinking exercise. However, it's essential that faculty provide students a list of acceptable news sources to avoid the cesspool of internet junk sites. This also allows students to become familiar with news sources new to them.

Faculty can encourage students to share their research and scholarship in essay-style quizzes with open-ended questions. By creating quizzes that have about five prompts each, with students allowed to pick three or four questions, students have control over their learning experiences. Questions such as: "What were some of the unusual effects of the Vietnam War upon US soldiers that were unique to this conflict?" Or "How did the Vietnam Conflict influence or alter standard treatment of drug addiction and mental health difficulties?" Such questions allow students an opportunity to not only refer to the class textbook and supplemental audio/visual materials, but also to their own research.

Another student favorite question on the essay-style quiz is the "Student's Choice" questions, where they are allowed to write about an aspect of the material covered in the unit that wasn't covered on any exams or that they wish to discuss in more depth. This technique gives them the chance to educate one another about what they've learned while keeping the focus on the classroom material. One example is:

> Student's Choice: What was the most interesting fact you learned during this unit that you did not know before? Your response must not address a topic addressed elsewhere on this quiz. Explain why you found this topic to be of interest. Cite sources, as appropriate. Four sentences minimum.

Asking students such questions provides unobtrusive, yet tangible, feedback about what themes and concepts are meaningful for students. This knowledge, in turn, provides helpful insight for future iterations of the course, including topics of emphasis in lectures, textbook selection, and audio/visual selection.

Conclusion

To be sure, using scaffolding in the history classroom has been a successful approach in the History of the Vietnam Conflict class. However, it cannot be implemented without extensive planning by the faculty. The length of term, points per assignment, and method of delivery are all important points to consider. Regardless, these considerations offer new ways to introduce students to the versatility of our discipline.

The most exciting part of the concept of scaffolding is that it truly does exist to let the students investigate topics of importance to them. It also encourages them to think of conducting "research" in new ways – they now have first-hand experience that it is far more than digging through the library stacks in search of some obscure book – and provides them ways to gain more expertise about their subject.

Finally, students who approach such projects with the goal to submit their work to a journal, historical society, archive, conference, or other entity where the project can live on after the course concludes provide a tangible example of how our profession can shape the scholars and decision-makers of the future.

Notes

1 Wood, David, and Heather Wood. "Vygotsky, Tutoring and Learning." *Oxford Review of Education 22*, no. *1* (1996): 5–16.
2 Vygotsky, L. *Thought and Language*. Cambridge, MA: MIT Press, 1934/1936.
3 Shvarts, Anna, and Arthur Bakker. "The Early History of the Scaffolding Metaphor: Bernstein, Luria, Vygotsky, and Before," *Mind, Culture, and Activity 26*, no. *1* (2019): 4–23.
4 McNiff, Jillian, and Thomas J. Aicher. "Understanding the Challenges and Opportunities Associated with Online Learning: A Scaffolding Theory Approach," *Sport Management Education Journal 11* (2017): 13–23.
5 Of particular use is Catherine McLoughlin's article, "Learner Support in Distance and Networked Learning Environments: Ten Dimensions for Successful Design," *Distance Education, 23*, no. *2* (2002): 149–162. She delves into the various types of scaffolding that can be applied in many disciplines.
6 See Beed, Penny L., Hawkins, E. Marie, Roller, and Cathy M. "Moving Learners toward Independence: The Power of Scaffolded Instruction." *The Reading Teacher, 44*, no. *9* (1991): 648–656, for a thorough discussion of how the method of faculty withdrawal in scaffolding can be a useful tool to foster learner independence.
7 Larkin, Martha J. "Providing Support for Student Independence through Scaffolded Instruction," *Teaching Exceptional Children 34*, no. *1* (2001): 30–34.

Chapter 17

Interactive Timelines as the Center of Class Discussion

Brandon Morgan

Several years ago, I began assigning a collaborative, interactive timeline in my New Mexico History course as a means of de-centering the discussion board from online coursework. I started teaching online in the fall of 2010 when a former graduate advisor reached out to see if I would be willing and able to teach an online section of New Mexico History that needed an instructor at the eleventh hour. I was still ABD, working as an adjunct at a community college, and had never taught an asynchronous online class.

Experienced colleagues gave me a rough crash course and a guidebook to online teaching. They taught me the main role of the instructor in an online format was to make sure the students demonstrated they were doing something with the assigned materials. Accordingly, I constructed a course based on several New Mexico history texts and centered weekly work on highly regimented discussion board assignments. I required students to post minimum-250-word responses to questions based on the readings, followed by 100-word responses to at least two peers.

A 2021 study by Howard E. Gardner and Wendy Fischman found that more than half of surveyed students considered college a transactional experience rather than a vehicle for developing vital skills in critical thinking and research.[1] Although most college history instructors emphasize the latter as the purpose of our courses, we often design assignments and activities that instead place students in transactional learning experiences. Paulo Freire called this the banking model of education. Learning "becomes an act of depositing, in which students are the depositees and the teacher is the depositor." To study, he noted, "is not to consume ideas, but to create and recreate them."[2]

Many history instructors, and college teachers more generally, become frustrated with the rote, transactional nature of interactions on the discussion board. My first experience with online teaching and learning was transactional. I'm sure students in that course were dissatisfied with the experience. As I continued teaching online, I worked to move the online learning experience beyond a digitized correspondence course. I wanted to feel as if I was actively teaching. I wanted students to learn history through interactive engagement with the past.

DOI: 10.4324/9781003258414-21

Experiences at various professional conferences helped me recognize I needed to discover my pedagogical values so I could redesign my courses to be more interactive and engaging for students. As I studied critical pedagogy and critical digital pedagogy, Paulo Freire's work stood out to me. I considered ways I could create spaces in my lower-division online courses where students could interpret historical arguments and create new understandings of our shared past together as a group.

Admittedly, I've come to recognize that discussion board activities are what you design them to be. The discussion board itself is not inherently transactional, dull, or contrived, but sometimes the assignments I planned were. When I created "post-250-words-and respond-with-two-100-word-replies" assignments, the discussion board became a transactional space. But when I stepped back to ask questions about what purpose discussion assignments should serve, the same discussion board became a site for creativity and historical thinking. When my goal was to generate more authentic types of conversation around historical issues, for example, I changed the assignment to one that required students to ask open-ended follow-up questions of one another's posts. Shifting the course toward an interactive timeline allowed me to use discussion boards differently. As our interactive timelines became a space for practicing historical thinking skills and making arguments about the significance of past events, I utilized the discussion board in more creative ways to allow students to apply the critical evaluation skills they developed on the timeline and in other course activities.

Pedagogical Considerations

I settled on a collaborative, interactive timeline to allow lower-division history students to create their own interpretations of historical figures, events, and themes. The timeline became a digital space where students worked together to post entries on key historical moments in New Mexico History. Following the success of that course, I adapted the assignment for my Modern Latin American History survey.

As I conceptualized the timeline assignment, I knew I wanted students to understand the dynamic nature of the field of history through our work together online. I thought that a timeline could be a good vehicle through which they could explore the choices that historians make as they select topics, evaluate evidence, and offer interpretations of the past. Admittedly, as I first mapped out a timeline assignment, I didn't recognize the level of scaffolding the analysis I envisioned would require.

In my experiences at conferences as varied as the American Historical Association's annual meeting, Blackboard World, the Rocky Mountain Council on Latin American Studies conference, and the Digital Pedagogy Lab, I gleaned new ways to think about digital tools. One of the most important early takeaways that informed my thinking about digital timelines was the idea that pedagogy should guide our use of technology rather than the other way around. In 2012 and 2013, the EdTech industry was growing in leaps and bounds. Like most instructors, I was bombarded with ads for different platforms and technology solutions for online students. That was also the heyday of the MOOC, the Massive Open Online Course. Pressure to implement technology in the classroom, whether in-person or fully online, ran high.

In that context, I welcomed the call to pause and ask questions about why and how I might use technology in my history classes. I was (and still am to a certain extent) what the EdTech promoters might call an "early adopter." My face-to-face survey classes were technology enhanced, meaning that students accessed most course materials and submitted their work via the learning management system. Based on a session at Blackboard World 2013, I decided to use Twitter with students as a means of conducting a first round of commentary and brief back-and-forth about readings and course materials. Student responses to Twitter have been decidedly mixed, much like that of the general public. After a couple of years using Twitter with students, I recognized and attempted to address the more problematic elements of the platform, including lack of privacy, the company's use of personal data, and the ubiquity of trolling.

When I decided to rework my courses to de-center the discussion board, however, I was ready to think a bit more critically about digital tools. In contrast with my implementation of Twitter, a pedagogical goal guided my work on creating a timeline assignment: that students begin to recognize the dynamic nature of the field of history and that they take tentative steps toward making interpretations of their own. I had no specific digital platform in mind for the timeline assignment. Instead, I attempted to design an activity that could connect to Thomas Andrews and Flannery Burke's Five Cs of Historical Thinking (change over time, causality, context, complexity, and contingency). Early in the semester, students read and comment on Andrews and Burke's essay and we discuss the significance of these in the practice of studying the past, as well as the five skills the American Historical Association highlighted as essential: chronological thinking, historical comprehension, historical analysis and interpretation, historical research capabilities, historical issues-analysis and decision-making. Together, these provide students a conceptual framework for thinking historically for class assignments.[3]

In completing the timeline assignment, students necessarily grapple with most, if not all, of the Five Cs. Please see the condensed example instructions sheet at the end of this chapter for more details about the assignment.

Students start with the Identification Step, which requires them to identify and claim a topic they would like to research further. Because one of the goals is to help students recognize the constructed nature of history, students are free to choose any topic relevant to the current timeframe and/or themes that we're studying. To support students who are less sure of what topic they might want to choose, the instructions guide them to identify a person, place, or theme that particularly stood out to them as they completed the assigned readings and videos for the current unit. Once they choose a topic, students add a placeholder to the timeline to prevent multiple entries on the same historical figure or event. (If left to their own devices, a third of my New Mexico History class would choose Billy the Kid in Unit 4.)

The placeholder is important because it allows students to secure their topic before completing the research and writing phase of the assignment. Previous class activities prepare students to identify relevant and credible sources online to support their work. The timeline entry itself consists of two to three paragraphs that provide an overview of the topic, an explanation of what unique interpretation or perspective the research sources add to our understanding of the topic, and an explanation of the topic's historical significance. Understanding historical significance can be difficult because doing so calls for interpretation and argument. As students work to understand the context of the topics they choose in light of competing perspectives and historical contingency, they recognize that explaining historical significance requires them to take a stand and make a historical interpretation.[4]

Even with preparative activities and scaffolding, it takes practice and effort for students to learn how to make a strong case for historical significance. The timeline assignment gives students so inclined opportunities to revise and resubmit. In addition to the narrative feedback I send them to push them to deepen their historical thinking skills, the second phase of the assignment, the Connection Step, puts students into conversation with one another about the entries they added to the timeline.

The Connection Step asks students to locate a peer's entry on the timeline that has some sort of connection to their own. The goal is to get them to think on their own about how the figures, events, and themes we study fit together. I also don't want to make them think that there are only certain types of connections that provide insights into our understanding of the past. This closing part of the assignment is an opportunity for them to once again make an argument to explain and justify the choice of connection that they've made. Depending on the topic, some connections seem readily apparent, such as connecting entries on Pat Garrett and Billy the Kid or connecting Cortés and Moctezuma. Others require a bit more explanation and argumentation, but whatever the connection, students must include a justification for their choice. The Connection Step gives students the opportunity to understand that historians make choices about the details and ideas they include in their arguments.

The Technology

Once I had an assignment in mind, I needed to find a digital platform that would support it. I knew that several different digital timeline platforms existed – that was part of the reason I chose this type of assignment, but I wasn't sure which one would be best. Based on my ongoing experiences using Twitter and another platform called Storify with students, I had a few priorities in mind:

- Ease of onboarding and regular use.
- Privacy for student data and their ability to manage their own digital presence.
- An ethically run company behind the platform.
- Capacity to include text, images or videos, and hyperlinks.

During an introduction to digital history session at the AHA annual meeting in 2015, one of the participants introduced Knight Lab's open-source TimelineJS platform. As I reviewed their website and the features of the platform, it met most of the criteria I had in mind except for the first one. Because I wanted students to collaborate on a single timeline, and because TimelineJS uses Google Sheets on the backend to build the timeline, I wasn't sure that students would readily be able to work with that platform unless I provided extensive training and support.

As I reviewed digital timelines, I recognized that I would have to be something of a support person no matter which platform I chose. I had been reading some of the research indicating that the idea of the digital native was a myth, and I had also observed that reality in working with my own online students.[5] Although many of them had grown up in a world where smart devices, laptops, and the internet were a daily reality, most had not been trained to use technology for learning. Additionally, the student population at my community college is highly diverse in terms of socioeconomic background, race, and age. Many needed at least some guidance and support for using our course learning management system. I had to find a user-friendly platform that I would be capable of teaching to them and that wouldn't get in the way of the learning experience I was envisioning.

The best option that I found in 2015 was a platform called Tiki-Toki. It works so well that I continue to use it. Unlike TimelineJS, Tiki-Toki contains a native editing feature, so students do not have to figure out where to enter their information into a Google Sheet to get it to display correctly on the timeline. The FAQ and Help resources for Tiki-Toki are also robust so I only had to create support materials to explain the specific ways that we will use the platform together as a class. I consistently let students know I am available to field questions about getting started with the platform, since most have no experience with Tiki-Toki. Any digital platform will have a learning curve for new users, but the curve for Tiki-Toki is low enough that learning it doesn't impede the pedagogical purpose of the timeline assignment.

I have continued to use Tiki-Toki for a collaborative digital timeline with my students over the years and created a FAQ sheet to address the questions students tend to ask. I also separated my onboarding video into a few shorter clips that focus on specific topics like how to login to our course timeline, how to get images to display correctly on the platform, where to look for credible and reliable sources, and how to be sure that you have addressed historical significance in the Identification Step. Overall, student responses to the timeline have been positive. Most report that they enjoy the visual nature of the assignment and that it has helped them to see connections between events that they might not have understood from the other course materials alone.

Takeaways and Room for Improvement

Although the digital timeline assignment created a more engaging and interactive center for my online classes, it is not perfect. Despite my best efforts, a few students never quite get the hang of adding their work to Tiki-Toki. Sometimes they add information in the wrong locations, making their entries harder to read and interact with. I don't worry as much when the issues are generally aesthetic, and the students are still able to engage with the historical thinking process as they complete the assignment. When they are not able to navigate the timeline and it becomes an obstacle, I reach out and do everything possible to help.

A wider ranging issue with the assignment has been that the Connection Step doesn't work quite as I had envisioned it. Students do interact with and read one another's posts, but they don't always evaluate each other's work in the substantive ways I laid out above. They develop the ability to write strong justifications for the connections they've made, but they do not often comment on their classmates' selection of sources or interpretations of historical significance. Both of those points can be addressed, I think, through a revision of the instructions for the assignment and the addition of scaffolded activities to prepare students for that type of peer review on the timeline.

Although Tiki-Toki is still available, I've learned to design assignments that are technology agnostic. Digital platforms come and go. For some time between 2010 and 2014, students in my classes used Storify to create digitally enhanced annotated bibliographies for research topics of their choosing. When Storify went away, I had to scramble to find a replacement since I had designed an assignment around that platform. Ultimately, I used Adobe Spark (now Adobe Express), and reworked the annotated bibliography assignment to reflect the platform change.

As with any learning activity and assignment, there is room for improvement. I've included a copy of the instructions that I provide to my New Mexico History students. Those could be adapted, revised, and reworked to fit a timeline tool other than Tiki-Toki. Although I chose not to use it for the reasons mentioned above, Timeline JS could be a good option in circumstances different from those at my institution. One of my colleagues has also had success using Sutori for student timelines, and students have successfully used Adobe Express and ChronoZoom for digital projects that center on chronology.

Timeline Assignment Example: Survey of New Mexico History

Learning competencies: Identify and describe key events from several different moments in New Mexico's past, paying special attention to their historical significance. Identify and analyze connections between historical figures and events. Consider the ways in which historical narratives and knowledge are constructed. Identify missing perspectives. Collaborate with classmates and instructor to construct a timeline of New Mexico History from the time of the region's earliest inhabitants to the present.

Over the course of this term, we will complete a detailed timeline of New Mexico History using Tiki-Toki (tiki-toki.com). You will need to login to the class Tiki-Toki account to make your contributions to the timeline. Use the login credentials below (you do not need to create your own Tiki-Toki account).

Our regular timeline contributions will produce a (relatively) complete timeline of New Mexico's past by the end of the term.

Instructions: Each timeline contribution consists of two steps: Identification and Connection. Please follow the instructions below and view these video tutorials:

- Assignment tutorial video: https://bit.ly/AssignmentTutorial (17:12).
- Tutorial: How to login to our timeline on Tiki-Toki: https://bit.ly/NMHLogin (3:16).
- Tutorial: Adding your entry to our Tiki-Toki timeline: https://bit.ly/AddEntry (11:00).

Identification step (60 points possible): In this step you will identify a person, event, or theme relevant to the elements of New Mexico History we are studying in the current Unit. Do not choose a topic someone else has already completed.

Once you've claimed a topic:

1 State its name or title and its specific date range.
2 Provide the URL or citation of the source you consulted (Wikipedia and similar sources are not allowed). Be sure to verify the credibility and reliability of your source.
3 Provide the URL of a video and/or image to illustrate the person, theme, or event you've chosen.
4 Write a paragraph or two summarizing what you learned from your source and explaining the historical significance of the person, event, or theme as it relates to New Mexico history.

Connection step (40 points possible): Locate one of your classmates' timeline contributions that relates to yours. Write a brief paragraph explaining how your classmate's contribution relates to your own. Be sure to use the connection to evaluate the historical significance of both topics.

Notes

1. Gardner, Howard E. and Wendy Fischman. "Does Truth Have a Future in Higher Education," *Studies in Higher Education 46*, no. *10* (2021): 2099–2105. Cited in Blakely, Judith, Michael Jazzar, and Michelle McCraney. "The Discussion Board: How Faculty Can Make Discussions Authentic and Not Transactional," Faculty Focus, Magna Publications, July 20, 2022. www.facultyfocus.com/articles/online-education/online-student-engagement/the-discussion-board-how-faculty-can-make-discussions-authentic-and-not-transactional/?st=FFWeekly%3Bsc%3DFFWeekly220720%3Butm_term%3DFFWeekly220720. Accessed July 23, 2022.
2. Freire, Paulo. *Pedagogy of the Oppressed*. New York: Continuum, 2000, 72; and Freire, Paulo. *The Politics of Education: Culture, Power, and Liberation*. Westport, CT: Bergin & Garvey, 1985.
3. Andrews, Thomas and Flannery Burke. "What Does It Mean to Think Historically?" *Perspectives on History* (2007). www.historians.org/publications-and-directories/perspectives-on-history/january-2007/what-does-it-mean-to-think-historically. Accessed July 30, 2022; and American Historical Association. "Historical Thinking Skills," www.historians.org/teaching-and-learning/teaching-resources-for-historians/teaching-and-learning-in-the-digital-age/the-history-of-the-americas/the-conquest-of-mexico/for-teachers/setting-up-the-project/historical-thinking-skills. Accessed July 30, 2022.
4. Gannon, Kevin. "Objective History is Impossible, and that's a Fact." The Tattooed Professor blog, May 9, 2016. https://thetattooedprof.com/2016/05/09/objective-history-is-impossible-and-thats-a-fact. Accessed August 1, 2022.
5. Eynon, Rebecca. "The Myth of the Digital Native: Why It Persists and the Harm It Inflicts," in *Education in the Digital Age: Healthy and Happy Children*, ed. T. Burns and F. Gottschalk. Paris: OECD Publishing, 2020.

Chapter 18

Using Omeka to Bring Women's History to Online Learners

Brigitte Billeaudeaux and Christine Eisel

Introduction

One of the biggest challenges instructors of online asynchronous courses face is finding ways to improve and enhance student engagement. The goals of the project described in this chapter were to better engage students in a general education US women's history course as they conducted primary and secondary source research and analysis, to improve students' information literacy, and to publish students' work on a public-facing platform – a more meaningful way to memorialize student research that traditional research papers may not offer.[1] Working in teams, the 21 students in this course constructed an Omeka digital exhibit featuring Tennessee women's lives.[2] Building on archival materials curated from the University of Memphis Libraries Special Collections, student teams biographized and contextualized women's lives throughout 19th- and 20th-century Tennessee history, reflecting social, economic, and political trends in ways that demonstrate how women were central to creating, maintaining, and challenging cultural norms.

As we constructed the project, we became aware of potential challenges and determined ways to address them, including how to make non-digitized local archival material available to students, how to manage potential team problems as they worked together, how to give students agency over the entirety of the project, and how to integrate a digital humanities project into the larger course content and learning goals so that the project outcome aligned with stated course learning outcomes. What follows is our process of putting the project together both from a teaching perspective and from an information science perspective, as well as a few things we have learned along the way.

Omeka

Omeka is an online platform for creating digital exhibits. Omeka.net hosts sites on its own server. At the time we built this exhibit, Omeka offered, for free, the ability to create one site with multiple plugins and five design options.[3] Using Omeka enabled students to upload digitized archival material and narrative essays with full citations, gave them the opportunity to learn new skills as they created metadata for each piece of evidence, and encouraged them to consider carefully archival material to highlight that best expressed their team's part of the exhibit.

Making Special Collection Archives Available to Distance Learning Students

As we looked for a way to translate the curriculum in a History of Women in America course into a digital humanities project, we were initially inspired by a public history project published in an article in *The American Historian*.[4] The premise of the project as explained in the article was to bring together digital tools and digitized primary source materials so that students could build history projects that would be publicly available. Their result is a historical website that uses primary resources and geographical information systems (GIS) to drive home the history of the Blue Ridge Parkway. Because of the complexity that GIS can present to novices, we discussed other ideas as we developed a manageable and publicly available project that would explore women's history in Tennessee. Based on positive previous experiences, we settled on using Omeka to create collections students could populate with archival material, historical narratives, and basic metadata, establishing a class site that could be cross-promoted through the history department and the library. Faculty at the University of Memphis had not attempted this type of project at the University of Memphis; students would not necessarily have to step onto campus to complete the project, and we would provide groups with subject-specific content around which they could research and build their collections for the digital exhibit. Students would have creative input in website design. The course instructor would direct student groups through different class modules to help keep the content and curriculum relevant, while the librarians would work on providing the class with sets of curated and digitized materials. We brought on to the project student interns to assist with digitizing archival material.

We tailored content exhibited according to themes the class covered throughout the course's curriculum and reflected Special Collections holdings. We chose seven topics: Activism, Civic Life, Domesticity, Education, Entertainment, Media, and Politics.

Methodology for Selection

The University Libraries' Special Collections department has long been involved with digitizing materials from its archives for use outside of its archives. Previously, the department focused primarily on scan on demand projects. This primarily consisted of "one off" requests and the odd large volume job from patrons. In 2008, the department began preparing for more planned and directed digitization. By 2010, appropriate staff were in place to move forward with creating curated projects using collections housed in the archives. More recently with the hire of the department's Preservation Librarian, the focus has moved from selected digitizing of individual items to including finding aids. This is a new venture, but an important one as the Special Collections department strives to make more content available through the library's catalog and its content management system (CMS).

Adding finding aids to the digital repository began in late summer and early fall of 2014. In selecting collections' finding aids to include on the CMS, quantity over quality – i.e., relevance to the collection – was preferred. Library staff selected the shortest and most accessible content to ensure library patrons a variety of materials. Several of the Special Collections department's new finding aids and collections were a good fit for the topics developed for this class.

For the Women in American History Omeka project, the librarians and instructor met on several occasions to discuss the criteria for inclusion of materials students could use for the project. Based on our holdings, we developed seven topic areas to keep student groups small and manageable. Items needed to be easily digitizable, so oversized materials were kept to a minimum and materials in very poor condition were excluded. Collections for each topic needed enough material so that students could produce narratives that tied content back into the curriculum.

Unfortunately, there were very few relevant items already digitized when we started this project. This meant we had to take swift action to identify appropriate materials that would fit with the seven topics, ensure enough time to digitize materials, and locate already digitized materials and make them available to students with enough time for them to complete evaluation and selection for inclusion in each group's project.

Based on the seven topic areas, some primary source materials immediately came to mind, most notably the Katherine Lawless Compton papers and the Meriwether family papers.[5] The Lawless Compton papers feature the work of women who broke barriers by engaging in civic work previously performed exclusively by men. The activities in which Lawless Compton engaged demonstrate the centrality of women's participation in Memphis civic activities.[6] The Meriwether Family papers have long been known for the contents pertaining to Minor Meriwether, a Confederate civil engineer; the works of Elizabeth Avery Meriwether provide a valuable record of Tennessee women's professional and domestic activity.[7] Finding aids were already available online for these collections; the background information that is provided in the scope and content notes of the aids proved to be important to the students as they contextualized the sources. Where topics lacked relevant content, we looked to other digitized collections, particularly portions of the department's newspaper morgue, to provide content for students. In some instances, we directed students to the Internet Archive where the University of Memphis Libraries houses materials owned by the university, including oral histories and the university's now defunct annuals.

While some topics were very easy to connect to primary sources, pulling and digitizing items for other topics was more difficult. Special Collections has over 600 manuscript collections and tens of thousands of photographs and paper manuscript items. This is in addition to the 60,000 books housed in the department. All the materials became fair game for the project.

In the end, we selected individual items from approximately nine collections. We created over 500 scans for this project. Manuscript materials, books, and images made up the bulk of the scanned material. From these, students ultimately chose items to create 79 records for the project exhibit. Each student group used varying levels of items that were provided to them. One group even looked beyond the items provided to them and located an oral history on the Special Collections department's Internet Archive site to include in their collections.

The Project as Part of the Course

Students accessed project directions via our online learning platform, Desire 2 Learn (D2L). We broke down the project into manageable sections:

- Getting Started.
- Secondary Resources.
- Working with Primary Resources.
- Writing Your Essay.
- Building the Exhibit.

"Getting Started" gave students a brief explanation of the project and directed them to choose their topic preferences based on the categories we established. Once we assigned topics, we created a course discussion forum for each group in which they could share ideas, concerns, and progress. They also could bring to our attention any questions or concerns in their group forums, via an "Instructor's Board," or in an "Ask the Librarian" forum. Together, these discussion forums allowed each of us to communicate with students directly.

The next step, "Secondary Resources" directed students in each group to collaborate on a working annotated bibliography for their topic. We gave each group some parameters based on what we had already found in the collections, especially concerning date ranges, but we avoided reining them in too much so that they could develop enough context and increase their understanding of their topic on a broader scale. We created for each group a dropbox in D2L where they could submit their completed annotated bibliographies and peer reviews in which they evaluated their own and each other's work.

In the third step, "Working with Primary Sources," we instructed students on how to access the zip files of scanned documents in their dropbox, to go through the archival material that had been scanned and uploaded for them, and to create a collection of sources that they would like to use for their topic in the exhibit. They were asked to consider which of the scanned items were most relevant to the secondary research they had done, those which were most visually interesting, and those around which they could build a narrative. Students wrote brief descriptions of each item selected. Students again collaborated on this in their groups and submitted to me via their groups' D2L dropbox a list of sources that included a description of each. Students again submitted peer reviews of their own and each other's work.

In step four, "Writing Your Essay," we instructed students to write narrative essays designed to introduce their group's collection and to edit as necessary their document descriptions. Students also created the metadata for each item they chose. This proved to be the most challenging part of the project. Once again, they submitted their work to their designated D2L dropboxes along with peer reviews. This part of the project required students to make the most revisions to their work – a few students wrote great narratives and descriptions; others struggled and needed several critiques before we accepted a finalized version.

"Building the Exhibit" was the last step. Earlier in the semester, we directed students to several examples of open access Omeka exhibits to give them an idea of what we would be creating. In a discussion forum, they gave input on design. We explained to students the importance of writing clear and focused metadata for each piece of archival evidence their teams chose for their part of the exhibit – metadata that would make each item searchable and useful to other researchers.[8] We created for students a series of technical directions for creating the metadata using Dublin Core and instructed them to use the "Ask the Librarian" discussion forum to post any questions or problems they faced. Students learned about copyright issues, gained a better understanding of the importance of provenance, and gave careful thought to the organization and flow of their project.

Embedding the Librarian

Early in our project development, we saw the necessity to embed the librarian so she could take a more hands-on approach in the course compared to librarian participation in other courses at the university.[9] In addition to providing curated content to be culled by class groups, the librarian provided in-depth explanations on how to create the digital humanities project by creating a variety of supportive materials designed to help students along in the digital metadata and electronic publishing processes, including written tutorials, videos, and a mock-up Omeka site to assist students. The librarian was available for face-to-face interactions with the students from the class when they needed more in-depth explanation or assistance with concepts, content, and record creation. While the course was completely online, most students in the class were in Memphis and the Memphis metro area and had access to campus. Making these resources available helped in a lot of aspects and several students took advantage of the face-to-face opportunities provided. Some of the more abstract concepts that students were least familiar with posed the biggest challenges. Instruction on metadata, archival material review, and using Omeka were the most common reasons students came to Special Collections for help.

Challenges

There were challenges to consider in collaborating and creating this project for students. For the librarian, the biggest challenge was selecting and digitizing a variety of collections in a relatively brief span of time, and then finding a way to make it easily accessible to students. We found it necessary to quickly make decisions regarding the comprehensiveness of each group's collection. Rather than creating a comprehensive collection of items for topic areas, we kept and digitized the most relevant items, and omitted more tertiary items.

Other challenges revolved around not knowing the skill level of each student since this was both a general education course and an upper division course. Designing uncomplicated instructions on how to add content to the project webpage and writing vital metadata, and creating a space to hold the archival material that was easily accessible to students, required thoughtful planning.

Lessons Learned

This project was a first for both the History Department and the University Libraries at the University of Memphis. While large-scale collaborations have been part of the culture at the University of Memphis, no two departments had ever taken on a digital humanities project using primary source materials from university-owned archives. There were many lessons learned from conducting this project:

1. Have a plan and devise it early. The librarians involved in this project knew enough about the Special Collections holdings that together we were able to come up with seven topics for students to pursue.
2. Model good collaboration skills for students. We divided the work between the librarians and course instructor in ways that drew on their strengths, which students were then able to model as they collaborated in ways that drew on each team member's strengths. This is an important lesson for students. Working across departments demonstrated to students that scholarship is not done in isolation. We were very open with them on the collaboration taking place in developing the assignment so that they felt more comfortable collaborating in their groups on their particular topics.

3   There is a fine line between too much and not enough material. Approximately 15 percent of the provided content was used in the final product of the project. This is not including sources that were located from other areas of University of Memphis Libraries' owned digital content. Different groups used varying percentages of materials that were given to them. The best attempts were made to make packages of resources full and fluid.

4   Students still struggle with information literacy, primary source literacy, and research. Students expressed difficulty in finding sources for their topic areas. Once resources were located many students expressed difficulty in relating literary resources to the primary source materials and vice versa.

5   Expect the unexpected. We had an idea of some of the archival material we could make available to students, yet the librarian found some real treasures in the archives, including items that clearly demonstrated to students Memphis's segregated past. Curating items for the use of others sometimes led to disappointments, as some of the more interesting items were not well-suited to the topics we had already created.

6   Be wary of discipline-related jargon. Throughout the semester the students were tasked with providing various posts and reading responses as a part of class participation. When it came time to begin creating narratives, students felt and expressed anxiety about this task. They had been doing this all semester long but using the term "narrative" seemed to throw them. They all had a collective "Aha" moment when they understood that the short essays they had been writing weekly were preparation for the larger project, and much of their anxiety dissipated.

7   Students know less about the subject matter than we, as instructors, often imagine. Using primary sources often allows students to create more personal connections with historical material.[10] When students first started looking at their archival material, they were often surprised at what they found. When asked to provide some initial thoughts as they started to look through the material, their responses were telling. One student in the "Activism" group spotted the Crenshaw material right away. She recalled she thought immediately "suffrage"; it never occurred to her to consider more local and more personal issues like the connection between water, sanitation, and poverty. Another student in the group working on "Politics" also wrote she had assumed anything political would be connected to suffrage. She was surprised to see newspaper clippings from the 1970s; somehow, to her, women were not politically motivated after 1920. One of the students in the "Education" group was surprised at the activity of Memphis area women in the National PTA; her immediate thoughts on education went to women becoming educated, rather than women working to reform education on such a large scale.

In the end, we hope that the students in this course learned from this project. We believe it can serve as a model for other distance-learning courses by encouraging students to use the resources that are available to them in new and creative ways. We observed that having the students work with artifacts on women who had a Memphis connection made studying US women's history even more personal for the learners in this course. The project enhanced the development of their research and writing skills, improved their information and primary source literacy, and showcased University Libraries' Special Collections.

Notes

1. Litterio, Lisa M. "Digital Humanities in Professional and Technical Communication: Results of a Pedagogical Pilot Study." *Technical Communications Quarterly 30*, no. 1 (2021): 77–88.
2. The completed exhibit, "Making an Impact: The Lives of Tennessee Women," is located at https://umhist4851.omeka.net/.
3. Options for Omeka exhibits have changed since creating this exhibit. See www.omeka.net/ for current pricing and options. Note that while Omeka.org offers more design options, plugins, and space, it requires users to have their own server.
4. Mitchell Whisnat, Anne and Pamela Lach. "Building the Unbuilt Parkway: Digital Public History in the Classroom." *The American Historian 1* (2014): 16–18.
5. The Katherine Lawless Compton papers finding aid is available at https://digitalcommons.memphis.edu/speccoll-findingaids/49/. The Meriwether Family papers finding aid is available at https://digitalcommons.memphis.edu/speccoll-findingaids/107/.
6. For the exhibit collection on "Civic Life," see https://umhist4851.omeka.net/items/show/95; students highlighted several documents from the Katherine Lawless Compton papers.
7. For the exhibit collection on "Domesticity," see https://umhist4851.omeka.net/collections/show/10; students highlighted several documents from the Meriwether collection.
8. Mussell, Jim. "Doing and Making History in the Digital Age." In *History in the Digital Age*, ed. Toni Weller, 79–94. New York: Routledge, 2013, 83.
9. Carlson, Jake, and Ruth Kneale. "Embedded Librarianship in the Research Context: Navigating New Waters." *College & Research Libraries News 72*, no. 3 (2011): 167–170.
10. Lee, John K. "Digital History in the History/Social Studies Classroom." *The History Teacher 35*, no. 4 (2002): 503–517.

Appendix 1: Sample Course Design Agreement and Related Documents

The enclosed documents are offered as general guidance and a starting point for new online course developers, instructors, and program managers. All will need some modification and/or addition to suit local laws and university policy. None should be taken as specific legal advice. Laws vary by location and change over time. Consult your school's legal office and other relevant officials for specific advice and assistance in crafting copyright agreements and related documents for your program.

Document 1: Sample Copyright Agreement

COPYRIGHT LICENSE AGREEMENT
Educational Course Materials

This Agreement made the ___day of _____, 20__, by and between the University of [NAME] (hereafter called "the Institution") and [FACULTY NAME].

THE AUTHOR AND THE INSTITUTION AGREE THAT:

1. **Rights GrantedNonprofit Educational Uses.** The Author hereby grants to the Institution for the full term of this Agreement the non-exclusive right to copy, distribute, display, perform, transmit, and publish for nonprofit educational purposes the educational course materials entitled: [Course # and name] (hereinafter called "Work").
2. **Description of the Work**
The Work which is the subject of this Agreement includes development of the online course and materials within it.
3. **Delivery of the Work**
    a The Author will prepare and deliver to the Institution on or before [Date of completion] the completed Work (with all illustrations, charts, graphs, and other material, including syllabi, handouts, assignment instructions, etc., in the medium mutually agreed upon for the Work) in form and content satisfactory to the Institution.
    b If the Author fails to deliver the Work on time, the Institution will have the right to terminate this Agreement and to recover from the Author any progress payments made in connection with the Work. Upon such termination, the Author may not have the Work published elsewhere until such progress payments have been repaid.
    c The Author will teach this course the first semester the Institution offers it. Afterward, the Author, if a fulltime faculty member of the Institution, shall have first right of refusal to teach the first section of the course each semester it is offered. This right is dependent upon:
        i Satisfactory performance in the online environment.
        ii Staffing issues.
        iii Satisfactory results from the course review process.
4. **Quoted Material**
With the exception of short excerpts from others' works, which constitute fair use, the Work will contain no material from other copyrighted works without the written consent of the copyright holder. The Author will obtain such consent at his or her own expense after consultation with the

Institution and will file them with the Institution at the time the Work is delivered. Any obligations associated with permissions will be the responsibility of the Author.

5. **Copyright**

    The Author authorizes the Institution to register copyright in the Work in the Author's name in the United States and elsewhere as the Institution may elect.

6. **Author's Warranty**

    The Author[s] warrant they are the sole owner of the Work and have full power and authority to make this Agreement; that the Work does not infringe any copyright, violate any property rights, or contain any scandalous, libelous, or unlawful matter. The Author[s] will defend, indemnify, and hold harmless the Institution and/or its licensees against all claims, suits, costs, damages, and expenses that the Institution and/or its licensees may sustain by reason of any scandalous, libelous, or unlawful matter contained or alleged to be contained in the Work or any infringement or violation by the Work of any copyright or property right; and until such claim or suit has been settled or withdrawn, the Institution may withhold any sums due the Author[s] under this Agreement.

7. **Consideration**

    In consideration of this Agreement, the Institution shall pay the Author[s] the sum of $[XXXX.XX] upon delivery and acceptance of the Work. The Institution shall also provide the Author access to Institution facilities and use of Institution resources such as computers and network access to complete the Work.

8. **Subsidiary Rights**

    Nonprofit Educational Uses. The Institution has been granted a limited right to use the Work for nonprofit educational purposes only and therefore does not need subsidiary rights, and all such rights are retained by the Author[s]. The Author[s] maintains the right to the material in the course. Should the Author[s] leave the University the Author[s] will have the right to use the material elsewhere. However, the University retains the right to use the course through its educational programs.

9. **Revisions**

    The Author[s] shall retain the right to revise the Work during the term of this Agreement in accordance with academic standards. The Author[s] further agrees to update the Work within ninety (90) days upon the receipt of a written request from the Institution. The provisions of this Agreement shall apply to each revision of the Work by the Author[s] as though that revision were the Work being published for the first time under this Agreement. In the event the Author[s] is unable or unwilling to provide a revision within ninety (90) days after the Institution has requested it, or should the Author[s] be deceased, the Institution may have the revision made by another person.

10. Term and Termination

a This Agreement shall remain in effect for five (5) year(s) unless terminated earlier in accordance with this Section 10. Upon expiration of the term and any renewal term(s) agreed upon pursuant to Section 10(c), or upon earlier termination in accordance with Section 10(b), the rights granted in the Work shall revert to the Author, subject to retention by the Institution of the non-exclusive, perpetual right and license to use the Work for internal nonprofit educational purposes and to use the structure and organization of the Work as a guide for the creation of a new course.

b In the event that either Party shall be in default of its material obligations under this Agreement and shall fail to remedy such default within sixty (60) days after receipt of written notice thereof, this Agreement shall terminate upon expiration of the sixty (60) day period.

c Upon the expiration of the term of this Agreement, the parties may agree to renew this Agreement for an additional five-year term, upon the same terms and conditions as set forth herein.

11. Options/Contracts with Third Parties

Nothing contained in Section 10 shall affect any license or other grant of rights, options, or Agreements made with third parties prior to the termination date or the rights of the Institution in the income resulting from such Agreements.

12. Amendments

The written provisions contained in this Agreement constitute the sole and entire Agreement made between the Author and the Institution concerning this Work, and any amendments to this Agreement shall not be valid unless made in writing and signed by both parties.

IN WITNESS WHEREOF, the parties have duly executed this Agreement as of the date first written above.

Author:

University Representative:

Document 2: Sample Course Planning Worksheet

As you develop and organize your online course and create your syllabus, consider the topics below.

Learning Objectives

What will students learn in your course? What are the overarching themes and ideas in your course? What should students take away with them after completing your course? What will students need to do and learn to be successful in your course? How will they develop their ability to think critically, research, and related skills in your course?

Topics

What topics will be covered in your course? How do these relate to your learning objectives? Clearly indicating relationships between the topics you will cover and your learning objectives will help students stay focused as they work their way through your course, participate in class discussions, and write their essays and other major assignments.

Course Content

What materials will your course contain? These can range from primary documents, selections from secondary sources, photos, and other graphics to audio, text, or video lectures. Consider how course materials will support your learning objectives. Be sure to consider copyright and intellectual property issues when choosing your course content. Make sure your course materials meet the accessibility criteria of your university with text descriptions of graphics, captions for videos, transcripts for audio files, and so on.

Course Activities and Assessments

What will students do in your course? How will they engage with course materials? Common activities in history courses include weekly participation in online discussions, quizzes on readings, essay questions, and research papers of varying lengths. Keep in mind both your own workload and that of the students. Quizzes are oftentimes consuming to create, but convenient afterward if automatically graded within your learning management system (LMS). Some instructors favor detailed grading rubrics for discussion participation and essays, while others eschew them. Regardless, the more detailed your instructions are to students, the better. It is a good idea to reinforce specific assignment instructions to students in regular emails, discussion posts, or course announcements.

Modules

As you develop your course topics, activities, and materials, consider how you will organize your course. What will be taught when and in what order? Most online courses are divided into modules (often assigned weekly), each with associated course materials and student activities, such as discussion posting, essays, or other assignments. Use the same structure to organize each module, noting assigned reading, course materials, assignments, and other important matters.

LMS Tools

Before you get too far into developing your course, assess the LMS you are using and make sure it supports teaching the course the way you wish. If not, you may have to rethink how you approach some course activities and adjust them to fit the limitations of your university's LMS.

Document 3: Online Course Design Checklist

Course Introduction

Was an introductory email sent to students letting them know how to find and log into the course?
Are there instructions explaining to students which internet browsers are compatible with the university's LMS and (if necessary) how they should be configured, such as setting them to "accept cookies?"
Can students easily find information on how to navigate the course and access its materials?
Do students know how to contact their instructor within and outside the LMS?
Do students know how to contact technical support?

Course Organization

Are layout, fonts, and related characteristics uniform and consistent through the course?
Any typos, grammatical errors, etc.?
Is course content organized logically and consistently into topics, modules, etc.?
Does the course's first module contain the syllabus and other important introductory material?
Are course assignments easily found and clearly explained? Do they include instructions on how to submit them through the LMS?
Are instructions for participating in class discussions posted?
Are specific due dates for assignments posted? Are they consistent, such as always having assignments due at the same time of day, such as 11:59pm?
Does the course use a mix of different instructional strategies?
Does the course follow universal design principles and adhere to university standards for accessibility?

Communication

Are students asked to introduce themselves at the beginning of the course?
Is there a dedicated discussion area for student questions?
Are students encouraged to interact with one another and the instructor?

Student Assessment

Are assignment instructions clear and consistent?
Are there a variety of assignments that reflect different approaches to learning?
Do students receive timely and useful feedback on their work through the semester?

Appendix 2: Website and Additional Resources

Accessibility Checklists

Blackboard Help—Accessibility Checklist: https://help.blackboard.com/Ally/Ally_for_LMS/Instructor/Improve_File_Accessibility/Accessibility_Checklist. This minimal checklist provides support for Blackboard. A link to a PDF checklist produced by Ally, an accessibility checking software, can also be found on this page.

Brightspace—Accessibility Checklist: https://brightspacecommunity.force.com/s/article/Improve-Your-Course-with-Brightspace-Accessibility-Checker. An overview of accessibility features and fixes for the Brightspace LMS.

Canvas Course Evaluation Checklist 2.0: https://docs.google.com/document/d/1c6cv_95IT2MpYn2oy9HhNFnvJdODWsAqv3ovqtfSITc/template/preview. This checklist provides guidelines for evaluating a class in Canvas that can be used as a starting point for online classes offered in other LMSs.

Canvas Course Evaluation Checklist—Mobile App Design: https://docs.google.com/document/d/1D2NjociFTdFtZScgrzg217RUhFzjTIjPIXXAB3Hm7BU/edit. This checklist is designed to assess how compatible an instructor's class is with mobile devices.

Moodle Help Guide—Mt. Holyoke College: https://guides.mtholyoke.edu/moodle/accessibility. This LibGuide provides basic accessibility tips for Moodle in a convenient checklist format.

UDL—Universe Checklists: https://enact.sonoma.edu/c.php?g=789377&p=5650629. A list of checklists that address various topics, such as creating accessible syllabi, checking documents for accessibility, and making slides in PowerPoint accessible. Note: as of this publication, not all of the links on the site were active.

Accessibility Tools

Accessible Templates for PowerPoint—Microsoft website: https://templates.office.com/en-us/accessible-powerpoint-template-sampler-tm16401472?ui=

en-US&rs=en-US&ad=UShttps://templates.office.com/en-us/accessible-powerpoint-template-sampler-tm16401472?ui=en-US&rs=en-US&ad=US. This website offers downloadable, accessible templates for PowerPoint.

Building Accessible Tables: www.dallascollege.edu/about/accessibility/guidelines/pages/building-tables.aspx#:~:text=What%20Makes%20a%20Table%20Accessible%3F%201%201.%20Include,5%205.%20Don%27t%20Use%20Screenshots%20of%20Tables.%20. This Dallas College website has set-by-step instructions for how to make tables in Word, Excel, PowerPoint, and eCampus, as well as guidance on alt tags, transcripts, headings, and other accessibility support. Note: many of these features are not yet available in Google Docs.

California Community Colleges Accessibility Center: https://cccaccessibility.org/alternate-media/ms-office-pdf. Suggests best practices and provides resources for making documents, including PDFs, accessible.

Guidelines for Accessibility for Mac Products (Keynote, Pages, etc.): https://support.apple.com/en-us/HT210563. This website provides a general overview of how to make accessible documents in Mac office software.

Make Your Document or Presentation More Accessible—Google Docs: https://support.google.com/docs/answer/6199477?hl=en. This website suggests ways to make Google Docs more accessible.

Make Your Excel Spreadsheets Accessible—Microsoft website: https://support.office.com/en-us/article/make-your-excel-documents-accessible-to-people-with-disabilities-6cc05fc5-1314-48b5-8eb3-683e49b3e593. Same as the above, but for Excel. Instructions on how to make spreadsheets accessible across various systems.

Make Your PowerPoints Accessible—Microsoft website: https://support.office.com/en-us/article/make-your-powerpoint-presentations-accessible-to-people-with-disabilities-6f7772b2-2f33-4bd2-8ca7-dae3b2b3ef25. In addition to what you can find in the Help guide for PowerPoint, this website explains how to make PowerPoint presentations accessible across various systems, including Mac, Android, and Windows.

Make Your Word Documents Accessible—Microsoft website: https://support.office.com/en-us/article/Make-your-Word-documents-accessible-to-people-with-disabilities-d9bf3683-87ac-47ea-b91a-78dcacb3c66d. Similar to the above but for Word documents. Provides instructions for how to make Word documents accessible across systems including Mac, Android, and Windows.

WCAG website: www.w3.org/TR/coga-usable/#background. A comprehensive source for information on making websites accessible. Click on "Making Content Usable for People with Cognitive and Learning Disabilities" for specific examples and scenarios.

WAVE Web Accessibility Tool: https://wave.webaim.org. Downloads a plugin for your browser (that is, a browser extension) that checks webpages in an LMS or other websites for accessibility. Helps identify problems that accessibility software in LMSs may miss.

Web Accessibility Tutorial: Content Structure: www.w3.org/WAI/tutorials/page-structure/content. This website offers a tutorial on how to edit HTML to create accessible web pages.

Annotation Tools

Hypothes.is is a social annotation tool that lets students collaboratively highlight and mark-up documents, websites, and other media: https://web.hypothes.is.

Color Contrast Checkers for Accessibility

Color Contrast Analyser: www.tpgi.com/color-contrast-checker/. Downloads an application that allows you to check for color accessibility by using the eyedropper to select the colors being compared.

WebAIM Contrast Checker: https://webaim.org/resources/contrastchecker/. Allows users to enter foreground and background colors to check for accessibility.

Gaming

CUNY Games Network offers a host of readings and other resources on game-based learning: https://games.commons.gc.cuny.edu/.

Reacting to the Past (RTTP) offers detailed, immersive classroom games on historical topics with accompanying textbooks and supporting materials: https://reacting.barnard.edu/.

Games in College Classrooms, Facebook group: www.facebook.com/groups/1773710516258929.

Flippity.net has lots of widgets for creating puzzles and other games or game elements.

Ludii Games offers many classic board games online including several ancient and medieval games, such as Aksadyuta, Hnefatafl, and Mehen: https://ludii.games.

Board Game Arena allows you to play a number of popular board games online, including several on history or historical events, such as Polis, on the Peloponnesian War, and Through the Ages, an abstract Civilization-style game that surveys political, social, and technological developments: https://boardgamearena.com/.

Open Educational Resources

American Yawp: www.americanyawp.com. One of the first open, collaboratively assembled textbooks, and still going strong.

CampusGrotto.com—Audio Textbooks: https://campusgrotto.com/audio-textbooks.html. Written for students, this website offers a number of suggestions for converting books, including textbooks, into audio formats, with suggestions for software and devices.

Galileo Open Learning Materials: https://oer.galileo.usg.edu/history-textbooks/. Textbooks for the US survey, Western Civilization, and World History.

OER Commons: www.oercommons.org. A large collection of open access books and shorter materials for college courses.

OER Knowledge Cloud: www.oerknowledgecloud.org. A searchable database and repository of articles and books on open access educational resources.

Open Textbook Library: https://open.umn.edu/opentextbooks. Based at the University of Minnesota, they offer history texts for both survey and several upper division courses.

Bibliography

1940 Statement of Principles on Academic Freedom and Tenure. www.aaup.org/file/1940%20Statement.pdf. Accessed December 24, 2020.

Ahmed, Amer. "'Glocal' Justice: Toward an Equity Imperative in International Education." Keynote Address at WISE Connect Symposium, Winston-Salem, NC, February 11, 2022.

Ali, A., and D. Smith. "Comparing Students' Performance in Online versus Face-to-Face Courses in Computer Literacy," *Competition Forum* 12 (2014): 118–123.

American Historical Association. "Historical Thinking Skills," www.historians.org/teaching-and-learning/teaching-resources-for-historians/teaching-and-learning-in-the-digital-age/the-history-of-the-americas/the-conquest-of-mexico/for-teachers/setting-up-the-project/historical-thinking-skills. Accessed July 30, 2022.

Anderson, Benedict. *Imagined Communities.* Revised Edition. New York: Verso, 1991.

Anderson, M., J. Goodman, and N. Schlossberg. *Counseling Adults in Transition: Linking Schlossberg's Theory with Practice in a Diverse World*, 4th ed. New York: Springer, 2012.

Anderson, Monica and Jingjing Jiang. "Teens, Social Media, and Technology 2018." n.d. www.pewresearch.org/internet/2018/05/31/teens-social-media-technology-2018. Accessed May 31, 2018.

Andrews, Thomas and Flannery Burke. "What Does It Mean to Think Historically?" *Perspectives on History* (2007). www.historians.org/publications-and-directories/perspectives-on-history/january-2007/what-does-it-mean-to-think-historically. Accessed July 30, 2022.

Angelo, Thomas A., and K. Patricia Cross. *Classroom Assessment Techniques: A Handbook for College Teachers.* San Francisco, CA: Jossey-Bass, Wiley, 1993 and 2012.

Association of American Colleges & Universities. "Global Learning VALUE Rubric." n.d. www.aacu.org/initiatives/value-initiative/value-rubrics/value-rubrics-global-learning. Accessed October 23, 2021.

Ayers, Edward L. "The Pasts and Futures of Digital History." The University of Virginia, 1999. www.vcdh.virginia.edu/PastsFutures.html. Accessed May 31, 2018.

Beed, Penny L., Hawkins, E. Marie, andCathy M. Roller "Moving Learners toward Independence: The Power of Scaffolded Instruction." *The Reading Teacher*, 44, no. 9 (1991): 648–656.

Bennett, Liz. "Putting in More: Emotional Work in Adopting Online Tools in Teaching and Learning Practices." *Teaching in Higher Education* 19, no. 8 (2014): 919–930.

Bennett, Milton J. "A Developmental Approach to Training for Intercultural Sensitivity." *International Journal of Intercultural Relations* 10, no. 2 (1986): 179–196.

Berg, Richard, et al. "Leveraging Recorded Mini-Lectures to Increase Student Learning," *Online Classroom* 14, no. 2 (2014): 5–6. www.csusb.edu/sites/default/files/upload/file/Leveraging_Recorded_Mini-Lectures_to_Inc.pdf.

Bergstrand, Kelly, and Scott Savage. "The Chalkboard versus the Avatar: Comparing the Effectiveness of Online and In-Class Courses." *Teaching Sociology* 41, no. 3 (2013): 294–306.

Biggs, J. and Tang, C., *Teaching for Quality Learning: What the Student Does*, 4th ed. Berkshire: Open University Press, 2011.

Blakely, Judith, Michael Jazzar, and Michelle McCraney. "The Discussion Board: How Faculty Can Make Discussions Authentic and Not Transactional," Faculty Focus, Magna Publications, July 20, 2022. www.facultyfocus.com/articles/online-education/online-student-engagement/the-discussion-board-how-faculty-can-make-discussions-authentic-and-not-transactional/?st=FFWeekly%3Bsc%3DFFWeekly220720%3Butm_term%3DFFWeekly220720. Accessed July 23, 2022.

Bloom, Benjamin S. *Taxonomy of Educational Objectives: The Classification of Educational Goals*. London: Longman Group, 1956.

Bloom, J. "Developmental Advising Definitions." NACADA Clearinghouse of Academic Advising Resources, March 20, 2014. https://nacada.ksu.edu/Resources/Clearinghouse/View-Articles/Developmental-advising-definitions.aspx. Accessed July 23, 2022.

Bogost, Ian. "Gamification is Bullshit," 2011, http://bogost.com/writing/blog/gamification_is_bullshit. Accessed November 22, 2022.

Bogost, Ian. "Why Gamification is Bullshit," in *The Gameful World: Approaches, Issues, Applications*, ed. Stephan Walz and Sebastion Deterdig, 65–79. Cambridge, MA: The MIT Press, 2014.

Bollinger, Doris, Fethi Inan, and Oksana Wasilik. "Development and Validation of the Online Instructor Satisfaction Measure." *Journal of Educational Technology & Society* 17, no. 2 (2014): 183–195.

Booth, Alan. *Teaching History at University: Enhancing Learning and Understanding*. New York: Routledge, 2003.

Boud, D. and Falchikov, N., "Aligning Assessment with Long-Term Learning," *Assessment and Evaluation in Higher Education* 31, no. 4 (2006): 399–413.

Bowman, Nicholas A. "Can 1st-Year College Students Accurately Report Their Learning and Development?" *American Educational Research Journal* 47, no. 2 (2010): 466–496. https://doi.org/10.3102/0002831209353595.

Budhai, Stephanie, and Williams, Maureen, "Teaching Presence in Online Courses: Practical Applications, Co-Facilitation and Technology Integration," *The Journal of Effective Teaching* 16, no. 3 (2016): 76–84.

Burgstahler, Sheryl. "What Higher Education Learned about the Accessibility of Online Opportunities during a Pandemic." *Journal of Higher Education Theory and Practice* 21, no. 7 (2021): 160–170.

Burke, Brian. *Gamify: How Gamification Motivates People to Do Extraordinary Things*. Brookline, MA: Bibliomotion, 2014.

Calder, Lendol. "Uncoverage: Toward a Signature Pedagogy for the History Survey," *The Journal of American History* 92, no. 4 (2006): 1358–1370.

Caldwell et al., eds. "Web Content Accessibility Guidelines." www.w3.org/TR/WCAG20. Accessed June 20, 2022.

California State University. "UDL-Universe: A Comprehensive Faculty Development Guide." https://enact.sonoma.edu/c.php?g=789377&p=5650608. Accessed June 20, 2022.

California Virtual Campus-Online Education Initiative (CVC-OEI) Professional Development Workgroup. "Peer Online Course Review." https://onlinenetworkofeducators.org/course-design-academy/pocr-resources. Accessed June 20, 2022.

Canning, Elizabeth A., Katherine Muenks, Dorainne J. Green, and Mary C. Murphy. "STEM Faculty Who Believe Ability Is Fixed Have Larger Racial Achievement Gaps and Inspire Less Student Motivation in Their Classes." *Science Advances* 5, no. 2 (2019). www.science.org/doi/full/10.1126/sciadv.aau4734.

Carlson, Jake, and Ruth Kneale. "Embedded Librarianship in the Research Context: Navigating New Waters." *College & Research Libraries News* 72, no. 3 (2011): 167–170.

Carnes, Mark. *Minds on Fire: How Role-Immersion Games Transform College*. Cambridge, MA: Harvard University Press, 2014.

Carnevale, Dan, and Jeffrey R. Young, "Who Owns Online Courses? Colleges and Professors Start to Sort It Out," *Chronicle of Higher Learning*, December 17, 1999.

Carter, Genesea and David Korostyshevsky, "Valuing Process Over Product: Using Writing to Teach History in the Undergraduate History Classroom," *Teaching History: A Journal of Methods* 46, no. 1 (2021): 10–22. https://openjournals.bsu.edu/teachinghistory/article/view/3204.

Castro, Joy. "On Becoming Educated." *The Scholar and Feminist Online* 8, no. 3 (2010). https://sfonline.barnard.edu/polyphonic/castro_01.htm.

Caudle, L., and T.H. Paulsen. "Evidence of Critical Thinking in a Capstone Course." *NACTA Journal* 61, no. 3 (2017): 208–218.

Cerezo, Alison and Amaranta Ramirez, "Navigating New Terrain: Sexual and Gender Diverse College Students Who Are the First in Their Families to Attend College," in *Affirming LGBTQ+ Students in Higher Education*, ed. D.P. Rivera, R.L. Abreu, and K.A. Gonzalez, 162–163. Washington, DC: American Psychology Association, 2022.

Chapdelaine, Robin, and Megan Toomer, "Experiential Learning in Ghana: Decentering the White Voice." *Radical Teacher* 121 (2021): 5–14.

Coates, Hamish, "Leveraging LMSs to Enhance Campus-Based Student Engagement," *EDUCAUSE Quarterly* 1 (2005): 66–68.

Cohen, Daniel J., and Roy Rosenzweig. "No Computer Left Behind." *Chronicle of Higher Education*, February 24, 2006. www.chronicle.com/article/no-computer-left-behind. Accessed November 22, 2022.

Condie, Rae, and Kay Livingston. "Blending Online Learning with Traditional Approaches: Changing Practices." *British Journal of Educational Technology* 38, no. 2 (2007): 337–348.

Crookston, B.B. "A Developmental View of Academic Advising as Teaching." *NACADA Journal* 14, no. 2 (1994): 5. Article reprinted from *Journal of College Student Personnel* 13 (1972): 12–17.

Crow, Kevin L. "Four Types of Disabilities: Their Impact on Online Learning." *Techtrends* 52, no. 1 (2008): 51–55.

Dalton, Elizabeth M., *et al.* "Inclusion, Universal Design and Universal Design for Learning in Higher Education: South Africa and the United States." *African Journal of Disability* 8: a519.

Darby, Flower and James Lang. *Small Teaching Online*. San Francisco, CA: Jossey-Bass, 2019.

Deardorff, Darla K. "Identification and Assessment of Intercultural Competence as a Student Outcome of Internationalization." *Journal of Studies in International Education* 10, no. 3 (2006): 241–266.

Delahunty, Janine. "Connecting to Learn, Learning to Connect: Thinking Together in Asynchronous Forum Discussion." *Linguistics & Education* 46 (2018): 12–22.

Delaney, Kevin, "Balancing in Light of the Purposes of Copyright: Whether Video Music Lessons Constitute Copyright Infringement," *Communication Law and Policy* 20, no. 3 (2015): 261–285.

Deslauriers, Louis, Logan S. McCarty, Kelly Miller, Kristina Callaghan, and Greg Kestin, "Measuring actual learning versus feeling of learning in response to being actively engaged in the classroom," *Proceedings of the National Academy of Sciences*, 116, no. 39 (2019): 19251–19257.

Dimitrov, Nanda, and Aisha Haque. "Intercultural Teaching Competence: A Multi-Disciplinary Model for Instructor Reflection." *Intercultural Education* 27, no. 5 (2016): 437–456.

Douglass, Frederick. "What to the Slave Is the Fourth of July?" Speech, Rochester, NY, July 5, 1852. https://teachingamericanhistory.org/document/what-to-the-slave-is-the-fourth-of-july/. Accessed November 22, 2022.

Duncan, Heather E., and Suzanne Young, "Online Pedagogy and Practice: Challenges and Strategies," *The Researcher* 22, no. 1 (2009): 17–32.

Ebner, Rachel, "Tips for Fostering Students' Self-Regulated Learning in Asynchronous Learning Environments," *Online Education*, September 2, 2020. www.facultyfocus.com/articles/online-education/tips-for-fostering-students-self-regulated-learning-in-asynchronous-online-learning-environments. Accessed November 22, 2022.

ECampus. "Faculty: Best Practices with ECampus." https://go.view.usg.edu/d2l/le/content/2451986/viewContent/45952082/View. Accessed November 22, 2022.

Edgar, Dale, *Audio-Visual Methods in Teaching*. New York: Dryden, 1969.

Edison Research. *The Infinite Dial 2021*. March 11, 2021. www.edisonresearch.com/wp-content/uploads/2021/03/The-Infinite-Dial-2021.pdf. Accessed November 22, 2022.

Ensmann, Suzanne, Aimee Whiteside, Lina Gomez-Vasquez, and Ronda Sturgill. "Connections before Curriculum: The Role of Social Presence during COVID-19 Emergency Remote Learning for Students." *Online Learning Journal* 25, no. 3 (2021): 36–56.

Eynon, Rebecca. "The Myth of the Digital Native: Why It Persists and the Harm It Inflicts," in *Education in the Digital Age: Healthy and Happy Children*, ed. T. Burns and F. Gottschalk. Paris: OECD Publishing, 2020.

Faidutti, Bruno. "Postcolonial Catan," *Analog Game Studies* 2 (2017): 3–34.

Fiorella, Logan and Richard E. Mayer, "What Works and What Doesn't Work with Instructional Video," *Computers in Human Behavior* 89 (2018): 465–470.

Fisher, Douglas, and Nancy Frey. *Checking for Understanding: Formative Assessment Techniques for Your Classroom*, 2nd ed. Alexandria, VA: ASCD, 2014.

Ford, Bridget, Katherine Chilton, Christopher Endy, Michael Henderson, Brad A. Jones, and Ji Y. Son, "Beyond Big Data: Teaching US History in the Age of Student Success," *Journal of American History* 106, no. 4 (2020): 989–1011.

Freire, Paulo. *Pedagogy of the Oppressed*. New York: Continuum, 2000.

Freire, Paulo. *The Politics of Education: Culture, Power, and Liberation*. Westport, CT: Bergin & Garvey, 1985.

Frost, S.H. "Advising Alliances: Sharing Responsibility for Student Success." *NACADA Journal* 14, no. 2 (1994): 56.

Fry, Richard and Anthony Cilluffo. "A Rising Share of Undergraduates Are from Poor Families, Especially at Less Selective Colleges." www.pewresearch.org/social-trends/2019/05/22/a-rising-share-of-undergraduates-are-from-poor-families-especially-at-less-selective-colleges/. Accessed May 22, 2019.

Gannon, Kevin. "Objective History is Impossible, and that's a Fact." The Tattooed Professor blog, May 9, 2016. https://thetattooedprof.com/2016/05/09/objective-history-is-impossible-and-thats-a-fact. Accessed August 1, 2022.

Garcia, Antero. "Privilege, Power, and Dungeons & Dragons: How Systems Shape Racial and Gender Identities in Tabletop Role-Playing Games," *Mind, Culture and Activity* 24, no. 3 (2017): 232–246.

Garcia, Rita, Katrina Faulkner and Rebecca Vivian. "Systematic Literature Review: Self-Regulated Learning Strategies Using E-Learning Tools for Computer Science," *Computers & Education* 123 (2018): 150–163.

Gardner, Howard E. and Wendy Fischman. "Does Truth Have a Future in Higher Education," *Studies in Higher Education* 46, no. 10 (2021): 2099–2105.

Garon, Jon, "Ownership of University Intellectual Property," *Cardoza Arts and Entertainment Law Journal* 36, no. 3 (2018): 635–674.

Greenholtz, Joe F. "Does Intercultural Sensitivity Cross Cultures? Validity Issues in Porting Instruments across Languages and Cultures." *International Journal of Intercultural Relations* 29, no. 1 (2005): 73–89.

Hammer, Mitchell R., Milton J. Bennett, and Richard Wiseman. "Measuring Intercultural Sensitivity: The Intercultural Development Inventory." *International Journal of Intercultural Relations* 27, no. 4 (2003): 421–443.

Harman, Kristyn, "The Transformative Power of Digital Humanities in Teaching Family History Online," *Journal of University Teaching and Learning Practice* 15, no. 3 (2018). https://doi.org/10.53761/1.15.3.7.

Hobson, Tiffaney D. and Krista K. Puruhito, "Going the Distance: Online Course Performance and Motivation of Distance Learning Students," *Online Learning*, 22, no. 4 (2018): 129–140.

Hoffman, Steven, ed., *Teaching the Humanities Online, A Practical Guide to the Virtual Classroom*. London and New York: Routledge, 2011.

hooks, bell. *Teaching Critical Thinking: Practical Wisdom*. New York: Routledge, 2010.

Hovland, Kevin. *Shared Futures: Global Learning and Liberal Education*. New York: Association of American Colleges and Universities, 2006.

Hughes, Richard. "New Guidelines for SoTL in History: A Discipline Considers the SoTL Turn?" *Teaching History: A Journal of Methods* 44, no. 2 (2019): 34–43. https://openjournals.bsu.edu/teachinghistory/article/view/2371.

Hutchinson, Kristine H. "The Teach Act: Copyright Law and Online Education," *New York University Law Review* 78, no. 6 (2003): 2204–2240.

Infande, Al. "A Dozen Strategies for Improving Online Student Retention." *Higher Ed Teaching & Learning*, July 8, 2013. www.facultyfocus.com/articles/online-education/a-dozen-strategies-for-improving-online-student-retention. Accessed November 22, 2022.

Ishii, Kumi, Mary Madison Lyons, and Sabrina A. Carr. "Revisiting Media Richness Theory for Today and the Future," *Human Behavior and Emerging Technologies* 1, no. 2 (2019): 124–131.

J. Paul Getty Museum, "The Art of Three Faiths: Torah, Bible, Qur'an," Google Arts and Culture. June 15, 2022. https://artsandculture.google.com/story/aAVRFg2-TKDIKQ. Accessed November 22, 2022.

Jacob, Brian, Dan Berger, Cassandra Hart, and Susanna Loeb. "Can Technology Help Promote Equality of Educational Opportunities?" *RSF: The Russell Sage Foundation Journal of the Social Sciences* 2, no. 5 (2016): 242–271.

Jacobs, Gloria E., *et al.* "Production and Consumption: A Closer Look at Adult Digital Literacy Acquisition," *Journal of Adolescent and Adult Literacy* 57, no. 8 (2014): 624–627.

Jordan, Katy, "Initial Trends in Enrolment and Completion of Massive Open Online Courses," *International Review of Research in Open and Distance Learning* 15, no. 1 (2014): 133–160.

Judt, Tony. "The Past Is Another Country: Myth and Memory in Postwar Europe." *Daedalus* 121, no. 4 (1992): 83–118.

Karmelita, C. "Advising Adult Learners during the Transition to College." *NACADA Journal* 40, no. 1 (2020): 64–77.

Kebritchi, Mansureh, "Preferred Teaching Methods in Online Courses: Learners' Views." *Journal of Online Learning & Teaching* 10, no. 3 (2014): 468–488.

Kelly, T. Mills. *Teaching History in the Digital Age.* Ann Arbor, MI: The University of Michigan Press, 2016.

Kim, Yuna, "Developing a Work Ready Social Media Marketing Analytics Course: A Model to Cultivate Data-Driven and Multiperspective Strategy Development Skills," *Decision Sciences Journal of Innovative Education* 17, no. 2 (2019): 163–188.

King, M. "Developmental Academic Advising." *NACADA Clearinghouse of Academic Advising Resources.* November 5, 2012. https://nacada.ksu.edu/Resources/Clearinghouse/View-Articles/Developmental-Academic-Advising.aspx. Accessed November 22, 2022.

Kwall, Roberta Rosenthal, "Copyright Issues in Online Courses: Ownership, Authorship and Conflict," *Santa Clara Computer and High Technology Law Journal* 18 (2001): 1–34.

Landorf, Hilary, Stephanie Doscher, and Jaffus Hardrick. *Making Global Learning Universal: Promoting Success and Inclusion for All Students.* Sterling, VA: Stylus Publishing, 2018.

Lane, Lisa. "Making Course Management Systems Work," in *Teaching the Humanities Online: A Practical Guide to the Virtual Classroom*, ed. Steven Hoffman, 46–60. London and New York: Routledge, 2011.

Lane, Lisa. "Reducing Distance in Online Classes," in *Teaching the Humanities Online: A Practical Guide to the Virtual Classroom*, ed. Steven Hoffman, 13–25. London and New York: Routledge, 2011.

Lane, Lisa. "Constructing the Past Online: Discussion Board as History Lab." *The History Teacher* 47, no. 2 (2014): 197–207.

Lang, James M. *Small Teaching: Everyday Lessons from the Science of Learning.* San Francisco, CA: Jossey-Bass, Wiley, 2016.

Lareau, Annette. *Unequal Childhoods: Class, Race, and Family Life.* Berkeley, CA: University of California Press, 2011.

Larkin, Martha J. "Providing Support for Student Independence through Scaffolded Instruction," *Teaching Exceptional Children* 34, no. 1 (2001): 30–34.

Latourette, Audrey, "Copyright Implications for Online Distance Learning," *Journal of College and University Law* 32 (2006): 613–654.

Lawes, Carolyn J. "Talking Less but Saying More: Teaching US History Online." *Journal of American History* 101, no. 4 (2015): 1204–1214.

Lee, Amy, Robert Poch, Mary Katherine O'Brien, and Catherine Solheim. *Teaching Interculturally: A Framework for Integrating Disciplinary Knowledge and Intercultural Development.* Sterling, VA: Stylus Publishing, 2017.

Lee, John K. "Digital History in the History/Social Studies Classroom." *The History Teacher* 35, no. 4 (2002): 503–517.

Leibowitz, Wendy R., "Law Professors Told to Expect Competition from Virtual Learning," *Chronicle of Higher Learning*, January 21, 2000.

Library of Congress, US Copyright Office, *Circular 1, Copyright Basics,* revised December, 2019. https://copyright.gov/circs/circ01.pdf. Accessed May 31, 2018.

Library of Congress, US Copyright Office, *Circular 30, Works Made for Hire,* revised September, 2021. https://copyright.gov/circs/circ30.pdf. Accessed May 31, 2018.

Lindquist, Thea, and Holley Long, "How Can Educational Technology Facilitate Student Engagement with Online Primary Sources? A User Needs Assessment," *Library Hi Tech* 29, no. 2 (2011): 226–227.

Litterio, Lisa M. "Digital Humanities in Professional and Technical Communication: Results of a Pedagogical Pilot Study." *Technical Communications Quarterly* 30, no. 1 (2021): 77–88.

Lloyd, Steven, Michelle Byrne, and Tami McCoy. "Faculty-Perceived Barriers of Online Education." *MERLOT Journal of Online Learning and Teaching* 8, no. 1 (2012): 1–12.

Lowenthal *et al.* "Creating Accessible and Inclusive Online Learning: Moving Beyond Compliance and Broadening the Discussion." *The Quarterly Review of Distance Education* 21, no. 2 (2020): 1–21.

Luckhardt, Courtney. "Teaching Historical Legacy and Making World History Relevant in the Online Discussion Board," *The History Teacher* 47, no. 2 (2014): 187–196.

Lyons, John. "Teaching US History Online: Problems and Prospects." *The History Teacher* 37, no. 4 (2004): 447–456.

Lyons, John. *Teaching History Online.* New York: Routledge, 2009.

MacGregor, Neil. *History of the World in 100 Objects.* New York: Penguin, 2010.

Magada, A.J., D. Capranos, and C.B. Aslanian. *Online College Students 2020: Comprehensive Data on Demands and Preferences.* Louisville, KY: Wiley Education Services, 2020. https://universityservices.wiley.com/wp-content/uploads/2020/06/OCS2020Report-ONLINE-FINAL.pdf.

Makarenko, Erica, and Jac Andrews. "An Empirical Review of the Mental Health and Well-Being of Online Instructors." *The Journal of Educational Thought (JET)/Revue De La Pensée Éducative* 50, no. 23 (2017): 182–199.

Marra, Rose M., Joi L. Moore, and Aimee K. Klimczak. "Content Analysis of Online Discussion Forums: A Comparative Analysis of Protocols." *Educational Technology Research & Development* 52, no. 2 (2004): 23–40.

Martin, F., A. Ritzhaupt, S. Kumar, and K. Budhrani, "Award-Winning Faculty Online Teaching Practices: Course Design, Assessment and Evaluation, and Facilitation," *The Internet and Higher Education* 42 (2019): 34–43.

Mazzolini, Margaret, and Sarah Maddison. "Sage, Guide or Ghost? The Effect of Instructor Intervention on Student Participation in Online Discussion Forums." *Computers & Education* 40, no. 3 (2003): 237–253.

McAllister-Grande, Bryan. "Changing the Foundations of International Education: Fixing a Broken System and Working for Social Justice." *The Global Impact Exchange, Diversity Abroad* (2018): 16–19.

McCormack, Suzanne K. "Teaching History Online to Today's Community College Students." *Journal of American History* 101, no. 4 (2015): 1215–1221.

McGunagle, Doreen, and Laura Zizka. "Meeting Real World Demands of the Global Economy: An Employer's Perspective," *Journal of Aviation/Aerospace Education and Research* 27, no. 2 (2018): 58–76.

McKeachie, W., and M. Svinicki, *McKeachie's Teaching Tips: Strategies, Research, and Theory for College and University Teachers*. Boston, MA: Houghton-Mifflin, 2006.

McLoughlin, Catherine. "Learner Support in Distance and Networked Learning Environments: Ten Dimensions for Successful Design," *Distance Education*, 23, no. 2 (2002): 149–162.

McNiff, Jillian, and Thomas J. Aicher. "Understanding the Challenges and Opportunities Associated with Online Learning: A Scaffolding Theory Approach," *Sport Management Education Journal* 11 (2017): 13–23.

McWright, B.L. (2003). "Educational Technology at a Distance: Is Access to Technology Enough?" *Quarterly Review of Distance Education*, 4, 167–176.

Mehanna, Wassila Naamani. "E-Pedagogy: The Pedagogies of E-Learning." *Research in Learning Technology* 12, no. 3 (2004): 279–293.

Mendes, Philip, "Online Delivery of Education: Copyright Issues in Universities," *Journal of Law and Information Science* 11, no. 2 (2000–2001):196–217.

Miller, Grant R., and Shannon Lindsay Toth. "To Dismantle an Idle Past: Using Historiography to Construct a Digital Learning Environment." *The Social Studies* 103, no. 2 (2012): 73–80.

Miller, Khadijah, "Before We Begin, Preparing to Teach Online," in *Teaching the Humanities Online: A Practical Guide to the Virtual Classroom*, ed. Steven Hoffman, 3–12. London and New York: Routledge, 2011.

Minielli, Maureen and Ferris, Sharmila, "Using Electronic Courseware," in *Teaching the Humanities Online: A Practical Guide to the Virtual Classroom*, ed. Steven Hoffman, 26–45. London and New York: Routledge, 2011.

Minnesota Historical Society. "Primary vs Secondary Sources," YouTube video, 4:18, September 14, 2015. www.youtube.com/watch?v=TgU1BcDStK0. Accessed June 20, 2022.

Mintz, Steven. "Transitioning to Online Teaching: A How-To Guide," *Perspectives on History*, March 17, 2020. www.historians.org/publications-and-directories/perspectives-on-history/march-2020/transitioning-to-online-teaching-a-how-to-guide. Accessed June 20, 2022.

Mitchell Whisnat, Anne and Pamela Lach. "Building the Unbuilt Parkway: Digital Public History in the Classroom." *The American Historian* 1 (2014): 16–18.

Mtshali, Muntuwenkosi Abraham, Suriamurthee Moonsamy Maistry, and Desmond Wesley Govender. "Online Discussion Forum: A Tool to Support Learning in Business Management Education." *South African Journal of Education* 40, no. 2 (2020): 1–9.

Murphree, Daniel, and Kevin Mercer, "Flipping the University Classroom: A Three-Year Analysis of Methods and Impacts," *Teaching History: A Journal of Methods* 43, no. 2 (2019): 17–41.

Murray, Janet H. *Hamlet on the Holodeck: The Future of Narrative in Cyberspace*. Cambridge, MA: MIT Press, 1997.

Mussell, Jim. "Doing and Making History in the Digital Age." In *History in the Digital Age*, ed. Toni Weller, 79–94. New York: Routledge, 2013.

Nandi, Dip, Margaret Hamilton, and James Harland. "Evaluating the Quality of Interaction in Asynchronous Discussion Forums in Fully Online Courses." *Distance Education* 33, no. 1 (2012): 5–30.

National Center for Education Statistics. "Fast Facts." 2020. https://nces.ed.gov/fastfacts/display.asp?id=60. Accessed June 20, 2022.

National Research Council. *How People Learn: Brain, Mind, Experience, and School*, Expanded Edition. Washington, DC: National Academies Press, 2000.

Ni, Anna Ya. "Comparing the Effectiveness of Classroom and Online Learning: Teaching Research Methods." *Journal of Public Affairs Education* 19, no. 2 (2013): 199–215.

Office of Policy Development and Research. "Digital Inequality and Low-income Households." 2016. www.huduser.gov/portal/periodicals/em/fall16/highlight2.html. Accessed November 22, 2022.

Olson, Joann, and Rita Kenahan. "An Overwhelming Cloud of Inertia: Evaluating the Impact of Course Design Changes Following the COVID-19 Pandemic." *Online Learning Journal* 25, no. 4 (2021): 344–361.

Orellana, Anymir. "Class Size and Interaction in Online Courses," *Quarterly Review of Distance Education* 7, no. 3 (2006): 236–242.

Ospina-Delgado, Julieth, Ana Zorio-Grima, and María García-Benau. "Massive Open Online Courses in Higher Education: A Data Analysis of the MOOC Supply," *OmniaScience* 12, no. 5 (2016): 1401–1451.

Ou, Chaohua, David A. Joyner, and Ashok K. Goel, "Designing and Developing Video Lessons for Online Learning: A Seven Principle Model," *Online Learning* 23, no. 2 (2019): 82–104.

Pearcy, Mark. "Student, Teacher, Professor: Three Perspectives on Online Education." *The History Teacher* 47, no. 2 (2014): 169–185.

Perrotta, Katherine, and Chara Bohan. "A Reflective Study of Online Faculty Teaching Experiences in Higher Education." *Journal of Effective Teaching in Higher Education* 3, no. 1 (2020): 50–66.

Perrow, Margaret. "Strengthening the Conversation in Blended and Face-to Face Courses: Connecting Online and In-Person Learning with Crossover Protocols." *College Teaching* 65, no. 3 (2017): 97–105.

Punti, Gemma, and Molly Dingel. "Rethinking Race, Ethnicity, and the Assessment of Intercultural Competence in Higher Education." *Education Sciences* 11, no. 3 (2021): 110.

Qiu, M., J. Hewitt, and C. Brett. "Online Class Size, Note Reading, Note Writing, and Collaborative Discourse," *Computer-Supported Collaborative Learning* 7 (2012): 423–444.

Rivera, David P., Roberto L. Abreu, and Kirsten A. Gonzalez, eds. *Affirming LGBTQ+ Students in Higher Education: Perspectives on Sexual Orientation and Gender Diversity.* Washington, DC: American Psychological Association, 2022.

Robinson, Will. "Orientalism and Abstraction in Eurogames," *Analog Game Studies* 1, no. 5 (2014). https://analoggamestudies.org/2014/12/orientalism-and-abstraction-in-eurogames.

Robles, Marcel, "Executive Perceptions of the Top 10 Soft Skills Needed in Today's Workplace," *Business Communication Quarterly* 75, no. 4 (2012): 453–465.

Rodrigo, Covadonga, and Bernardo Tabuenca. "Learning Ecologies in Students with Disabilities." *Comunicar* 62, no. 28 (2020): 53–64.

Ross-Gordon, J.M. "Research on Adult Learners: Supporting the Needs of a Student Population that Is No Longer Nontraditional." *Peer Review* 13, no. 1 (2011): 26–29.

Rutherford, Teomara, Sarah Karamarkovich, Di Xu, Tamara Tate, Brian Sato, Rachel Baker, and Mark Warschauer. "Profiles of Instructor Responses to Emergency Distance Learning." *Online Learning Journal* 25, no. 1 (2021): 86–114.

Safar, A.H., and F.A. AlKhezzi. "Beyond Computer Literacy: Technology Integration and Curriculum Transformation," *College Student Journal* 47 (2013): 614–626.

Santrock, John W. *A Topical Approach to Life-Span Development*. New York: McGraw Hill Education, 2014.

Schaffhauser, Dian, "How MOOCs Make Money?" *Campus Technology*, March 20, 2019. https://campustechnology.com/Articles/2019/03/20/How-MOOCs-Make-Money.aspx?p=1 Accessed May 1, 2022.

Schneider, Vivian I., Alice F. Healy, Kenneth W. Carlson, Carolyn J. Buck-Gengler, and Immanuel Barshi, "How Much is Remembered as a Function of Presentation Modality?" *Memory* (2019): 261–267.

Schrum, Kelly, and Nate Sleeter. "Teaching History Online: Challenges and Opportunities." *Organization of American Historians Magazine of History* 27, no. 3 (2013): 35–38.

Schrum, Kelly, Nate Sleeter, *et al.*, "Teaching Hidden History: Student Outcomes from a Distributed, Collaborative, Hybrid Course," *The History Teacher* 51, no. 4 (2018): 574–596.

Scott, Joan Wallach. "The Evidence of Experience." *Critical Inquiry* 17, no. 4 (1991): 773–797.

Shepherd, Morgan M. and William Benjamin Martz, Jr., "Media Richness Theory and the Distance Education Environment," *The Journal of Computer Information Systems* 47 (2006): 114–122.

Shepherd, R., and Goggin, P. (2012). "Reclaiming 'Old' Literacies in the New Literacy Information Age: The Functional Literacies of the Mediated Workstation," *Composition Studies*, 40, 66–91.

Shiefelbein, Jill. "Media Richness and Communication in Online Education," Blog entry for Magna Publications, April 10, 2012. www.facultyfocus.com/articles/online-education/media-richness-and-communication-in-online-education/. Accessed November 22, 2022.

Shvarts, Anna, and Arthur Bakker. "The Early History of the Scaffolding Metaphor: Bernstein, Luria, Vygotsky, and Before," *Mind, Culture, and Activity* 26, no. 1 (2019): 4–23.

Simpson, Audra. "On Ethnographic Refusal: Indigeneity, 'Voice' and Colonial Citizenship." *Junctures* 9 (2007). https://junctures.org/index.php/junctures/article/view/66.

Sipress, Joel M., and David J. Voelker. "The End of the History Survey Course: The Rise and Fall of the Coverage Model." *Journal of American History* 97, no. 4 (2011): 1050–1066.

Sium, Aman, and Eric Ritskes. "Speaking Truth to Power: Indigenous Storytelling as an Act of Living Resistance." *Decolonization: Indigeneity, Education & Society* 2, no. 1 (2013): I–X.

Smith, Gregory, and Cynthia Brame. "Active Learning Cheat Sheet." https://cdn.vanderbilt.edu/vu-wp0/wp-content/uploads/sites/59/2019/04/22143029/Active-Learning-Cheat-Sheet.pdf. Accessed November 22, 2022.

Sorrells, Kathryn. *Intercultural Communication: Globalization and Social Justice*. Los Angeles, CA: Sage, 2016.

Stauss, Kimberly, Eun Koh, and Michael Collie. "Comparing the Effectiveness of an Online Human Diversity Course to Face-to-Face Instruction." *Journal of Social Work Education* 54, no. 3 (2018): 492–505.
Steed, Marlo, "New Media Design for Learning, An Argument for Curriculum Change," *The International Journal of Learning* 17, no. 3 (2010): 291–301.
Szabo, Zsuzsanna. "Better Together: Teams and Discourse in Asynchronous Online Discussion Forums." *Journal of Psychological & Educational Research* 23, no. 1 (2015): 73–88.
Szabo, Zsuzsanna, and Jonathan Schwartz. "Online Forum Discussions: They Will Respond the Way You Ask." *Journal of Psychological & Educational Research* 25, no. 1 (2017): 130–141.
Tackett, Timothy. *When the King Took Flight*. Cambridge: Harvard University Press, 2004.
Taft, Susan H., Tracy Perkowski, and Lorene S. Martin. "A Framework for Evaluating Class Size In Online Education," *Quarterly Review of Distance Education* 12, no. 3 (2011): 181–197.
Ter-Stepanian, Anahit. "Online or Face to Face?: Instructional Strategies for Improving Learning Outcomes in e-Learning." *International Journal of Technology, Knowledge & Society* 8, no. 2 (2012): 41–50.
Thomas, M., ed. *Deconstructing Digital Natives: Young People, Technology, and the New Literacies*. New York: Routledge, 2011.
Tienda, Marta. "Diversity ≠ Inclusion: Promoting Integration in Higher Education." *Educational Researcher* 42, no. 9 (2013): 467–475.
Tierney, William G. and Suneal Kolluri, *Diversifying Digital Learning: Online Literacy and Educational Opportunity*. Baltimore, MD: John Hopkins University Press, 2018.
Tierney, William G., Zoë B. Corwin, and Amanda Ochsner, eds. *Diversifying Digital Learning: Online Literacy and Educational Opportunity*. Baltimore, MD: Johns Hopkins University Press, 2018.
Ting, Yu-Liang. "Tapping Into Students' Digital Literacy and Designing Negotiated Learning to Promote Learner Autonomy," *The Internet and Higher Education* 26 (2015): 25–32.
Tomei, Lawrence A. "Impact of Online Teaching on Faculty Load: Computing the Ideal Class Size for Online Courses," *Journal of Technology and Teacher Education* 14, no. 3 (2006): 531–541.
Trammell, Aaron. "Misogyny and the Female Body in Dungeons & Dragons," *Analog Game Studies* 1, no. 3 (2014). https://analoggamestudies.org/2014/10/constructing-the-female-body-in-role-playing-games.
Twigg, Carol. *Who Owns Online Courses and Course Materials? Intellectual Property Policies for a New Learning Environment*. Troy, NY: Center for Academic Transformation at Rensselaer Polytechnic Institute, 2000.
Ubell, John. "Advice for Faculty Members about Overcoming Resistance to Teaching Online." *Inside Higher Ed*, December 13, 2016. www.insidehighered.com/advice/2016/12/13/advice-faculty-members-about-overcoming-resistance-teaching-online-essay. Accessed June 20, 2022.
US Copyright Office. "More Information on Fair Use." www.copyright.gov/fair-use/more-info.html. Accessed June 20, 2022.
Vecchiola, Carla. "Digging in the Digital Archives." *The History Teacher* 53, no. 1 (2019): 107–134.
Vivolo, John. "Understanding and Combating Resistance to Online Learning." *Science Progress* 99, no. 4 (2016): 399–412.

Voekler, David J. "Assessing Student Understanding in Introductory Courses: A Sample Strategy." *History Teacher* 41, no. 4 (2008): 505–518.

Vulaj, Elizabeth. "Copyright and COVID 19: Navigating Streaming Laws for Online Classes in the New Normal," *New York State Bar Association Journal* 92, no. 7 (2020): 36–39.

Vygotsky, L. *Thought and Language.* Cambridge, MA: MIT Press, 1934/1936.

Waring, Scott M. "Escaping Myopia: Teaching Students about Historical Causality." *The History Teacher* 43, no. 2 (2010): 283–288.

Wavle, S. and G. Ozogul. "Investigating the Impact of Online Classes on Undergraduate Degree Completion." *Online Learning Journal* 23, no. 4 (2019): 281–295.

Weimer, Maryellen. 2013. *Learner-Centered Teaching: Five Key Changes to Practice,* 2nd ed. San Francisco, CA: Jossey-Bass.

Whitaker, Jonathan, J. Randolph New, and R. Duane Ireland, "MOOCs and the Online Delivery of Business Education What's New? What's not? What now?" *Academy of Management learning & Education* 15, no. 2 (2016): 345–365.

White, J.W., A. Pascale, and S. Aragon. "Collegiate Cultural Capital and Integration into the College Community." *College Student Affairs Journal* 38, no. 1 (2020): 34–52.

Wiggins, Grant and Jay McTighe, *Understanding by Design.* Alexandria, VA: Association for Supervision and Curriculum Development, 2005.

Wilson, Lucinda M. and Deborah A. Corpus. "The Effects of Reward Systems on Academic Performance," *Middle School Journal* 33, no. 1 (2001): 56–60.

Wineburg, Samuel S. *Historical Thinking and Other Unnatural Acts: Charting the Future of Teaching the Past.* Philadelphia, PA: Temple University Press, 2001.

Wood, David, and Heather Wood. "Vygotsky, Tutoring and Learning." *Oxford Review of Education* 22, no. 1 (1996): 5–16.

Word for Mac Help Guide. "Improve Accessibility with the Accessibility Checker." https://support.microsoft.com/en-us/office/improve-accessibility-with-the-accessibility-checker-a16f6de0-2f39-4a2b-8bd8-5ad801426c7f#PickTab=macOS. Accessed June 20, 2022.

Yu, Eunjyu. "Student-Inspired Optimal Design of Online Learning for Generation Z." *Journal of Educators Online* 17, no. 1 (2020). www.thejeo.com/archive/2020_17_1/yu.

Zhang, Y. "Distance Learning Receptivity: Are They Ready Yet?" *Quarterly Review of Distance Education* 6 (2005): 45–53.

Zhang, Zhe (Victor). "Promoting Student Engagement with Feedback: Insights from Collaborative Pedagogy and Teacher Feedback." *Assessment & Evaluation in Higher Education* 47, no. 4 (2022): 540–555.

Zimmerman, B.J. "Attaining Self-Regulation: A Social Cognitive Perspective," in *Handbook of Self-Regulation,* ed. M. Boekaerts, P.R. Pintrich, and M. Zeidner, 13–39. San Diego, CA: Academic Press, 2000.

Zimmerman, B.J. "Investigating Self-Regulation and Motivation: Historical Background, Methodological Developments, and Future Prospects," *American Educational Journal* 45, no. 1 (2008): 166–183.

Zimmerman, B.J. "From Cognitive Modeling to Self-Regulation: A Social Cognitive Path," *Educational Psychologist* 48, no. 3 (2013): 135–147.

Zimmerman, B.J., and Kallen Tsikalas. "Can Computer-Based Learning Environments (CBLEs) Be Used as Self-Regulatory Tools to Enhance Learning?" *Educational Psychologist* 40, no. 4 (2005): 267–271.

Index

accessibility 3, 5, 15–22, 26, 34, 36–37, 40, 54, 88, 124, 159, 166, 169–169, 171
Adobe *Acrobat* 21
Adobe *Express* 151–152
Adobe *Spark* 151
advising, student 5, 33–40
Aicher, Thomas 140
Amazon.com 53
American Association of University Professors (AAUP) 27–28, 50–51
American Historical Association (AHA) 147–148
American YAWP 118, 172
Americans with Disabilities Act (ADA) 15, 37, 88
Anderson, Benedict 116–117
Andrews, Thomas 113, 148
annotation 89, 91–93, 104, 171
Apple 20, 53, 87
archives 137, 155–156, 159–160; National Archives 137
assessment *see* Learning assessment
Association of American Colleges and Universities (AAC&U) 51–52, 70
asynchronous classes 8, 10–11, 15, 17, 28, 35–36, 47, 63–65, 74, 78, 82, 86, 102–106, 112, 121, 124, 130–131, 146
audio 2, 20, 27, 46, 54, 130, 134, 144–145, 166
audio books 17–18
Avalon Project 118

Bakker, Arthur 139
Berry, Daina Ramey 119
Biggs, J. 63
blogs 28–29, 73, 97, 119
Board Game Arena 103, 171
Bogost, Ian 101–102

Bookshare 18
breakout rooms, *see* discussion boards, breakout rooms
budgeting 5, 7, 25–27, 29, 51
Budhai, Stephanie 61
Burke, Brian 101–102
Burke, Flannery 113, 148

Carnes, Mark 105
Castro, Joy 75
Cengage, *see* publishers, Cengage
chat 12, 14, 28, 38, 103
classrooms: flipped 91; hybrid 85, 91, 121; large 7, 26–28, 51, 109, 123–131; traditional 7–12, 15, 25, 27, 29–32, 34, 44–45, 47, 60–61, 70, 72, 74, 85–86, 88–89, 91, 94–95, 111–112, 114, 124, 139, 148, 158–159; virtual 5, 11, 15–16, 26, 28–31, 33–39, 61–2, 69–72, 74, 85, 112, 118, 123, 139
ChronoZoom 152
closed captioning 16, 20, 36–37, 54, 88, 166
Collaborative Online Intercultural Learning (COIL) 69
collaboration, *see* learning, collaborative
community building 2, 5, 10–11, 33, 25–28, 54, 70, 73–74, 101, 111, 129
compensation 7, 29
computer literacy 5, 26, 28–32
copyright 5–6, 49–55, 136, 158, 162–166
Copyright Acts: 1909 50; 1976 51–2; 1998 Digital Millennium Copyright Act (DMCA) 53; 2002 Technology, Education, and Copyright Harmonization (TEACH) Act 53–55
course management system (CMS), *see* learning management system (LMS)

creative commons license 47, 54
critical thinking skills 1–3, 47, 59–63, 72–74, 89, 94–95, 97, 109–112, 133–134, 136, 140, 144, 146, 148, 166
Crookston, B. 33
curriculum 70–72, 22, 59, 64–65, 75, 86, 112, 155–156

Darby, Flower 102–103
data collection and analysis 5–6, 25, 31–32, 44–45, 47, 90
deadlines 2, 11, 37, 105, 111–112
Desire 2 Learn (D2L), *see* learning management systems (LMS), Desire 2 Learn
developmental advising model 33–34
Dimitrov, Nanda 71
Discord 106
discussion 2–3, 9–11, 27–30, 43–44, 46, 60–63, 71–75, 78, 81–83, 86, 89, 91–96, 98–99, 102–104, 109–121, 123–131, 133, 136–138, 146–148, 158, 166–168
discussion boards 2–3, 10–11, 27–31, 43, 60, 63, 78, 89, 92–93, 99, 103–104, 106, 109–117, 123–128, 136–138, 140–143, 146–148; breakout rooms 103–104, 106, 126
discussion prompts 37, 74, 96, 98–99, 112, 114–121, 124–126, 129–130, 134–138, 141
diversity *see* students, diversity
Douglass, Frederick 119
Dublin Core 158
due dates 9–10, 45–46, 106, 142

Edison Research 119
Edpuzzle 81–83
edpuzzles 60, 78, 81, 83
email 9–12, 28–29, 35–38, 44–45, 81, 86, 98, 127–128, 166, 168
engagement, student 3, 5, 7, 25, 33, 37–38, 43–44, 47–48, 61, 63, 65–66, 70–71, 74, 76, 78, 82, 85, 87, 94–95, 112, 123, 129, 136–137, 146, 154
English as second language (ESL) 16, 124
evaluations: course 18, 46, 75, 91, 168; student 34, 190, 199, 112, 156
exhibits, online 78, 81–83, 154–158

Facebook *see* social media, Facebook
Faidutti, Bruno 102
fair use 6, 49, 52–55

feedback, *see* learning assessment
films, *see* video
Final Cut Pro 87
Fischman, Wendy 146
Fisher, Douglas 111
Flipgrid 106
Foner, Eric 115
Forgie, George B. 120
Freire, Paulo 146–147
Frey, Nancy 111

games 2–3, 59–60, 101–106, 171; board 102–103, 106; escape rooms 104; *Reacting to the Past* 60, 105, 171; role-playing 59, 102–103, 105–106; scavenger hunts 101, 104; storytelling 104; video 105
gamification 60, 65, 101–106
Garcia, Antero 102
Gardner, Howard E. 146
general education courses 1, 26, 31, 65, 86, 154, 159
geographic information system (GIS), *see* maps
Geography of Slavery in Virginia 80
Gilder-Lehrman Institute 119
global learning, *see* learning, global
Google Arts and Culture 82
Google Books 52
Google *Sheets* 83, 150
grading, *see* learning assessment

Haque, Aisha 71
Harman, Kristyn 63
Harper & Row Publishers, Inc. v Nation Enterprises 52
Harris, Leslie 119–120
Hegel, Georg 139
Hidden in Plain Sight 63
historical thinking 39, 78, 80, 89–91, 94–95, 113–115, 118–119, 121, 147–149, 151; five Cs 113, 115, 148
Hobbes, Thomas 115–116
Hutchinson, Kristine 53
Huzinga, Johan 101

incentive-based budget model (IBBM) 25–27
inclusivity 5, 16–18, 37, 124
Instagram *see* social media, Instagram
intellectual property 49–55
interaction 7–8, 27–28, 34, 36, 38, 43, 49–50, 60, 62, 86, 99, 103, 123–126,

128, 130, 146; instructor-to-student 2, 10–11, 28, 49–50, 78, 99, 111–114, 124–125, 136–137, 143, 158; student-to-student 2, 8, 10–11, 38, 43, 86, 99, 111–114, 124–125
Internet History Sourcebooks Project 118
internships 37, 39–40

J. Paul Getty Museum 82
Judt, Tony 71

Kahoots 102
Kanopy 53
Kelley, T. Mills 66

Lane, Lisa 62
Lang, James 85, 102–3
Lawes, Carolyn 61–62, 114, 118
learning; collaborative 63, 70, 73, 104, 146–147, 150; intercultural 69, 69–75; self-regulated 34, 64–66, 90, 134
learning assessment 10, 12, 18, 43, 50, 78, 89–91, 94–99, 128–130; exams 9, 45–47, 95, 99, 110–111, 128, 155, 158, 160, 166–167; peer evaluation 9, 17, 28, 99; quizzes 9, 43–47, 51, 54, 62, 80, 87, 90–92, 96, 101, 103–104, 111, 113, 143–144, 166; self-assessment 34, 90
learning management systems (LMS) 8–12, 19, 29, 49, 51, 53–55, 61, 81, 83–84, 104–106, 109, 117, 130, 134, 136, 148, 150, 156, 166–168; Blackboard 8, 30, 141; Canvas 8; Desire 2 Learn (D2L) 8, 157
learning objectives 10, 26, 29–30, 53, 60, 63–65, 70, 78–80, 82–83, 85, 87–88, 96–97, 102–104, 106, 125–126, 131, 133–134, 138, 140, 142, 154, 166
Lee, Amy 69–70, 75
Library of Congress 80, 118, 138
Lyons, John 111, 114

MacGregor, Neil 127
maps 43, 46–47, 80–81, 118, 134, 137
Marx, Karl 139
massive open online courses (MOOCs) 51, 118
McCormack, Suzanne K. 112, 115
McNiff, Jillian 140
Microsoft *Excel* 20, 170
Microsoft *PowerPoint* 11, 20–21, 43, 61, 143, 169

Microsoft *Office* 19–21
Microsoft *Word* 20–21, 30, 98, 170
Miller, Grant 118
MindTap 43, 47–48
Minnesota Historical Society 113
movies, *see* video
Murray, Janet H. 105

National Center for Education Statistics 15
National History Education Clearinghouse 113
Netflix 53

Omeka 110, 154–161
onboarding, *see* orientation, student
open educational resource (OER) 43, 47–48, 137
optical character recognition (OCR) 21
Orellana, Anymir 27
orientation, student 35–36, 50–51

Paine, Thomas 118
Pearcy, Mark 118
Pearson, *see* Publishers, Pearson
Peer Online Course Review (POCR) 17
Pew Research Center 21
plagiarism 8, 53, 63, 117
podcasts 62, 119–120
Prezi 143
primary sources 2–3, 40, 43, 46–47, 64, 66, 86, 89, 91–93, 96–97, 99, 104, 110–116, 118–121, 127, 133–138, 154–157, 159–161, 166
publishers 2–3, 6, 18, 22, 43–48, 53, 92, 134; Cengage 18, 43, 45; Pearson 43, 46

Quality Matters 91, 93
quizzes, *see* learning assessments, quizzes

Reacting to the Past, see Games, *Reacting to the Past*
retention, student 5, 25–27, 90
Revel 43, 46–48
Robinson, Will 102
Roosevelt, Franklin Delano 133–134
rubrics 48, 82–83, 91, 109, 127–128, 166

Salvatore, Nick 120
scaffolding 2, 72, 89, 109–110, 139–145, 147, 149
Schlossberg, Nancy K. 34
Schrum, Kelly 63, 113

secondary sources 2–3, 66, 96–97, 99, 112–113, 119, 125, 157–158, 166
Shvarts, Anna 139
Skype, *see* video conferencing, Skype
Slack 106
Sleeter, Nate 63, 113
Small Teaching 103–104
Small Teaching Online 85
Snapchat 30
social media 35–38, 47, 55, 86, 110; Facebook 38; Instagram 37–38; Twitter 148, 150
Softchalk 87
Sorrells, Kathryn 70, 72
Stanrock, John 133
Storify 150–151
story mapping 59–60, 80–81, 83
students 1–3, 5–12, 15–22, 25–32, 33–40, 43–55, 59–66, 69–75, 78–92, 94–99, 101–106, 109–121, 123–130, 134, 136–151, 154–161, 166, 168; diversity 16, 22, 27, 70, 102, 124; first-generation 18, 22, 26, 47, 75, 95; low income 16, 21, 31, 75, 94; non-traditional 16, 25, 31–32, 34; traditional 15–16, 25–28, 30–31, 43, 45, 66, 141; veterans 16, 75, 142–143; with disabilities 15–18, 37, 39, 88, 40
study abroad programs 37, 69
Suits, Bernard 101
Sutori 151
syllabus 10, 18, 21–22, 50, 54, 72, 104, 106, 125, 163, 166, 168–169
synchronous classes 10–11, 15, 28, 44–45, 86, 103–106, 121

Tang, C. 63
teaching assistants 91, 126, 131
TEDx 74
Tennessee Valley Authority (TVA) 134–136
textbooks 16–18, 43–48, 50, 53–54, 118, 120, 134; digital 43–47
TikTok 38
Tiki-Toki 83, 110, 150–152
Timeline JS 79, 83
timelines 60, 78–81, 83–84, 95, 110, 144, 146–153
Toth, Shannon 118
Trammell, Aaron 102
transcription 16, 20, 88, 120, 136, 166

Tsikalas, Kallen 64
Twigg, Carol 49–50
Twitter 148, 150

universal design 16–17, 20, 23, 102, 106, 168

Vecchiola, Carla 116, 118
video 2–3, 10–11, 15, 18–20, 37, 43, 46, 49, 53–54, 59–60, 62, 74, 79–81, 85–92, 94–96, 98–99, 113, 119–120, 130, 134, 137, 140, 150–152, 158, 166; films 49–50, 53–55, 60, 62, 81, 103, 135; lectures 43, 62, 87–92, 94, 96, 166
video conferencing 12, 14, 18, 28; Skype 12, 14, 36; Zoom 12, 14, 18, 36, 86, 103
Vietnam War 141–145
Virtual Jamestown 118
Voekler, David 117
Voluntary Product Accessibility Template (VPAT) 17–18, 23
Vygotsky, Lev 139

Walker, David 118–119
Waring, Scott M. 120
Wave Reader 18
Web Content Accessibility Guidelines 17
Wikipedia 152
Williams v. Weisser 50
Williams, Maureen 61
Wineburg, Sam 112, 137
Women in World History Primary Source Collection 118
Works Progress Administration (WPA) 134–135
writing 2, 8–9, 30, 35, 39, 47, 51, 59, 60–63, 65, 89, 95–98, 109–110, 126, 133, 136, 140, 142–143
writing assignments 30, 61–63, 65, 89, 95–98, 136, 142–143; essays 30, 47, 95, 99, 110–111, 128, 155, 158, 160, 166–167; journaling 28–29; research papers 17, 37, 39–40, 43, 79, 110, 141–146, 148–151, 154–155, 158–161

YouTube 38, 81, 87
Yuja 87

Zimmerman, Barry J. 64
Zinn Education Project 105
Zoom *see* video conferencing, Zoom

For Product Safety Concerns and Information please contact our EU representative GPSR@taylorandfrancis.com
Taylor & Francis Verlag GmbH, Kaufingerstraße 24, 80331 München, Germany

www.ingramcontent.com/pod-product-compliance
Lightning Source LLC
Chambersburg PA
CBHW061715300426
44115CB00014B/2692